PRINCIPAL DATES

1903		Stanley Setty (Sulman Seti) born in Baghdad
1919 December		Brian Donald Hume born in Swanage
1939 September	7	Hume joins the RAF
1941 May	13	Hume discharged from RAF following a serious flying accident in 1940 and an attack of cerebro-spinal meningitis
1942 June		Hume arrested at Northolt airport for fraud
1943 January		Hume takes premises at 620 Finchley Road
1947 December		Hume's first casual meeting with Setty
1948 September	9	Hume marries Cynthia Kahn
1949 January		Hume meets Setty in the Hollywood Club, and forms an association
July	17	A baby girl is born to the Humes
October	4	Setty disappears
	5	Hume disposes of two parcels by plane over the English Channel
	6	Hume disposes of third parcel in the same way
	21	Setty's torso found in Dengie Marshes
	28	Hume charged with murder of Setty
1950 January	18	Trial begins before Mr Justice Lewis
	19	Mr Justice Lewis taken ill. Trial restarted before Mr Justice Sellers
	26	Trial ends; jury disagree on murder charge. Hume pleads guilty to second indictment and is sentenced to twelve years' imprisonment as accessory
1958 February	1	Hume released from Dartmoor
May	25	Hume leaves England for Zurich
June	1–29	Hume's 'Confession' to the murder of Setty appears in the Sunday Pictorial
August	2	Hume commits robbery at the Midland Bank, Brentford
November	12	Second raid on the Midland Bank, now in the Great West Road

1959 January 30 Hume raids Gewerbe Bank of Zurich and kills Arthur Maag, Swiss taxidriver

September 24 Hume's trial begins in Switzerland

30 Trial ends; Hume is sentenced to life imprisonment

THE FIRST EPISTLE OF SAINT PAUL
TO THE CORINTHIANS

THE FIRST EPISTLE OF SAINT PAUL
TO THE CORINTHIANS

THE FIRST EPISTLE
OF SAINT PAUL
TO THE CORINTHIANS

JEAN HÉRING

Professor in the Faculty of Protestant Theology
in the University of Strasbourg

Translated from the Second French Edition by
A. W. Heathcote and P. J. Allcock

LONDON
THE EPWORTH PRESS

FIRST PUBLISHED IN 1962
REPRINTED 1964

© THE EPWORTH PRESS 1962

Book Steward
FRANK H. CUMBERS

PRINTED AND BOUND IN ENGLAND BY
HAZELL WATSON AND VINEY LTD
AYLESBURY, BUCKS

Dedicated to the memory

of

FRÉDÉRIC GODET

In so far as we love the Gospel, to that extent let us study the ancient tongues. And let us notice that without the knowledge of languages we can scarcely preserve the Gospel. Languages are the sheath which hides the sword of the Spirit, they are the chest in which this jewel is enclosed, the goblet holding this draught.

So although the Faith and the Gospel may be proclaimed by preachers without the knowledge of languages, the preaching will be feeble and ineffective. But where the languages are studied, the proclamation will be fresh and powerful, the Scriptures will be searched, and the Faith will be constantly rediscovered through ever new words and deeds.

MARTIN LUTHER

FOREWORD

THE FIRST EPISTLE of the Apostle Paul to the Corinthians touches on such varied and important questions, and contains in addition so many difficult passages, that it has aroused discussions which are as exciting as they are numerous. The commentator is therefore sorely tempted to set up a kind of symposium in which his predecessors could be given ample opportunity of speaking for themselves in order to expound their own ideas and argue among themselves. We have thought fit not to yield to this temptation. For it would lead to a very bulky work likely to discourage many readers—and purchasers. With the full agreement of the publishers responsible for this series of commentaries, we have been at pains to be concise and to reduce to a minimum the space given to controversy, whether initiated by ourselves or by others. 'Everything is permissible, but not everything is expedient.'

For the same reason, we have decided to jettison a cumbersome load of references of little value, rarely checked, often imprecise and sometimes inaccurate, which many scrupulous commentators drag along like a baggage-wagon. We think it better to quote sparingly but well, that is to give quotations and references of real value, *which have been previously verified.*

Divergent readings will be mentioned only when they are interesting from a philological or theological point of view, and each time the most important and characteristic authorities will be quoted. Of these, we have ourselves checked all quotations from the Fathers[1] and from the Vulgate. But so far as the other ancient versions and manuscripts are concerned, we rely on Tischendorf (Edition Octava Maior II [1872]), from which the quotations are taken, with the exception of those from the Chester Beatty Papyrus, P 46 (third century), which we have ourselves studied in facsimile in the fine Kenyon edition (Fasc. 3, Pauline Epistles, London, 1937), and which generally confirms the text of B (Vaticanus).

Quotations from the Old Testament refer, unless otherwise stated, to the Septuagint Version (ed. Rahlfs, 2 vols, Stuttgart, undated); when this version's numbering differs from that of the Massoretic text, as for example in the majority of the Psalms, the reference to the Hebrew text is given in parentheses. Similarly 3 Kings (1 Kings)

---

[1] If we often quote from the Fathers in MIGNE's *Patrology* and from secular authors in the TEUBNER series, it is not because these editions are necessarily the best, but that they are the only fairly complete ones which are readily available in the majority of libraries to our readers. The page-numbering of the Latin *Patrology* is that of the first edition, which is sometimes different from later ones.

refers to the Third Book of Kings in the LXX, and to the First in the Massoretic text.

Further, we think that the commentator's first task is to justify his translation, by keeping as closely as possible to the Greek text. We do not flatter ourselves that all our readers will be convinced, for there are many passages in which, strictly speaking, other translations are tenable. But we have striven, in such cases, to decide clearly for one or other of the possibilities, by avoiding ambiguous expressions. Only when the Apostle himself makes intentional use of vague or ambiguous wording have we tried to imitate him.

It goes without saying that we shall welcome any reasoned comments from our readers; but we reject in advance any criticism from those who are content to say merely that they 'prefer' another translation or interpretation, without advancing any serious exegetical reasons. We assume, moreover, that the reader has the Nestlé text at hand; when we diverge from it, we say so and explain why.

The commentator's second task is to remove, as far as possible, the great difficulties which Pauline thought or the linkage of its various elements presents to the modern reader. It is not for us to judge whether we have succeeded; we hope that at least we have not scamped any important problem.

Above all we should be happy to have shown how much greater the Apostle's teaching is in substance, in originality, and in utter heedlessness of later ecclesiastical or philosophical decisions, in a word, in *inspiration*, than we are sometimes led to suppose by the efforts of those who are a little too ready to fit it into some system or other. The Apostle, need it be said, recognizes no other master than the One whose witness and messenger he is.

STRASBOURG   J.H.
   31*st May* 1948

THE ENGLISH TRANSLATION embodies the addenda to the second French edition, together with other minor alterations made by the author. The translation of the text of the Epistle does not entirely follow the French translation given by Professor Héring, but at his request it has been made with attention to the Greek text, and on the basis of his own critical comments.

6*th September* 1960   A.W.H.

CONTENTS

INTRODUCTION

THE FOUNDING of the Corinthian Church is related in Acts 18[1-17]. There is nothing in Paul's Epistles to contradict that narrative, though they add to it somewhat. We learn, for example, that the conversion of Stephanas and his household was the first important success of the Apostle. The Church consisted predominantly of converted pagans. On this point also the information in Acts, according to which the Jews had generally showed themselves refractory to the preaching of the Apostle, and the information of the Epistle, in which Jews seldom figure, is mutually confirmatory.

The approximate date of Paul's first sojourn in Corinth is fixed by the famous inscription concerning Gallio, the procurator of Achaia, mentioned in Acts 18; the date lies between May 51 and May 52.[1]

Corinth, destroyed by Mummius and rebuilt under Julius Caesar and Augustus, had the reputation of being a wealthy city of loose morals (the word 'korinthiazesthai' was used for a dissolute life). So the Christians of Corinth, though of humble origin, were in some cases still rather-much inclined to licentious living.

After founding the Church, the Apostle Paul returned to Jerusalem, calling at Ephesus and Caesarea. Then he returned to Antioch. This was the end of what is usually called the Second Missionary Journey.

Some time later he returned to Ephesus, after passing through ta anōtera merē, that is the central plateau region of Asia Minor, including Galatia, expressly mentioned in 16[1]. The Apostle stayed in Ephesus for some time, as his preaching there was successful in spite of many obstacles (16[9]). In 4[19], he hopes to come again 'soon', but later he explains why he will still defer his visit for some time longer (16[8-9]). However, even when Chapter 4 was written, Timothy had been sent to Corinth; 16[10] confirms this fact, and is in accord with Acts 19[22]. Acts adds one interesting detail: Timothy went by land through Macedonia. This explains why our Epistle (or the first part of it, if the hypothesis developed later is accepted), which was to go by the shorter sea route, was expected to reach Corinth before Paul's fellow-worker.

If 15[32] alludes to the riot of Acts 19[23ff], then the second part of the letter must have been written after this incident.

Our Epistle had been preceded, moreover, by another also

---

[1] See *RB*(1913), pp. 36–7 (facsimile).—M. GOGUEL, *Introduction au N.T.*, IV.I.10ff.—CABROL and LECLERCQ, *Dictionnaire d'archéologie chrétienne et de liturgie*, III, art. 'Corinthe' (col. 2963ff).—JACKSON AND LAKE, *Beginnings of Christianity*, V.460–4.

probably despatched from Ephesus. The Apostle refers to it in 5^9. It is possible that a fragment has been preserved in 2 Corinthians 6^{14}-7^1.

What had happened in Corinth since the Apostle left? Discipline had considerably relaxed. The free-thinking group, also known as 'gnostics' *par excellence*, gave him a bad name, and adopted a very free attitude towards sexual matters and pagan sacrifices. Some women used the imperfectly understood Christian freedom to achieve a shocking degree of emancipation. At the other extreme, certain rigorists wondered whether they should not reject marriage and refuse to eat meat. Furthermore, the Corinthians showed an untoward preference for one or other of the apostles, for Paul, Apollos or Cephas (i.e. Peter), which ran the risk of dividing the Church. Some even contested the validity of Paul's apostolate, doubtless through the influence of false apostles, as in Galatia.

Other abuses arose neither from ill-will nor from gnostic arrogance, but simply from the fact that the Church lacked firm organization and was dominated by those who were inspired. Gatherings tended to become disorderly and tumultuous, as those of the spirit-filled have been in any age.

Into the bargain, the preaching of the resurrection was either ill-comprehended or denied, probably not only by the gnostics but also by other Greeks whose spiritualistic outlook hardly countenanced anything but survival of the soul. The Apostle heard about this situation partly through 'Chloe's people' (1^{11}), partly from Sosthenes (1^1) and from Stephanas, Fortunatus and Achaicus (16^{17}), as well as by the letter from Corinth carried by one or other of these and to which he refers at the beginning of Chapters **7** and **8**.

The authenticity of our Epistle, which was mentioned as early as the Epistle of Clement of Rome to the Corinthians $47^{1\text{ff}}$, has never been seriously questioned, except by extremists like Bruno Bauer and Delafosse (alias Turmel);[2] the latter thinks that he can detect extensive late Marcionite or Catholic interpolations; but they have convinced no specialist.

The unity of the letter, on the other hand, has given rise to considerable discussion. We know, in fact, that the Apostle sent not two, but at least four letters to Corinth. For besides the letter prior to 1 Corinthians which we have already mentioned, one is mentioned in 2 Corinthians 2^4, $7^{8-9,12}$, a letter marked by great severity and written in great distress, and which does not seem to be identical with 1 Corinthians.

Since we do not like to admit the loss of these letters, attempts have been made to trace them, at least in part, in the canonical epistles.[3]

[2] DELAFOSSE, *Commentaire de la première épître aux Corinthiens* (Paris, Rieder, 1925); cf. the critical study by M. GOGUEL in *RHPR*(1926), pp. 583–4.

[3] The Churches of Armenia are known to have preserved a third letter by Paul, as well as a letter addressed to Paul by the Corinthians, in addition to the two generally accepted Epistles. But they are compositions of no value. A French

But the most serious argument against the unity of 1 Corinthians is afforded by an examination of this long letter itself, certain parts of which accord ill with others, even if allowance is made for longer or shorter interruptions in its dictation. We cannot discuss here, or even mention, all the attempts to divide up this Epistle; these may be found set out in M. Goguel, *Introduction au N.T.*, IV.II.86ff. We may notice, as the most interesting ones, those of Johannes Weiss and of M. Goguel. According to the German scholar[4] 10^{1-23}, 6^{12-20}, 11^{2-34} along with 2 Corinthians $6^{14}-7^1$ belong to the first letter; whilst 7–9, $10^{24}-11^1$ and 12–15 form a second letter, and 1^1-6^{11} a third one which was despatched almost at the same time as the second. The verses of 16 may be allocated to the three letters (and a fourth and fifth may be traced in 2 Cor).

M. Goguel, on his part, attributes the same elements as Johannes Weiss (except for 10^{23}) to the first letter. The second letter would comprise 5^1-6^{11}, 7^1-8^{13}, $10^{23}-14^{40}$, 15^{1-58}, $16^{1-9,12}$; the third $1^{10}-4^{21}$, 9^{1-27}, 16^{10-11}. Other elements are indeterminate. (Three other letters may be found in 2 Cor.)

From the critical observations which are prompted by the composition of 1 Corinthians we may select the following as really important:

(1) The contradiction between **4**, where the Apostle speaks of his imminent arrival, and **16**, where he explains why his coming will be yet longer delayed.

(2) The contradiction between 10^{1-22}, which takes up a rigorist attitude over the question of pagan sacrifices, and $10^{23}-11^1$ which makes it principally a matter of concern for the weak, as does **8**. (For details see the commentary.)

(3) The resumption *ex abrupto* of the discussion about the apostolate in **9**, which seemed settled by **1–4**. A transition from **8** to **9** is lacking. Furthermore, the question is out of place. It is no more a matter of partisan spirits who prefer one apostle to another, but of opponents who challenge completely the validity of Paul's apostleship. If the letter received from Corinth during the writing of the Epistle brought the writer some information on the point, it is difficult to understand why he did not first deal with the capital issue before replying to the questions on marriage and sacrifices (from **7** onwards).

Since we shall doubtless be expected to give our own hypothesis about the composition of 1 Corinthians, we will advance one which seems to take cognizance of the points just raised, without involving us in a very extensive, and therefore rather hypothetical, editorial task. We would thus distinguish two letters:

translation of these will be found in A. CARRIÈRE and S. BERGER, *La correspondance apocryphe de saint Paul et des Corinthiens* (Paris, 1891), and a German translation in HENNEKE, *N.T.-liche Apokryphen* (Tübingen and Leipzig, 1904), I.388ff. They are not given in JAMES, *The Apocryphal New Testament* (Oxford, 1950).

[4] JOHANNES WEISS, *The History of Primitive Christianity*, I.323ff. This is a later work (1910) than his commentary.

(a) **1–8, 10²³–11¹, 16¹⁻⁴, ¹⁰⁻¹⁴.**

(b) **9, 10¹⁻²², 11–15,** the remainder of **16** (**13** being a special addition, on any view).

Let the reader carefully examine these two letters. He will find they are two coherent letters. The difficulties we have noticed are removed; for the passages which are contradictory belong respectively to the two distinct letters. Detailed exegesis will show, moreover, that we have not separated passages which support one another; thus, the two sections introduced by the phrase *panta exestin, all' ou panta sumpherei* (**6¹²** and **10²³**) are found in the same epistle. So the work of the editor is reduced to small dimensions:

(1) He has attached the second letter to the first, probably because its beginning had become illegible.

(2) He has carelessly attached **10²³–11¹** (which had perhaps been detached from the body of the first epistle with the final salutations) to **10¹⁻²²**, which treated of the same question.

(3) He has put together into a single chapter (**16**) the final remarks and the salutations of the two letters.

Thus the sequence of events according to our reconstruction was:

(a) First, the Apostle received a visit from Chloe's people, who told him verbally of the danger of schism in the Church.

(b) In addition, he received through the same people, or perhaps through Sosthenes, a letter from the Corinthians with their questions on problems of marriage and food offered to idols.

(c) All these questions Paul dealt with in his first letter (**1–8** and parts of **10** and **16**). He announced the visit of Timothy who was already, perhaps, on the way, and he promised his own visit in the near future. The reply was perhaps carried by Chloe's people.

(d) Then the Apostle received alarming news from Corinth, where the situation had worsened (questions about the validity of his apostleship, disorder in Church gatherings, denial of the resurrection); it was no doubt Stephanas who, after having taken Paul's part at Corinth, came to Ephesus to acquaint him with his anxieties.

(e) Paul now wrote a second letter, that which we call B, namely **9–15** and parts of **10** and **16**. Throughout it is more vigorous than the first (cf. the tone of **9, 11¹⁶**). No longer does the writer envisage an early visit, but he explains why fresh delays are inevitable. The letter may have been carried to Corinth by Stephanas and his companions, again mentioned in **16**. He hopes that it, too, will arrive before Timothy.

In the form in which the letter called 1 Corinthians is presented to us it is not easy to detect its subdivisions, because of many repetitions and digressions. By and large, five main parts may be distinguished:

(1) Discussions about cliques at Corinth and about true wisdom: **1–4.**

(2) Remonstrances about cases of immorality and litigation: **5** and **6.**

(3) Reply to the letter from the Corinthians concerning marriage and food offered to idols: **7** and **8**.

(4) The opponents of Paul at Corinth and the disorder in Church meetings: **9–14**.

(5) The resurrection of the dead: **15**. Chapter **16** is an appendix containing practical advice and final salutations.

BIBLIOGRAPHICAL COMMENTS

ALL WE CAN do here is to mention some particularly important studies that we recommend, without necessarily agreeing with all their opinions.

In Patristic literature sober and clear comments are to be found, particularly in the works of JOHN CHRYSOSTOM (*MPG*, Vol. LXI) and PSEUDO-AMBROSE, commonly known as AMBROSIASTER (*MPL*, Vol. XVII). With the writers of the Middle Ages there appear the comparatively original commentaries of ATTO DE VERCEIL (tenth century, *MPL*, Vol. CXXXIV), and of HERVÉ DE BOURG-DIEU (twelfth century, *MPL*, Vol. CLXXXI), whilst those of ST THOMAS AQUINAS, ingenious as they may be in collating texts, disappoint the reader who is seeking to keep close to the meaning of each particular passage (*Opera*, Paris, 1876, pub. Vivès, Vols XX and XXI).

The commentaries of LUTHER and of CALVIN are too well known to need commendation. We have cited Luther in the Erlangen Edition, Vol. XXII, and Calvin in the English translation by Pringle, *Commentary on the Epistles of Paul the Apostle to the Corinthians* (2 vols, 1848, 1849); the Latin edition of Calvin's commentary is found in the *Opera Calvini*, Vol. XLIX.

The writings of HUGO GROTIUS, very unusual when dealing with many other New Testament books, are of little interest for our Epistle. On the other hand, BENGEL's *Gnomon* (3rd and posthumous edn, 1773), intelligent as it is concise, retains its value, as does the commentary of WETTSTEIN (*Novum Testamentum Graecum*, II [Amsterdam, 1752]), a veritable thesaurus, which is often used as a source, but seldom checked.

The modern period has seen an excellent French commentary from the pen of FREDERIC GODET (E.Tr. A. CUSIN, *Commentary on St Paul's First Epistle to the Corinthians*, 2 vols [Edinburgh, 1886–7]); in spite of the progress in exegesis made since its time, it remains a classic because of its extreme conscientiousness and its instinctive lucidity.

In German we must pay some attention to the commentary of BACHMANN (1910—in the series *Kommentar zum N.T.*, edited by Th. Zahn), who sometimes unfortunately weakens the spontaneity of the Apostle's thought, no doubt so as not to shock the unconscious modernism of his conservative readers; then we have the commentary of LIETZMANN (*Handbuch zum N.T.* [3rd edn, 1931]), somewhat brief, but interesting from the philological and historical angles; and last and most important, that of JOHANNES WEISS (referred to as J.W.) (1910, 2nd edn unchanged 1925) (in H. A. W. Meyer's series *Kritisch-exegetischer Kommentar*), a very considerable

work and astonishingly objective in the sense that he is always concerned with recovering the Apostle's own meaning, even when he does not think it can be retained in modern theology, yet unfortunately careless over the many references, which often lack precision and accuracy. Many pertinent comments can also be found in the commentary by A. SCHLATTER bearing the title *Paulus, der Bote Jesu* (Stuttgart, 1934), even though this is rather a work of popularization.

Catholic commentaries have all been superseded by a recent French work by Father ALLO (1934—2nd edn 1956), in the collection *Etudes bibliques*, published by Lecoffre-Gabalda.

In English we must primarily mention the works by STANLEY, *The Epistles of St Paul to the Corinthians* (1876) and by A. T. ROBERTSON and A. PLUMMER (*International Critical Commentary* [1891]), which include a wealth of out-of-the-way information. Of those of Dutch scholars we may note BALJON, *De tekst der brieven van Paulus an de Romeinen, de Corinthiers*, etc. (Utrecht, 1884), which contains interesting textual suggestions.

So far as the relationship between Paul's thought and that of the rabbis is concerned, it is regrettable that the excellent Semitist and commentator on the Gospels, ADALBERT MERX, has published nothing on this Epistle. However, Vol. III of the commentary of STRACK–BILLERBECK, *Kommentar zum N.T. aus Talmud u. Midrasch* (Munich, Beck, 1926) renders great assistance if the quotations are checked, as well as the two parts of Vol. IV which contain interesting excursus, e.g. No. 29 ('This world, the days of the Messiah and the future world') and No. 32 ('Resurrection of some or of all the dead ?').

It would be unfair to overlook, apart from commentaries, certain more general works whose study is important for elucidating Pauline thought. By this we mean studies like WILLIAM M. RAMSAY, *St Paul the Traveller and the Roman Citizen* (1920), the great work called *The Beginnings of Christianity* by F. J. FOAKES–JACKSON and KIRSOPP LAKE (5 vols, London, Macmillan, 1920 onwards), the *Introduction au N.T.* by MAURICE GOGUEL (Paris, Leroux, 4 parts, 1922–6), also his *The Birth of Christianity* (Tr. Snape, London, 1953), as well as numerous articles by the same author in various reviews, especially in *RHPR* (*v.* Index in Nos 3 and 4, 1945); ALBERT SCHWEITZER's important study, *Die Mystik des Apostels Paulus* (Tübingen, 1930; E.Tr. *The Mysticism of Paul the Apostle* [London, 1931]), which is a sequel to his *Geschichte der Paulinischen Forschung* (1911; E.Tr. *Paul and his Interpreters* [London, 1912]), which has effectively reacted against the exaggerations of the so-called Religio-historical school chiefly represented by R. REITZENSTEIN (see particularly his *Die hellenistischen Mysterienreligionen* [Leipzig and Berlin, 2nd edn, 1920]).

Then we do not forget the *Dictionnaire de la Bible* by VIGOUROUX (5 vols, [1926–8]) with its supplement (in course of publication since 1928), nor the *Dictionnaire encyclopédique de la Bible* published under the direction of ALEXANDRE WESTPHAL (I [Paris, 1932], II

[Valence, 1935]), which amongst other articles contains those of HENRI CLAVIER on Paul and on the Epistles to the Corinthians. For anything remotely connected with archaeology the work to be consulted is by CABROL (Vol. 3 onwards, CABROL and LECLERCQ), *Dictionnaire d'archéologie chrétienne et de liturgie.*

Other studies dealing with more restricted subjects are cited at the appropriate places.—The edition of the Talmud used is the small edition by GOLDSCHMIDT in 12 vols (Berlin, 1930–6).—When BLASS is cited it always means BLASS–DEBRUNNER, *Grammatik des N.T.-lichen Griechisch* (5th edn, 1921, which is almost identical with the 4th edn of 1913).

Addendum. When the following was completed the fine study by W. D. DAVIES, *Paul and Rabbinic Judaism* (London, 1948) came into our hands. We regret that we have been unable to make use of it, but we call the attention of our readers to it.

Typographical note. The lines in italics at the head of the pages give the translation; the rest is commentary. It is inevitable that part of the commentary on a given page relates occasionally to a portion of the translation already given on a previous page. The reader is asked to take this point into account. [See translator's note at end of Foreword, p. viii.]

ABBREVIATIONS

ATANT	*Abhandlungen zur Theologie des Alten and Neuen Testaments*
ARW	*Archiv für Religionswissenschaft*
BZAW	*Beihefte zur Zeitschrift für die alttestamentliche Wissenschaft*
BZNW	*Beihefte zur Zeitschrift für die neutestamentliche Wissenschaft*
CTAP	*Cahiers théologiques de l'actualité protestante*
CSEL	*Corpus Scriptorum Ecclesiasticorum Latinorum*
DACL	*Dictionnaire d'archéologie chrétienne et de liturgie*
HDB	*Hastings Dictionary of the Bible*
DEB	*Dictionnaire encyclopédique de la Bible*
DTC	*Dictionnaire de théologie catholique*
EB	*Encyclopaedia Biblica*
EHPR	*Etudes d'histoire et de philosophie religieuses* (Strasbourg)
EJ	*Encylopaedia Judaïca*
ERE	*Encyclopaedia of Religion and Ethics*
ETR	*Etudes théologiques et religieuses* (Montpellier)
ET	*Expository Times*
GCS	*Die griechischen christlichen Schriftsteller der ersten drei Jahrhunderte*
HTR	*Harvard Theological Review*
JBL	*Journal of Biblical Literature*
JR	*Journal of Religion*
JTS	*Journal of Theological Studies*
Jud.	*Judaica*
MPG	*Migne, Patrology, Greek Series*
MPL	*Migne, Patrology, Latin Series*
NKZ	*Neue Kirchliche Zeitschrift*
RAC	*Reallexikon für Antike und Christentum*
RB	*Revue biblique*
RE	*Realenzyklopädie für protestantische Theologie und Kirche* 3rd edn
RGG	*Die Religion in Geschichte und Gegenwart*, 2nd edn
REG	*Revue des études grecques*
REJ	*Revue des études juives*
RHPR	*Revue d'histoire et de philosophie religieuses* (Strasbourg)
RHR	*Revue de l'histoire des religions*
RKAW	*Realenzyklopädie der klassischen Altertumswissenschaften*
RTP	*Revue de théologie et de philosophie* (Lausanne)
SAB	*Sitzungsberichte der Preussischen Akademie der Wissenschaften zu Berlin (phil.-hist. Klasse)*
TB	*Theologische Blätter*
TLZ	*Theologische Literatur-Zeitung*

TR	Theologische Rundschau
TS	Theologische Studien
TSK	Theologische Studien und Kritiken
TWNT	Theologisches Wörterbuch zum Neuen Testament
TZ	Theologische Zeitschrift
TU	Texte und Untersuchungen zur Geschichte der altchristlichen Literatur
ZAW	Zeitschrift für die alttestamentliche Wissenschaft
ZKG	Zeitschrift für Kirchengeschichte
ZNW	Zeitschrift für die neutestamentliche Wissenschaft
ZST	Zeitschrift für systematische Theologie
ZTK	Zeitschrift für Theologie und Kirche

CHAPTER I

(1) *Paul, called to be an apostle of Jesus Christ, through the will of God, and Sosthenes our brother, (2) to the Church of God which is at Corinth, composed of members who are sanctified in Jesus Christ, who are consecrated through being called, and who live in fellowship with all, wherever they may be, who invoke the name of our Lord Jesus Christ, their Lord as well as ours.*

1^{1-2}. (**1¹**) *'klētos'* = 'called' is duplicated by *'dia thelēmatos Theou'* = 'by the will of God',[1] and perhaps the latter should be deleted.

'Apostolos', a translation of the Hebrew שָׁלִיּחַ, = 'one who is sent', i.e. to preach the Gospel.[2] Paul grants this title also (expressly or implicitly) to Peter (**9⁵**, Gal 1¹⁸), James the Lord's brother (Gal 1¹⁹), Andronicus and Junias (Rom 16⁷), Apollos (**4⁶**), Barnabas (**9⁶**), and also to the Twelve (**15⁷**, 2 Cor 11⁵, 12¹¹, Gal 1¹⁷).

On the other hand, it is not given to Timothy, Titus, or to his other fellow-workers. Thus he seems to reserve it for missionaries called directly by Jesus Christ, probably through a vision and not by a human intermediary.[3]

For this reason the expression *'dia thelēmatos Theou'*, if it is retained, must not be thought to imply the existence of apostles called under other conditions. It is added in order to make clear that the sender of the letter is an apostle in the full sense of the word (i.e. one of the original missionaries), and not any sort of evangelist commissioned by a Church. The *'brother'* (i.e. the Christian) Sosthenes, is probably to be identified with the one-time chief of the synagogue mentioned in Acts 18¹⁷. We are ignorant of his precise share in the writing of the letter. For the contents, it does not seem to have been great, since Paul always speaks in the first person singular (in contrast to 1 and 2 Thess). However, Paul apparently dictated at least the first part of the letter (**1–8**) to him, perhaps even the entire letter, with the exception, of course, of **16²¹⁻⁴**, which according to **16²¹** he wrote with his own hand.

1^2. *'Ekklēsia Theou'* = קְהַל יְהוָה, here means the Christian com-

---

[1] Unlike Romans 1¹; cf. 2 Corinthians 1¹. *'Klētos'* is omitted by A, D, E, Cyril (*MPG*, LXXIV, col. 856).

[2] See ANTON FRIDRICHSEN, 'The Apostle and his message', in *Recueil de travaux* (published by the University of Uppsala), No. 3 (1947). Cf. *TWNT*, art. 'Apostolos'.

[3] See the excursus on the Apostolate in our commentary on *La seconde épître de saint Paul aux Corinthiens* (Neuchâtel, 1958).

(3) *Grace to you and peace from God our Father and the Lord Jesus Christ.* (4) *I do not cease to thank God for you because of the grace of God which has been given you in Christ Jesus.* (5) *For you have been enriched in him with all gifts, those of speech and those of knowledge,* (6) *in accordance with the testimony of Christ, which has been effectively presented in your midst.* (7) *This is why no endowment is lacking to you—you who await the revelation of our Lord Jesus Christ.* (8) *He it is who will also strengthen you to the very end, so that you may be without reproach in the Day of our Lord Jesus Christ.* (9) *God is faithful; through whom you have been called into fellowship with his son Jesus Christ our Lord.*

munity in Corinth. But the second part of **1²** (from '*sun pasin*' = 'with all those') stresses its incorporation within the ecumenical Church.

'*Klētois hagiois*' = 'those who are consecrated by being called' seems to be synonymous with '*hēgiasmenois en Iēsou Christō*' = 'those who are sanctified in Jesus Christ'. But there is a shade of difference: '*hēgiasmenois en Iesou Christo*' alludes to the body of Christ, to which the Corinthians belong by baptism, while '*hagios*'[4] lays stress rather on their separation from the world; moreover, neither of the two expressions has a strictly ethical connotation. It is noticeable that '*klētos*' and '*ekklēsia*' are derived from the same root: '*kaleō*'; it is God who calls and who joins together.

'*Hoi epikaloumenoi to onoma*', etc. = 'those who call upon the name', etc., is a circumlocution for 'Christians'; the word '*christianoi*' = 'Christians' is never used by the Apostle, though according to Acts 11²⁶ it may already have been familiar at that time in Antioch.[5]

1¹⁻³. The greeting 'Mercy and peace' was used in Judaism;[6] the Apostle Paul used it, in inverted form, in Galatians 6¹⁶ ('*eirēnē kai eleos*'). Usually he replaces '*eleos*' = 'mercy' by '*charis*' = 'grace', perhaps in order to come closer to the form of the Greek salutation '*Chaire*'. But it goes without saying that from his pen '*charis*' means the grace of God. It precedes the 'peace' of which it is the source.

1⁴⁻⁹. (**1⁴**) '*Peri*' = 'for you' is here synonymous with '*huper*', whilst '*epi*' = 'because of' indicates the reason—cf. 1 Thessalonians 3⁹.

'In Jesus Christ' not only means that grace is granted to believers through the intermediary of Jesus Christ, but is a reminder that this grace becomes effective through intimate communion with the risen

---

[4] Cf. Latin '*sacer*', which recalls '*secerno*', 'to separate'.
[5] On the various names for the Christians in Acts see Note 30 in Additional Notes, Vol. V of *The Beginnings of Christianity*, JACKSON AND LAKE.
[6] See Syriac Apocalypse of Baruch, 78.2; KAUTZSCH, *Pseudepigraphen des A.T.* (Tübingen, 1900), CHARLES, *Apocrypha and Pseudepigrapha of the O.T.* (Oxford, 1913), II.521.

Christ. Compare with the frequent expression 'to be in Jesus Christ', which is often used for belonging to His mystical body.[7]

1[5] explains the effect of grace upon the Corinthians and their two main endowments, namely their preaching gift (perhaps already we have a passing reference to the phenomena of glossolaly, cf. 12–14) and their receptivity to the teaching of the apostles. But the verse is particularly important by what it leaves unsaid: there is no reference to moral progress or to genuinely serious devotion—and with reason.

1[6]. 'kathōs' is difficult to translate; the point at issue is that the preaching of the Gospel was the cause of the Spirit's action, but there is also a reminder that the fruits of the Spirit will only be genuine when the Corinthians conform to the Gospel. 'Ebebaiōthē' cannot mean 'to strengthen, to establish with difficulty'. It was by the witness of the apostles that the Gospel was firmly established. This is a somewhat optimistic view, intended to encourage the healthy elements of the Church and to admonish the others. This polite way of reminding the Corinthians of what they ought to be is particularly clear in the next verse.

1[7]. Full endowment with all charismatic gifts is obviously most desirable, but not yet fully attained. 'Those who await . . .' is again a way of designating 'Christians'.[8] 'Revelation' ('apokalupsis') means the appearance of the Lord in all His glory. In the same way the Apostle speaks (Rom 8[19]) of the 'apocalypse' of the sons of God at the end of time, i.e. at the time when they will be raised up or transfigured.

1[8]. The prayer to the Lord to make the Corinthians Christians without reproach, worthy of receiving Him, is not superfluous in view of the moral condition of the Church. In 10 the Apostle reminds them again, expressly, that salvation may be lost.—'The Day of the Lord' ('hēmera kuriou') is a translation of the Hebrew יוֹם יְהֹוָה, a frequently used term of Jewish prophecy and apocalyptic.[9] It refers to the day of Divine judgement.[10] Moreover, as always with Paul, 'kurios' certainly means Jesus Christ.

---

[7] Cf. DEISSMANN, *Die N.T.-liche Formel in Christo Jesu* (1893); E. WEBER, '*Die Formel in Christo Jesu u.d. paulin. Christusmystik*', *NKZ*, XXXI(1920).213–60; A. SCHWEITZER, *The Mysticism of Paul the Apostle* (E.Tr., 1931), pp. 119–30.

[8] On the importance of this expectation in the religious life of the early Christians see G. BALDENSPERGER, '*Trois études sur le christianisme primitif*', *RHPR* (1939), pp. 195–222.

[9] The classic first reference is Amos 5[18].

[10] Cf. the German expression: '*Gerichtstag*'. On what this judgement might mean for the Christian, see below, 3[15].

(10) *But I beg you, brothers, by the name of our Lord Jesus Christ, all to be in accord, and not to tolerate cleavages in your midst, but be in harmony in one spirit and in one judgment.*

(11) *Indeed, it has been reported to me by Chloe's people that there are disputes amongst you.*

(12) *Now I say this, because each of you speaks thus: 'I am for Paul', or 'I am for Apollos' or 'I am for Cephas', (but I am for Christ).* (13) *Is Christ divided? Or is it Paul who has been crucified for you? Or was it in the name of Paul that you have been baptized?*

1⁹. 'Faithful' (*'pistos'*) recalls that God fulfils His promises. Here it is a matter of the promises concerning the entrance of Christians into the Kingdom. They are not unconditional, in so far as addressed to the individual; yet God does not abandon His Church. *'Di' hou'* = 'through whom' is surprising; *'huph' hou'* would be expected. But God is not only the author of salvation, He also prepares the way to it.

1¹⁰. 'I beg you' (*'parakalō'*). The Vulgate translates by *'obsecro'* ('I intreat you'), which is perhaps a little too strong. But it is wise to remember that effective power was attributed to the name of Jesus. By invoking this name the apostles healed the sick[11] and baptized converts,[12] and by it the Father was to be addressed in prayer.[13] *'Schismata'* means 'fissures'. So it is not a quesion of groups separated from the Church, but of cliques within the local community. The expression is not quite synonymous with *'haireseis'* = 'divisions, heresies', a term which stresses peculiar teachings. It is rather a matter of groups gathering round particular people. The terms 'spirit' (*'nous'*) and 'judgement' (*'gnōmē'*) must not be taken with too much of an intellectualist meaning: what is in mind are dispositions of spirit, which should be harmonized (*'katartizō'*).

1¹¹. Chloe is a nickname of the goddess Demeter, often given to slaves.[14] Here a free person is meant, since she has others in her service. Some or all of these were probably Christians and they had the opportunity to come to Ephesus. We do not know whether they belonged to the Corinthian community or had merely passed through the place.

1¹²⁻¹³. (1¹²) John Chrysostom,[15] whilst admitting the existence of parties at Corinth, does not think they would have dared to claim association with Paul, Apollos, Cephas or Christ. The Apostle may

[11] Mark 9³⁸, 16¹⁷, Luke 9⁴⁹, 10¹⁷, Acts 4¹⁰,¹², 16¹⁸, 2 Thessalonians 3⁶.
[12] Acts 2³⁸, 10⁴⁸.
[13] John 14¹³⁻¹⁴, 15¹⁶, 16²⁴⁻⁶. The classic work on this point is by HEITMÜLLER, *Im Namen Jesu* (1903).
[14] Cf. HORACE, *Odes*, III.IX.9.
[15] *MPG* LXI, col. 23.

have invented this situation to show where they were in danger of going, when the spirit of division was rife in a community. It seems hard to support this view; for there is nothing to suggest that the Apostle is speaking of what might be or of what is not actual. So we must examine the four parties as they are depicted by the author.

(1) *The Paul party* was perhaps made up of Christians who had been converted by the Apostle's preaching, as told in Acts 18.

(2) *The Apollos party* preferred this apostle to Paul, no doubt because of his great eloquence. The Acts of the Apostles in fact calls him a fine preacher (*'anēr logios'*), and adds further that he was 'well-versed in the Scriptures' (i.e. in O.T. exegesis; cf. Acts 18²⁴). The same passage (18²⁴⁻⁸) gives some curious information about his past: he was a Jew of Alexandria, who had received the 'baptism of John the Baptist' and who already knew something of the life and work of Jesus (*'ta peri tou Iēsou'*), but who still had to be instructed in Christian doctrine by Aquila and Priscilla whom he met at Ephesus (cf. Acts 18¹⁻²). Some other disciples of John the Baptist were also to be found in that city (Acts 19¹⁻⁷). Perhaps the Apollos party was composed of people baptized by him (cf. 1¹⁷). Since the Apostle Paul always speaks of Apollos with much esteem and affection, we may assume that he himself did not hold with this cleavage.

(3) *The Peter party*. The text has 'Cephas' (as 3²², 9⁵, 15⁵, Gal 1¹⁸, 2⁹,¹¹), which is only a rendering of the Aramaic word *'Kepha'*, the Greek translation of which would be *'Petros'*. There can be no doubt about the identification of this Cephas with Simon Peter the apostle. However, as we know nothing about a visit of Peter to Corinth,[16] this party must have been made up of Jewish Christians from Palestine, who had perhaps been baptized by Peter (cf. 1¹⁷).

(4) *The Christ party*. This is one which has most perplexed scholars. Are we to suppose that there may have been at Corinth a considerable number of Christians who had known Christ 'in the flesh' and had been converted by Him, or, later, by James His brother? Or, on the other hand, are we to think of spiritualistic gnostics who recognized no authority apart from the Spirit of Christ?[17] But the chief difficulty is of a logical nature. The Apostle seems to be reproaching the Corinthians for using the names of Paul, Cephas and Apollos, and not Christ, in whose name they had been baptized. Thus he should have presented those who were 'for Christ' as the model and advised

---

[16] See M. GOGUEL, *RHPR*, XXIV(1934).461–500.
[17] An opinion supported by W. LÜTGERT, *'Die Freiheitspredigt und Schwarmgeister in Korinth'* (in: *Beiträge zur Förderung Christlicher Theologie*, XII.3 [Gütersloh, 1908]), and by ALLO. But although it may be easy to prove that a spiritualistic party existed, it is hard to establish its identity with the 'Christ party'.

(14) *I thank God that I have baptized no one, except Crispus and Gaius*; (15) *so that no one can allege that you have been baptized into my name.* (16) *I baptized also the family of Stephanas. Apart from*

the others to join this party.[18] But in fact he judges these as severely as the others, treating all the parties alike.

Perdelwitz[19] has made an ingenious conjecture: he would read 'Crispus' ('*krispos*') for 'Christ' ('*christos*'). The confusion would have been easier from the similarity of the names when written in uncials, which were the only characters used in the most ancient manuscripts. Now Crispus was a Corinthian Jew, the chief of the synagogue, who was converted and baptized by Paul (1[14], Acts 18[8]). It is possible that he played an important part in the Church; but he has never been looked upon as an apostle, so that one might be surprised at seeing him figure alongside Paul, Peter and Apollos (cf. the casual reference to Crispus in 1[14]). We would prefer to suppose that a copyist has brought into the text the gloss by a Christian (perhaps even by Sosthenes) who was angered by these schisms and could not help exclaiming: 'As for me, I am for Christ.' Otherwise, if the text is held authentic, the interpretation by von Dobschütz[20] must be accepted, which sees the phrase as a kind of parenthesis expressing the opinion of the writer of the letter. This is not impossible, although the opposition between his attitude and that of the others should have been expressed more clearly in the construction of the phrase: e.g. by writing 'but I myself say . . .'

1[13], by its rhetorical questions, is a reminder that Christ alone is the head of the Church. 'His object', says Calvin, 'is to maintain Christ's exclusive authority in the Church, so that we may all exercise dependence upon him, that he alone may be recognized among us as Lord and Master, and that the name of no individual be set in opposition to his.'[21]

When we think about these truths it is hard not to be astonished that Christians, familiar with this epistle, have thought it well to accept the name of 'Dominicans' or 'Franciscans', 'Lutherans', 'Calvinists', or 'Wesleyans'.

1[14-17]. (1[14]) *'Crispus'*, see 1[12]. Gaius is probably the same person as

---

[18] This is what some commentators have fancied they read in the text. ATTO DE VERCEIL (*MPL* CXXXIV, col. 296 B): *ostendit etiam illos solummodo in fide perseverasse, qui se non ullius hominis, sed Christi discipulos dicebant, quos et superius laudat.* (Copied almost word for word from AMBROSIASTER, *v. MPL* XVII, col. 186 D). Unfortunately this praise is never given by Paul. CALVIN (*Commentary on the Epistles of Paul to the Corinthians*, I.67) also thought that those who 'retained Christ as their Master' were 'in a sounder condition than the others'. But Paul does not say this.

[19] *TSK* (1911), pp. 180–204.

[20] *Die urchristlichen Gemeinden* (Leipzig, 1902), p. 58.

[21] Comm. N.T., E. Tr. I.66.

that, I do not know that I baptized anyone else. (17) *For Christ did not send me to baptize, but to proclaim the Gospel, and that without using the eloquence of philosophy, for fear that the cross of Christ should be deprived of its efficacy.*

mentioned in Romans 16[23] as the host of Paul and of 'the whole Church'. The fact of his being referred to by his *praenomen* alone may indicate that he was a freed slave.

1[16]. Stephenas is mentioned again in 16[15,17]. Acts does not speak of him.

The argument of 1[14–17] implies that many of the Corinthians believed there was a kind of mystic relationship between the baptizer and the baptized. Such a belief is not surprising because in many of the mystery religions[22] the initiating individual was called the father of the initiate. It is true that in these cults the 'father' was also the instructor of the initiated. But since in the early Christian Churches instruction was generally given in common, it is understandable that the idea of mystic parentage should attach itself especially to baptism, which was more often administered individually.[23]

Now Paul is glad that he has baptized only very few people at Corinth, thereby removing every appearance of justification for such a superstitious attachment to his person. Yet it was not from fear of such misunderstanding that, in general, he abstained from baptizing; it was because this was not his vocation. This separation of the charism of preaching from that of the administration of baptism may astonish us, for Matthew 28[19–20] seems to equip each disciple with the power to preach and to baptize. But supposing that this formula goes back to Jesus Himself (which is not proved) and that Paul knew of it (which is even more doubtful), he may have interpreted it as the statement of a number of charismatic endowments which need not be united in the same individual, in accordance with his discussion about the diversity of gifts. In any case, we must accept as a fact this separation of ministries in the Pauline Churches. It goes without saying that there was nothing absolute about it, and it is equally obvious that the stress upon the Apostle Paul's entire devotion to the ministry of the Word does not imply any shadow of disrespect for other gifts (*v.* 11) nor any indifference about Christian baptism (*v.* Rom 6).

1[17] provides the transition to the following section. It reminds us that the Apostle, after his check at Athens (where he had adopted the

[22] Particularly in the case of the cult of Isis, the Phrygian mystery religions, the cult of Mithras and of some Hypistarians, according to REITZENSTEIN, *Hellenistische Mysterienreligionen* (2nd edn, Leipzig and Berlin, 1920), pp. 27ff.

[23] We know that in the Catholic Church the idea of mystic parentage attaches even to the relationship of godfather and godmother with their godchild, so that this association presents an obstacle to marriage (*Tridentinum Sessio* 24, *Decretum de Reformatione Matrimonii,* Ch. 2).

(18) *For instruction about the cross is foolishness to those who are going towards destruction; but to us who are on the way of salvation it is the manifestation of the power of God.* (19) *For it is written:*

> '*I will destroy the philosophy of the philosophers, and I will nullify the reason of men of understanding*'.

(20) *Where is the philosopher? where is the rabbi? where is the sophist of this present world? Has not God made foolish this world's wisdom?*

(21) *For the world did not recognize God by the divine wisdom (displayed in creation) through the instrumentality of philosophy. Hence God determined to save those who became believers through the foolishness of the preaching (about the cross).* (22) *For Jews, on the one hand, demand miracles, and Greeks, for their part, seek for philosophy;* (23) *but we ourselves preach Christ crucified, which is a scandal to Jews and folly to pagans,* (24) *but which for us the elect, both Jews and Greeks, is indeed Christ—God's power and God's wisdom.* (25) *Truly, the foolishness which comes from God is wiser than men, and the weakness of God is stronger than men.*

language of philosophy, according to Acts 17), had decided to change his method in evangelizing the Corinthians: he had spoken bluntly and directly of the Cross of Christ.

1^{18-25}. '*Logos*' means not only 'word', but also 'instruction'. It is highly characteristic of Paul's soteriology that he does not speak of 'the saved' (which would be '*sesōsmenoi*'), but of those who are being saved ('*sōzomenoi*'). Salvation is not yet gained in its totality, in so far as the world of the resurrection, also called the 'future age', has not appeared. Whilst waiting for it, the elect are on the way to the Kingdom of God, just as the rest of men go towards destruction ('*hoi apollumenoi*'). Note also that in 1^{21} it is a question of those who are '*pisteuontes*' and not of the '*pisteusantes*' (i.e. of those who make a faith-decision and not of those who have already become 'believers', the decision being made when a man is touched by the preaching).

1^{19}. The quotation from Isaiah 29^{14} does not correspond exactly to the text of the LXX, either because the Apostle quotes from memory, or because he has used another translation, as in 14^{21}. In agreement with the parallelism of members in Hebrew poetry, the terms '*sophoi*' (philosophers) and '*sunetoi*' (understanding men) are almost synonyms. Neither the one nor the other has a pejorative sense in itself, as Calvin has rightly stressed: 'The right order of things was assuredly this, that man, contemplating the wisdom of God in his works, by the light of the understanding furnished him by nature, might arrive

at an acquaintance with him.'[24] It is easier to draw a distinction between '*sophos*', '*grammateus*' and '*sunzētētēs*' in **1²⁰**. The first is the Greek wise man, i.e. the philosopher; the second, the Jewish scholar or doctor of the Law; the third, the only one to have a pejorative sense, is a 'disputer', i.e. a sophist, whether Greek or Jewish. But account must also be taken of the article by Eric Peterson,[25] who draws attention to the striking resemblance between this Pauline passage and certain verses in Baruch 3, to be found in Greek in the LXX.[26] Peterson, however, does not believe that St Paul was directly dependent upon Baruch, but, following the researches of H. St J. Thackeray[27] he thinks that both Paul and Baruch were using a homiletical fragment based on Jeremiah 8¹³–9²⁴, which was a passage expounded, so it seems, on the Day of Atonement. Like Baruch, Paul may have been directing his polemic against the wisdom of the great ones of this world. Yet it would seem that he was also aiming his diatribe at Greek philosophers.

But Peterson goes on to draw a curious conclusion from his enquiry. Because Baruch is familiar with a wisdom taught and practised by the worldly-wise, Peterson thinks that **2⁸** cannot refer to supernatural beings. Yet, even supposing that Paul had followed Baruch on this point, our fourth argument in favour of the supernaturalistic explanation would lose none of its weight (though the '*archontes tōn ethnōn*' could be angels) and the other arguments also would seem to retain their value.

In classical Greek the verb '*mōrainō*' has an intransitive sense ('be silly', 'foolish'). But already the LXX had given it the sense of a Hebrew Hiphil (= 'drive mad', see particularly Isa 19¹¹). 'This age' ('*ho aiōn houtos*') is a basic concept of Jewish apocalyptic. It means our present world, in opposition to the future world ('*ho aiōn mellōn*', in Hebrew הַזֶּה הָעוֹלָם, as over against הַבָּא הָעוֹלָם).

While sin and corruption reign in the former, the latter will involve the absolute reign of God and the incorruptibility of the elect. This chronological juxtaposition of two 'aeons' has nothing in common with the superimposition, dear to the Greeks, of two co-existent

---

[24] Comm. N.T. E. Tr., I.84.

[25] '*1 Korinther 1.18 und die Thematik des jüdischen Busstages*' (*Biblica*, XXXII [1951].97ff).

[26] The expression '*sunzētētēs tou aiōnos toutou*' (1²⁰) recalls '*ekzētountes tēn sunesin epi tēs gēs*' ('those who seek for understanding on the earth'—Baruch 3²³). Similarly, the '*archontes tōn ethnōn*' of Baruch 3¹⁶ remind us of the '*archontes tou aiōnos toutou*' in 2⁸. The use of the verb '*exelexato*' (and the context) in 1²⁷ is reminiscent of Baruch 3²⁷, '*ou toutous exelexato*'. Finally, the exclamation '*pou sophos; pou grammateus*' is not without parallel in the expression in Baruch 3¹⁴, '*pou estin phronēsis, pou estin ischus*', where '*ischus*' corresponds somewhat with '*dunamis*' in 1²⁴.

[27] *The Septuagint and Jewish Worship* (The Schweich Lectures, 1920; 2nd edn, London, 1923), pp. 95ff.

worlds, namely the eternal world of Ideas and the temporal world
here below. Thus every attempt to interpret the biblical pattern of
the two worlds (present and future) in the light of the opposition
between time and eternity, as theologians influenced by Kant sometimes suggest to us, is a betrayal of biblical theology.[28] The expression
'the world' used at the end of **1²⁰** is synonymous with 'this world' or
'this age'. The 'divine Wisdom' which should have enabled the
philosophers to know God, is that inscribed in created things
according to Romans 1¹⁹⁻²⁰ (cf. Ecclus 1¹⁹, Wis 7 and 8, and Prov 8³⁰).
But from whence does the Apostle derive the notion that in principle
men were capable of attaining to God by contemplation of the
world? Is he alluding to ancient philosophers (Plato? Aristotle?)
who might have been less foolish than their contemporaries to be
met in Athens or Tarsus (Epicureans, Stoics)? But there is no indication that the condemnation of empirical philosophy is not general,
or even that Paul knew about the wise men of earlier Greece. Certainly it was the reading of the Old Testament (cf. e.g. the famous
Psalm 18 [Hebrew 19] which inspired this. In any case, at the
present time, men needed a new revelation, because they could not
read the book of nature. This second revelation was made primarily
through the focal event of Christ's crucifixion—which must not,
however, be separated from His resurrection, as we are shown in **15**.

1²¹. Since philosophy does not understand these events, it is declared
obsolete and at the same time it becomes stupid and futile. It is true
enough that philosophy, in its turn, passes the same condemnatory
judgement upon the manifestation of the divine Wisdom in Christ;
but the Christian has experience of the supernatural power released
by the Cross, and this settles the question on the practical level.

1²²⁻⁴. Why were the Greeks, or at least their philosophers, unable
to believe in Christ crucified? The polemic of a Celsus or Porphyry[29]
shows us why: a God ignominiously condemned and executed could
not be taken seriously, and the fact that there was no cult devoted
to Prometheus (the sole prefiguration of Christ in Greek religion) is
most significant. For the Jews, on their side, a crucified Messiah was
an insult to their messianic hopes, which were essentially political.

[28] See J. Héring, *Le Royaume de Dieu selon Jésus et Paul* (Paris, 1937; 2nd
edn [phototype], Neuchâtel, 1959). We may be allowed to quote some lines: 'It
is not because God is infinite and man finite, that God had to send his Son . . .
it is because God is Holy and man a sinner. It is not because God dwells in
Eternity, while the world is in time, that God does not exercise effective dominion
over the world; it is because the world lives aimlessly in a state of corruption and
revolt. Thus, one must not introduce alien metaphysical notions. . . . Indeed,
man's eschatological hope, according to the Apostle, contains no hint of the
suppression of an opposition between the finite and the infinite' (loc. cit.). Cf.
O. Cullmann, *Christ and Time*, (Tr. Filson, London, 1951).

[29] Cf. Labriolle, *La réaction païenne, Etude sur la polémique antichrétienne du
Iᵉʳ au VIᵉ siècle* (Paris, 1934).

A suffering Messiah was completely unknown at that period. It was
only in the third century of our era that, under the influence of
Christianity, some traces of such a conception appear in Judaism,
and we have to come down to the period of Charlemagne to find it
in a more developed form. It must be noted carefully that no Jew of
Paul's time would have entertained the idea of identifying the Man
of Sorrows in Isaiah 53 with the Messiah.[30]

1²⁵. In this verse, which makes transition to the following passage,
'the foolishness of God' ('*to mōron tou Theou*') naturally means 'the
so-called foolishness of God'. The same is true of the 'weakness'.

General note on **1¹⁸⁻²⁵**.

Matters are complicated somewhat by the fact that not only does
the Apostle distinguish two forms of wisdom, the divine and the
human, but that each of them in turn appears in a favourable light,
according to the standpoint—and the time—from which they are
viewed. The relationships involved are certainly not simple; and,
moreover, the divine wisdom is manifested successively in two
entirely different ways.

We may clarify the situation thus: human wisdom (philosophy)
is not, in principle, a futility. We have just said that it was equipped
for recognizing God in nature. But it fell short in the task. Therefore
God has degraded it. The first manifestation of divine wisdom, that
in nature, is also superseded, and to a certain extent pushed into the
background, by the Cross, which reveals something more profound
about the divine nature, namely God's love for men and His plan
for delivering them from the powers of evil.[31]

The opposition between human and divine wisdom (and also the
two successive manifestions of divine wisdom) is somewhat reminiscent of the gnostic doctrines of Valentinus, who opposed a superior
wisdom to an inferior wisdom. But where Valentinus used personification, Paul was content to speak of powers and of qualities.
Even the personification of 'Sophia'—and of folly—in what is usually
called the Jewish Wisdom literature (chiefly Proverbs, Wisdom of
Solomon, Ecclesiasticus) is avoided in Paul's usage which is as sober
as it is vigorous. Only in Christ does Wisdom become personified
(**1²⁴ end,³⁰**). The opposition between foolishness and Wisdom, which
change places for the believer, is taken up again in 3¹⁹ᶠᶠ.

The expression '*Theou sophia*' at the end of **1²⁴** signifies literally
'Theosophy'; but such a translation is avoided because it often
suggests doctrines which are non-Christian. **1²⁶⁻³¹** show the truth of
the affirmations in **1²⁵** by referring to the peculiar composition of the

---

[30] On this subject see our article, '*Messie juif et Messie chrétien*', in *RHPR*
(1938) Nos 5–6, with the literature there cited.

[31] See Colossians 2¹⁴⁻¹⁵, which is the best introduction to the Apostle's
soteriology.

*(26) For consider your calling as Christians, my brothers, and you
will see that among you there are not many wise according to the
flesh, not many men of power, not many of noble birth. (27) But God
chose what is foolish in the world's sight to confound the wise, and
what is feeble in the world to shame what is strong; (28) God chose
what is base and despised in the world, he chose what does not exist
to bring to nothing what does exist, (29) so that no creature should
boast before God.*

Corinthian Church. It consisted almost entirely of uncultured
people.

1^{26-9}. In this passage we twice encounter the term *'sarx'* = 'flesh',
in different senses. The first time (*'sophoi kata sarka'*, 1^{26}) it is synonymous with *'kosmos'* ('world'). What is wise according to 'the flesh' is
esteemed by the world, which itself lacks the divine wisdom. On the
second occasion (1^{29} ᵉⁿᵈ, *'hopōs mē kauchēsētai pasa sarx'*) the term
is synonymous with 'creature', as often in the LXX (= Hebrew
בָּשָׂר).[32]

The genitive *'tou kosmou'* ($1^{27,28}$) is grammatically a possessive
genitive. But it implies the idea of 'according to the world's judgement'. The opposition between *'ta mē onta'* ('what does not exist,
what is of no consequence') and *'ta onta'* ('what exists') is reminiscent of Plato's terminology, but it is doubtful whether the Apostle
knew this.[33] In any case, the meaning of the passage is clear. Divine
wisdom chooses men according to other categories and standards of
value than the world. Hence, no one can vaunt himself that he has
been chosen for qualities esteemed by men, like erudition, social
influence or position. This argument is strongly reminiscent of a
verse in the Book of Jeremiah: 'Let not the wise man glory in his
wisdom, neither let the mighty man glory in his might, let not the
rich man glory in his riches' (9^{22} LXX; 9^{23} Hebrew).

So the preaching of the Cross has won 'simple' people, whilst the
more philosophical discussion held at Athens had not even won the
erudite.[34] It is to be observed that again the author writes in rhythmical prose: he uses anaphora in 1^{26} (the threefold repetition of
'ou polloi') like the popular Greek orators, whom he does not seem
to despise as did the genuine philosophers[35]—at least so far as their
style is concerned; 1^{27} is constructed in the manner of Hebrew poetry
(parallelism of members), and to some extent also 1^{28}.

[32] See Genesis $6^{12,17,19}$, $7^{15,16,21}$, $8^{17,21}$, Isaiah $40^{5,6}$, and many other texts.
[33] The LXX uses the term *'mataioi'* for certain people; but the meaning is not
the same as here.
[34] As J. WEISS remarks, this passage reminds us a little of the famous prayer of
Jesus in Matthew 11^{25}, only the Apostle brings out the privilege of the *'mē onta'*.
[35] See below on 7^{17-18}. On the other hand, we have also long known that the
'gnosticism' of the scholars had a counterpart in popular gnosis, which was no
less arrogant. So it must not surprise us to find so many 'gnostics' among the
ordinary folk at Corinth.

(30) *Thanks to Him you have your existence in Christ Jesus. It is he who has become for us wisdom coming from God, as well as justification, sanctification and redemption, (31) so that, as the Scriptures say, 'let him who boasts, boast in the Lord'.*

1^{29}, in which this flight of oratory culminates, even contains a flagrant Hebraism (frequent also in the LXX): '*mē . . . pasa*' = לֹא כֹּל ('that every creature should not vaunt itself'); in classical Greek '*hopōs mēdemia*' or '*mēpote tis*' ('so that no creature should boast').

1^{30-1}. These verses give the positive counterpart to the preceding statements, and they end with a free citation of Jeremiah 9^{23} (9^{24}).

To be 'in Christ', a favourite expression of the Apostle's, does not simply mean a kind of community of ideas or of feelings with Christ, but refers to a new form of existence, as we can see here; one which 2 Corinthians 5^{17} will express in a classic phrase: 'If any man is in Christ, etc. . . .'[36] The use of the preposition '*en*' ('in') is justified by the real belonging of the Christian to the body of Christ. The equivalence of this ontological truth in the realm of psychology is expressed by the phrase: 'Christ in me, in us, in you'. Christ is present in the whole body of Christians, as well as in each member thereof.[37]

We already know from 1^{24} that Christ incarnates the divine Wisdom (see also Col 1^{15-20}). But, going beyond the immediate subject which he set out to expound, the Apostle uses the opportunity to summarize, in one powerful sentence of testimony, the whole work of Christ:

(1) He justifies us ('*dikaiosunē*')—that is, He wipes out our past sins (*v.* Rom 3 and 4);

(2) He sanctifies us ('*hagiasmos*') by effective attachment to Himself from now on (cf. 2 Thess 2^{13}, 1 Pet 1^2);

(3) He redeems us ('*apolutrōsis*') from the powers of darkness, of which we had become slaves, to make us citizens of the future Kingdom of God (Rom $6^{17,20}$, Col 1^{13}, 2^{14}).

This form of expression ('Christ was made unto us wisdom from God', etc.) may be compared with the famous declarations of the Johannine Logos ('I am the Resurrection and the Life', etc.).

[36] See our Commentary on Second Corinthians *ad locum*; also F. NEUGEBAUER, '*Das Paulinische in Christo*', in *New Testament Studies* (January 1958), pp. 124–38.
[37] See ALBERT SCHWEITZER, *Mysticism of Paul the Apostle*, especially pp. 122–30.

CHAPTER II

(1) *Also, when I came to you, brothers, I did not come to announce to you the divine mystery with the prestige of rhetoric or philosophy.* (2) *For I had decided to know nothing while I was among you except Jesus Christ, or to be exact—Jesus Christ crucified.* (3) *Also I was present with you in a condition of great weakness, fear and trembling;* (4) *and my discussions and preaching were not aimed at philosophical persuasion but at a demonstration of the power of the Spirit,* (5) *so that your faith should not rest upon human philosophy, but upon the power of God.*

2^{1-5}. The anaphora '*kagō—kagō*', at the beginning of 2^1 and 2^3, may be observed, which marks an affectionate style. '*Huperochē*' (2^1) literally means 'a prominent point, eminence'; the translation 'prestige' by the Synodale Version is excellent.—'*Logos*' and '*Sophia*' ('word' and 'wisdom') refer respectively to the arts of the rhetorician and philosopher, which the Apostle had decided to relinquish in order to preach simply the Cross of Christ (cf. 1^{17}).—In a general sense, the impression he made was not due to his personal qualities. He seems to have been rather of a retiring nature, perhaps also hampered by his affliction (2 Cor 10^{10}), and by his unimpressive appearance, which the Acts of Paul and Thecla §3 describe thus: 'A man little of stature, thin-haired upon the head, crooked in the legs, of good state of body, with eyebrows joining, and nose somewhat hooked, full of grace'[1]—scarcely a flattering portrait and certainly not hagiographic. In any case, this great weakness ('*pollō*' [2^3] must be connected with the three nouns: '*astheneia*', '*phobos*', '*tromos*' = 'weakness', 'fear', 'trembling') conforms with what was said in 1^{27}.

If nevertheless the preaching of Paul at Corinth was highly successful that could only have been due to the power of God's Spirit which animated it. '*Pneumatos*' and '*dunameōs*' in 2^4 are subjective genitives indicating the powers which have won the assent of his listeners. Yet it must be observed that 'Spirit' and 'Power' are not two distinct factors (it is a case of '*hen dia duoin*').

The reading '*marturion tou Theou*' = 'the testimony of God' (Nestlé) at the end of 2^1 does not give an acceptable sense. If '*tou Theou*' is an objective genitive, it is scarcely in place, since it was to the Cross of Christ that the Apostle bore witness. Could it be a subjective genitive? In that case we should have to think of God testifying (to whom?) by the crucifixion, which is obscure and hardly

---

[1] M. R. JAMES, *The Apocryphal New Testament* (Oxford, 1924), p. 273.

(6) *Nevertheless, amongst mature Christians we do teach a wisdom, but it is not the wisdom of this age nor of the rulers of this age, who are on the way to destruction;* (7) *on the contrary, we teach a mysterious divine wisdom, which has been hidden until the present time but which already, before the ages, God had destined to our glory.* (8) *None of the rulers of this age knew this wisdom, otherwise they would not have crucified the Lord of glory.*

Pauline. So we have preferred to adopt the reading '*mustērion tou Theou*' = 'the mystery of God'.[2] For the fact of the Cross can be truly spoken of as a mystery of divine Providence (cf. 2^{7-8}, Col 1^{25-9}, 2^2, 4^3, Eph $3^{4,9}$, 6^{19}). It follows also from 4^1 that the Apostle had divine mysteries to administer.

Another difficulty is created by the text which Nestlé accepts for 2^4: the expression '*en peithois sophias logois*' is inadmissible, because it presupposes an adjective '*peithos*', which does not exist. Although this is the reading attested by the most ancient MSS, we prefer '*en peithoi sophias*'[3] (*peithoi* = dative of the noun *peithō* = persuasion). It has the advantage of being correct linguistically, clear, and dependent upon the expression: '*en apodeixei pneumatos*' = 'in demonstration of the Spirit'. From this was derived by a slip in dictation (dittography of a sigma) the reading '*en peithois sophias*', given by F and G. To make this more comprehensible '*peithois*' was taken as an adjective and the substantive '*logois*' was added.[4]

2^{6-7}. What exactly is the wisdom mentioned here? It is certainly not human wisdom. Then it is part of the divine wisdom which is foolishness in the eyes of men. What is involved is a superior stage of Christian teaching, a kind of Christian theosophy ('*theou sophia*', 2^3). As such it was reserved for a Christian élite, just as the philosophy of the time appertained to an élite amongst pagans. There is therefore superimposed here, upon the opposition between pagan and Christian wisdom (in a general sense), an opposition between Christian wisdom (wisdom here in a more restricted sense) and elementary Christian teaching. It is no longer pure and simple teaching of the Cross which is meant, but a more profound mystery (*v.* infra, 2^{7-8}). Notice the use of the verb '*lalein*' = 'speak', which must denote private teaching as against '*kērussein*' = 'preach'.

[2] This was already pointed out by WESTCOTT and HORT and is attested by P 46 (the papyrus is in poor condition, but '*ērion tou Theou*' can be read distinctly), ℵ, A, C, Pesh., Coptic, ANTIOCHUS of Ptolemais (*MPG* LXXXIX, col. 1580 A), AMBROSE (*MPL* XV, col. 1747 B), AUGUSTINE (*MPL* XXXVIII, col. 874), AMBROSIASTER (*MPL* XVII, col. 202 B), and some minuscules.

[3] With BLASS (§47.4, §112, §474.4), following MS 18, ORIGEN *Contra Celsum*, Bk VI, Ch.2 (KOETSCHAU, p. 71), where one group of MSS read '*peithoi*' as *Contra Celsum*, I, Ch. 62 (KOETSCHAU, p. 114), and ATHANASIUS (*MPG* XXVII, col. 477 B), a reading presupposed also by the manuscripts f and g of the Old Latin, as well as by AMBROSIASTER ('*praedicatio mea non in persuasione humanae sapientiae*', *MPL* XVII, col. 193 A).

[4] Other less interesting readings are given by TISCHENDORF, *N.T.Graece*, edn VIII, maior II, p. 465.

Who are the '*teleioi*' = 'the mature'? They are not Christians who have arrived at perfection, for that cannot be reached before the obtaining of 'glory'. But they are Christians who are spiritually adult, as is shown by the contrast to '*nēpioi*' (3^1), i.e. very young children. This idea is clarified by what follows. We may note at once that the term '*teleioi*' is borrowed from the vocabulary of the mystery religions, which, to judge from Philo, were not unknown to the Judaism of the Dispersion.[5] But whilst in the case of these mysteries, baptism *ipso facto* conferred the character of '*teleios*', this is most certainly not so in the Apostle's thought. Furthermore, according to the gnostics, only one who had become a '*teleios*' was saved. For St Paul, on the contrary, salvation in the measure that it is realizable on earth is granted straight away to mere beginners, provided that they have faith and are associated with the body of Christ by baptism and the Eucharist. At the same time, it is certain that any true Christian will aspire to progress and grow towards the ideal of perfection, which implies a deepening of faith and a more profound comprehension of Christian truths.

2^{7-8} gives us a glimpse of this instruction which was reserved for 'adults'.[6] To understand these verses we must first ask who are the 'rulers of this age' ('*hoi archontes tou aiōnos toutou*'). With Origen[7] and Theodore of Mopsuestia[8] and in contradistinction to Chrysostom[9] we think that this expression must be linked with '*archōn tou kosmou toutou*' (Jn 12^{13}, 14^{30}, 16^{11}), where there is no question that supernatural powers are meant. If this is so, there is then here no reference to Pontius Pilate or the Roman emperors, but to powers of the invisible world. This seems to be supported by:

(a) the parallel text of Colossians 2^{15}, where Christ triumphs by the Cross over hostile powers, called '*archai kai exousiai*'; as well

[5] See in particular R. REITZENSTEIN, *Hellenistische Mysterienreligionen* (2nd edn) pp. 191ff, E. BREHIER, *Les idées philosophiques et religieuses de Philon d'Alexandrie* (1919), pp. 242–6, and also GOODENOUGH, *By Light, Light* (New Haven and London, 1935).
For the term '*teleioi*': N. HUGEDÉ, *La métaphore du miroir*, pp. 177–84 (Neuchâtel, 1957).—On '*exousiai*' and '*stoicheia*' see the article by B. N. WAMBACQ, 'Per eum reconciliare . . .' *RB* (1948), pp. 35ff.
[6] That is, we link '*en mustēriō*' with '*sophian*' (as BACHMANN) and not with '*laloumen*' (like J. W.).
[7] *De principiis*, III.3.2 (*MPG* XI, col. 315 AB).
[8] '*Archontas de tou aiōnos toutou legei de tas ponēras dunameis. Ei de houtoi ēgnoēsan, pollō mallon hoi anthropoi di' hōn hoi daimones ton kurion estaurōsan.*' (He calls the evil powers '*archontas*'. If these themselves were ignorant how much more were also the men by the intermediary of whom the demons crucified the Lord.) THEODORE of Mopsuestia is cited from K. STAAB, *Paulus-Kommentare aus der griechischen Kirche*, p. 174 (*N.T.-liche Abhandlungen*, ed. Prof. MEINERTZ, Munster, XV [1933]). The work of STAAB is important, because he makes use of the catenas embodying fragments of lost commentaries.—So far as ORIGEN is concerned, another text is found in *Contra Celsum*, VIII, Ch. 5 (KOETSCHAU II.224).
[9] *MPG* LXI, col. 55.

as by Romans 8[38], where the *'archai'* (along with other supernatural powers) are mentioned as being likely to hinder the work of Redemption;

(*b*) the fact that the Roman Empire was looked upon by the Apostle as a providential and beneficent power (Rom 13[1–7]);

(*c*) possibly also by the use of the verb *'katargein'* (2[6]), which is sometimes a technical astrological term for the nullifying of an astral influence by a superior power;[10]

(*d*) the fact that they diffuse a wisdom, i.e. teaching, which is in no way characteristic of the political powers.

We are concerned, then, with astral powers, directly related to the *'stoicheia'* = 'the elements' of Galatians.[11] There is nothing to show that the Apostle ranked these among the beings which were evil by nature, like the *'daimones'* of 10[20–2] or like Satan or Beliar. All we are told is that they were opposed to the Gospel. But they would not have been, had they possessed divine wisdom. For in such a case, they would have known that it was not in their own interests to crucify the Lord, since his death struck a terrible blow at their rule (Col 2[15]). Some scholars[12] further think that they did not even recognize the Lord, recalling in this connection the gnostic (oriental) myth of a god who deceived the 'devil' by hiding his identity.[13] It is not impossible that this idea is presupposed by our text; but it is not expressed; and, furthermore, we cannot think that the identity of Christ belonged to the teaching reserved only for those Christians who were *'teleioi'*.

Nor is anything said directly about the motive which drove the 'dominions' to kill the Lord.[14] But Romans 8[38] is significant in this connection: these powers felt that Christ threatened their dominion by introducing into the world a force (the love of God) superior to the 'fate' which they controlled. (Belief in the power of the stars over 'this world' was sometimes shared by Christians, but it was thought that their death-knell had sounded.) A measure of parallel with Mandaean religion may be noted, for which the stars, influential as they were in this world, had similarly become powers hostile to true

---

[10] Cf. REITZENSTEIN, *Poimandres* (Leipzig, 1904), p. 353.

[11] The supernatural character of the *'exousiai'* does not prevent them making use of the political powers, without the latter necessarily being conscious of the fact; on this see O. CULLMANN, *Königsherrschaft Christi und Kirche im N.T.*, pp. 44–8 (in *Theologische Studien*, ed. K. BARTH, No. 10, 1941). A French edition of this work appeared as *Cahier Biblique* of '*Foi et Vie*' in 1941.

[12] LIETZMANN, p. 12, ORIGEN, on Matthew 16[8] (LOMMATZSCH, IV.27).

[13] On this see in particular BOUSSET, *Hauptprobleme des Gnosis* (Göttingen, 1907), pp. 258ff, and [S. IGNATIUS, *Ep. to the Ephes*. 19; as well as the *Ascension of Isaiah*, X.11ff (ed. CHARLES [London, 1900], p. 70).

[14] Or, according to LIETZMANN, the unknown, anonymous spoil-sport. For these 'powers' see also the important article by WAMBACQ, '*Per eum reconciliare*', *RB*(1948), pp. 35ff; this writer has well understood the unusual character of these beings.

(9–10a) *It is to us, on the contrary, that God (as Scripture says)
has revealed by the Spirit 'things which the eye has not seen, and the
ear has not heard, and which have not entered into man's consciousness,
but which God has prepared for those who love him'.*

religion.[15] The expression 'Lord of glory' (2[8]), seems to have been
borrowed from the apocalyptic thought of Enoch, in which this
title is given to God (v. *Eth. Enoch*, 22[14], 25[3,7], 27[3,4], 63[2], 75[3]).
'The hidden wisdom' there involves teaching about Christ's
struggle with the opposing powers of the spiritual world. Chapter 15
of this letter shows us another aspect of this teaching, namely its
eschatological side. We need not be too surprised to find the Apostle
lifting the veil, after having treated the Corinthians as '*nēpioi*', 3[1].
In the first place, it is not certain that he has said everything in this
letter; and further, there is perhaps a measure of exaggeration in 3[1]
for pedagogical reasons. 'I am indeed kind to give you this teaching
—really you do not deserve it.'

2[9–10a]. The conjunction '*gar*' (beginning of 2[10]) must be linked with
'*alla*' (begining of 2[9]), '*alla gar*' = 'but on the contrary'. 'Those who
love God' (hardly a Pauline expression, but belonging to the quotation) are opposed to the 'powers' who know nothing of the divine
wisdom. Yet the Christians themselves only understand these
mysteries in so far as the Holy Spirit reveals them to them. The
quotation, which includes 2[9] (except for the introductory words
'*alla kathōs gegraptai*' = 'but as it is written'), is made up of three
lines, the first two stressing the impossibility of attaining the revelation by sensory perception or by imagination ('*non in mentem venerunt*',
Bengel), for to Semites the heart was very often the organ of
thought.[16]
    From what book was this text borrowed? The only canonical
source which could be considered is Isaiah 64[4] (EVV). But it only
presents a slight parallel: 'For from of old men have not heard, nor
perceived by the ear, neither hath the eye seen a God beside thee,
which worketh for him that waiteth for him'.[17] Must we suppose
with Jerome[18] that the Apostle only wished to give here a paraphrase
of the prophetic text? But the word '*gegraptai*' must introduce a
textual quotation.[19] So an apocryphal book has been suggested. In
fact, Origen found the words in the 'Apocalypse of Elijah', a work

---

[15] See CHARLES PUECH, *Le Mandéisme* in: *Histoire générale des religions*, pub.
under the direction of MAXIME GORCE and RAOUL PORTIER (pub. Quillet),
II.67ff(1945).
[16] See KITTEL, *TWNT*, art. '*Kardia*'.
[17] So the Massoretic text; the LXX diverges still farther from our quotation.
[18] On Isaiah 65[4], *MPL* XXIV, col. 622 BC.
[19] The Bab. Talmud, fol. 99a (GOLDSCHMIDT IX.75), gives a vaguely similar
text: 'Apart from thee, O God, no eye has seen what he will do for the one who
hopes in him.'

(10b) *For the Spirit searches out all things, even the deep things of God.* (11) *Indeed, who knows what is in man except the human spirit which is in him?*

(12) *As for us, we have not received the spirit of the world, but the Spirit which comes from God, so that we know the blessings God has granted us.* (13) *We talk of these things, not amongst people instructed in human philosophy, but amongst those who are instructed in the truths of the spirit; we explain spiritual truths to spiritual men.*

(14) *The natural man does not receive the truths which come from the Spirit of God; for they are foolishness to him and he cannot understand them, because they can only be judged spiritually.* (15) *But the spiritual man judges all things, without himself being judged by any one.* (16) *For 'who knows the mind of the Lord, so as to instruct him'?— But as for us, we have the mind of Christ.*

since lost.[20] Jerome[21] knew that tradition, but opposed it as heretical. It is by no means unlikely that the Apostle should quote from an apocryphal apocalypse to support a 'hidden' truth. Does not the Epistle of Jude expressly cite the book known as *Ethiopic Enoch* (part of which is preserved in Greek)? It is true that in the Synoptic Gospels almost nothing but the Law and the Prophets—and, when necessary, the Psalms (*v.* Lk 24[44])—are quoted as canonical. But that only shows that Palestinian Jews held narrower views on this point than Jews of the Dispersion. Moreover, it is known that the Apostle, who was profoundly influenced by Jewish apocalyptic, was more than once inspired by non-canonical tradition, though he rarely quotes from it as *Scripture* (*v.* infra 10[11]). Marc Philonenko has recently drawn attention[22] to a passage of Pseudo-Philo[23] in which it is said: '*Ex eo quod oculus non vidit nec auris audivit, et in cor hominis non ascendit.*' . . . The textual similarity is striking, but it throws no light on the origin of the phrase.

2[10b–16]. This most important passage, which contains the great charter for Christian theologians, presents several grammatical difficulties which we must first resolve.

(1) At the beginning of 2[11] the Nestlé text reads: '*Tis gar oiden anthrōpōn ta tou anthrōpou*', etc. = 'Who among men knows what is in man?' But it is not a matter of distinguishing one man from amongst others, but one part of the man himself, namely his spirit. The difficulty can be resolved if '*anthrōpōn*' is deleted.[24] It is true that

[20] See *MPG* XIII, col. 1769C: '*In nullo enim regulari libro hoc printum invenitis nisi in secretis Eliae prophetae.*'
[21] *MPL* XXII, col. 576.
[22] *TZ* (Bâle) 'Year 15' (1959), pp. 51–2.
[23] *Liber Antiquitatum Biblicarum*, 26.13. The passage is certainly later than the time of Paul. It is to be found in *Publications in Mediaeval Studies*, Vol. X (Indiana, 1949), by GUIDO KISCH (*v.* p. 188).
[24] With A,17, Ethiop. and Cyril (*MPG* LXXIV, col. 301 A). (P 46 is defective.)

the masculine '*tis*' still needs explanation, but we can suppose that the human spirit is personified by analogy with the Spirit of God.

(2) What exactly is meant by 2[13a]: '*En didaktois anthrōpinēs sophias logois?*' '*didaktos*' = 'he who' (or 'what') 'has been taught'. The usual translation is: 'In words taught by human wisdom.' But the genitive '*sophias*' can only have this sense (even if we stretch a point) if '*didaktos*' were a noun. Then with Blass (§183) we should have to delete the word '*logois*', introduced by a misunderstanding (rather like 2[4]). If we do not resort to this conjecture, we can only take the genitive as designating the object of the teaching: 'learned discourses in philosophy.'[25]

However, Blass's conjecture seems to us to be acceptable, because '*didaktos*', taken as a masculine substantive, agrees better with the only possible sense of '*pneumatikos*' at the end of the verse. If this word were taken as a neuter it would imply a third, an essentially logical, difficulty; in this case it is not so much the absence of the noun '*logos*' which would be awkward, for the substantive could be understood. But what follows shows that the Apostle means the opposition between natural and spiritual men. Hence it is much more natural to take this word as a masculine substantive and to translate it as we have done (setting forth spiritual truths amongst spiritual people). Indirectly Blass's treatment of 2[13a] becomes very probable; therefore we take '*en didaktois anthrōpinēs sophias*' as depending on '*en teleiois* (2[6]) = 'amongst people instructed in human philosophy' (or by human philosophy).[26]

Once again the natural man[27] is contrasted with the spiritual man. The former sees but folly in the divine wisdom. The second recognizes it according to the measure of the Holy Spirit's work in him. In principle, all Christians have received the Spirit. Yet only in the '*teleioi*', here called '*pneumatikoi*' = 'spiritual men', in a strong sense, has the Spirit truly become a principle of knowledge. For this reason spiritual men are also spoken of in opposition to 'babes' or to 'fleshly men'.—Demonstration of the exceptional abilities of spiritual men is by analogy: no one knows what is within a man (not even his fellow), but the spirit of that man himself. ('*Hominem ne homo quidem alter cognoscit*', Bengel.) '*A fortiori*, none can know God but the Spirit of God, which is also the Spirit of Christ. But we have received the same. So there is therefore no limit imposed by any external authority (ecclesiastical or epistemological) on the Christian theologian ('he is judged by no one'), provided he remains faithful to the Spirit. In that case, he can even search out the divine essence

---

[25] As 1 Maccabees 4[7]: '*didaktoi polemou*' = 'instructed in matters of war'.

[26] ORIGEN, *Contra Celsum*, IV, Ch. 71 (KOETSCHAU, p. 314), and VII, Ch. 11 (K., p. 163), seems to presuppose the reading '*pneumatikōs*'. In principle this would be possible. But it is not attested elsewhere, and, moreover, '*pneumatikois*' gives a very acceptable sense.

[27] Here called '*psuchikos*', as often among the gnostics, in conformity with the usual meaning of '*psuchē*' = 'the life-principle of animals and men'.

('*eraunan*' = '*ereunan*' = 'search out'). A boldness truly gnostic in the highest sense of the term! But what Christian is there who can boast that he always allows himself to be led by the Spirit? So then, it is an ideal rather than an established fact. As for the problem how the Spirit can indwell many men without losing His universality, this is a question raised only by a typically rationalist line of reasoning. Probably it springs from 'human wisdom', which is why the Apostle does well not to consider it.

The quotation in 2^{16a} comes from Isaiah 40^{13}. The Apostle's concern always to link his teaching with the Old Testament (although the Old Testament does not yet contain the hidden wisdom), distinguishes the gnosis of the Apostle from that of the 'gnostics' (in a pejorative sense). Another distinctive mark is that while for the 'gnostics' entire wisdom is innate in spiritual men and is necessary for salvation, for Paul it is the result of the development of a Christian who already possesses the assurance of salvation (by justification), but who can only enjoy more fully the gifts of grace as he advances along the way of perfection.

CHAPTER III

(1) *For my part, brothers, I could not speak to you as to spiritual but only as to fleshly people, as to Christian babes.* (2) *I offered you milk, not solid food, for you were not yet able to bear it. Neither to the present time are you able to bear it,* (3) *for you are still fleshly.*

Indeed, so long as dissensions rage amongst you, are you not still fleshly people who live after the manner of men? (4) *For when one of you says 'I am for Paul' and another 'I am for Apollos', are you not still merely human?* (5) *What is Apollos really? What is Paul? Servants (of Christ), who led you to the faith, each in accordance with the gifts the Lord granted him.* (6) *It is I who planted, it is Apollos who watered, but it is God who caused the growth.* (7) *This is why the planter is nothing and the waterer is nothing, but God who caused the growth (is everything).* (8) *Planter and waterer—it's a matter of indifference; but each shall receive his own wages, according to his own work.* (9) *For we are fellow-workers with God, and you are God's garden, God's house.*

3^{1-9}. This is no place to try to distinguish between the meaning of 'psuchikoi' and 'sarkinoi';[1] here the terms are synonyms. If the Apostle uses here the term 'fleshly' it is in order to remind the Corinthians (often arrogant and taking themselves for truly spiritual men) of their moral inferiority. We shall meet sad instances of this in Chapters 5 and 6. For the present, the writer insists, a second time, on the impropriety of dissensions ('eris' = 'strife', 'contention'; 'zēlos' = 'the fanaticism with which it is pursued'). These schisms, centred around human beings, are the clearest sign of the unredeemed and purely human mentality of the members of the Church. But whilst in Chapter 1 the Apostle insisted on unity of the faith through baptism in the name of the Lord, here he stresses unity within the Christian life, which can only develop under God's blessing.

Paul and Apollos (for save for 3^{22} Peter does not come into the picture; he has played no part or but little part in the development of the society) are only God's gardeners (the figure: Israel = the garden or vineyard of God, is common in the Old Testament); it is God who gives the plants the power to grow. True enough, Paul does not put himself on quite the same plane as Apollos; he, Paul, founded the Church in which Apollos has laboured. However, by the side of God neither has any standing.—We may notice that it does not seem possible to take, as the Synodale Version does, 'ho auxanōn' = 'he

---

[1] As the Gnostic VALENTINUS does, dividing men into three groups; spiritual, natural, and bodily (fleshly) men. See DE FAYE, *Gnostiques et Gnosticisme* (pub. Geuthner, Paris, 1925), pp. 57ff.

(10) *According to the grace of God given to me, I laid the foundation like a wise architect, and another built upon it. But let each take care how he builds.* (11) *It is true that, so far as the foundation is concerned, no one can lay any other than that which is already laid, which is Jesus Christ.* (12) *But if anyone builds on this foundation with gold, silver, precious stones, or with wood, hay, straw,* (13) *the work of each one will be revealed.*

For the Day of Judgment will disclose it, because it will be accompanied by fire. And the fire will test the quality of each one's work. (14) *If what has been built by anyone survives, he shall receive a reward;* (15) *if anyone's work is burned up by the fire, he will be deprived of a reward; nevertheless he himself will escape, but like a man who has passed through fire.*

(16) *Do you not know that you are the temple of God and that the spirit of God dwells in you?* (17) *Now, if anyone destroys the temple of God, God will destroy him. For the temple of God is holy, and it is you who are this temple.*

who caused to grow' (3^7) as an attribute. It has already been said that God causes the growth. And now it is the action of the apostles which is to be compared with that of God; thus '*auxanōn*' is in apposition to '*Theos*' = 'God'. We are not, perhaps, over-stressing with the translation 'God is everything'—in comparison with whom Paul and Apollos are nothing—instead of the more literal 'God is something'.

$3^{8–9}$ introduces the idea of the apostles' responsibility before God. The following verses ($3^{10–15}$) develop the theme in more detail.

$3^{10–15}$. '*Themelion*' means the foundations laid by the architect, not the ground built upon. 3^{11} makes two assertions about this:

(1) Once the foundations are laid, the building can only be done thereupon, without adding others; that is to say, Paul alone is responsible for establishing the foundations.

(2) There can be no doubt about the choice of foundations: Christ alone can so serve.

On these foundations the successors and collaborators of the Apostle have built with materials whose solidity the 'day' will reveal, i.e. the day of the Lord, a technical term for the Day of Judgement. This will be accompanied by fire ('*en puri apokaluptetai*', where '*en*' is probably a Semitism for 'with',[2] the subject of the verb being '*hēmera*' = 'the day'). Yet it is not a question of a purifying fire (no purgatory!), but of one which destroys worthless material. What becomes of the architects? Their salvation is not under discussion, for it is not acquired by works (Rom 3^4). But their rank in the hierarchy of the Kingdom will not be the same. Those whose works

[2] Cf. the expression, '*en doxē elthein*' (Mk 8^{38}, 10^{37}, 13^{26}), a synonym for '*meta doxēs*'. However, see also on this subject our note on '*en rhabdō*' at 4^{21}.

(18) *Let no one deceive himself: if anyone among you thinks himself wise in this world, let him become a fool, so that he may become wise.* **(19)** *For the wisdom of this world is foolishness with God. Indeed, it is*

go with them[3] will be distinguished by a reward (as Mt 25[21,23]), the rest will not have it. '*Zēmioun*' normally, in fact, does not mean 'punish', but 'to deprive someone of something'. '*Mercede excidet, non salute*' (Bengel); cf. 2 Corinthians 5[10].

The writer seems, however, to exclude himself from this quest for reward, having been content himself to lay the foundations. The comparison of the Last Judgement to a fire was a commonplace of Jewish apocalyptic.[4] The idea appears to have been of Mazdaean origin,[5] as well as the belief that the righteous will pass through the fire unharmed.

3[16-17]. '*Naos Theou*' = '*ho naos Theou*' = 'the temple of God' (there is only one); the article is absent not only because '*naos*' is attributive, but also because it is a reflection of the Hebrew 'construct state'.

J.W. is surprised by the assertion that the Spirit indwells people to whom the quality of being 'spiritual' is denied; but it must be remembered that all Christians, including those called 'babes', have received the Spirit, even if He is not yet fully displayed in them. Nor is the identification of the Church with the perfect Temple of the last times[6] surprising. But it is hard to see who could profane or try to destroy ('*praesens de conatu?*') this temple. In the preceding passage only builders and not destroyers were in view, except for the fire which only fulfils its function. Furthermore, what follows takes us back to the problem of two forms of Wisdom, and has no reference to 3[16-17]. So, without going so far as to call them interpolations (as J.W. does for 3[16]), we may nevertheless ask whether they are in their proper place. Some would prefer to place them at the end of Chapter 6. But such conjectures are always hazardous, and it would be better to suppose that the writer is already thinking of the scandals denounced in Chapters 5 and 6.

3[18-23]. We already know the two equations: worldly wisdom = foolishness before God; divine wisdom = foolishness in the eyes of men. Here (3[18]) we learn that the philosophers are not totally

[3] So Revelation 14[13], 2 Esdras 7[35] (CHARLES, *Pseudepigrapha*, II.583).
[4] Cf. Isaiah 31[9], 43[2], Malachi 3[1-2] and 4[1ff] (LXX numeration); Psalms of Solomon 15[4,5ff] (CHARLES, *Pseudepigrapha*, II.646); Test. of Abraham, Ch.13 (in J. A. ROBINSON, *Texts and Studies*, II.II.93); Apoc. Baruch (= 2 Bar) 48[39] (CHARLES, op. cit., p. 507), and for the Baptist (according to Mt 3[10-12], Lk 3[9]). It is similarly implicit in 2 Thessalonians 1[8], 1 Peter 4[12] and Didache 16.
[5] Cf. NATHAN SÖDERBLOM, *La vie future d'après le Mazdéisme à la lumière des croyances parallèles dans les autres religions*, (Annales du Musée Guimet, IX, [1880], and CH. AUTRAN, *Mithra, Zoroastre et la Préhistoire du christianisme* (Paris, Payot, 1935).
[6] Isaiah 28[16ff], Eth. Enoch 91[13] (CHARLES, *Pseudepigrapha*, II.264), Jubilees 1[17] (CHARLES, ibid., p. 12).

written: 'He it is who seizes the wise in their knavery' (20) and again:
'The Lord knows the thoughts of the wise, he knows that they are futile.'
(21) So let no one boast of men. For all things are yours, (22) whether
Paul, Apollos or Cephas, whether the world, life, death, the present or
the future—all is yours, (23) but you are Christ's, and Christ is God's.

rejected. They can acquire true wisdom, if they reject the false and
accept the risk of being accused by men of being fools. The text takes
new point when we remember that for the Cynic brotherhood and
the Stoa—especially in later times—the term *'mōros'* = 'madman',
'fool', was almost a technical term for all who were opposed to
philosophy (or to their brand in particular). The two quotations
of 3[19b and 20] are borrowed respectively from the Book of Job (5[13])
and Psalm 93[11] (EVV 94[11]). But, in the first of these, the participle
'katalambanōn' of the LXX is replaced by the stronger verb *'dras-*
somenos' (= 'grasp with the hand', from a root *'drak'*, found also
in the substantive *'drax'* = 'handful'), whilst *'phronēsis'* is replaced
by the more pejorative word *'panourgia'* = 'knavery', 'wile'. Perhaps
Paul had read Job in another translation than the LXX. In the
quotation from the Psalm, we notice a curious divergence from the
LXX text (and from the Massoretic!). In the latter it is the passions
of men in general which are under consideration and not those of
philosophers in particular. Is Paul applying the biblical text to a particular case? However, this method of changing the traditional text
is not a habit of his. We might suppose an error of memory, or that
here again another translation than that of the LXX was in his
hands. But we are inclined to accept the reading *'tōn anthrōpōn'* =
'of men' here in the Pauline passage.[7] In that case, contrary to what
is generally thought, the reading *'sophōn'* = 'of the wise' would be
a correction by a copyist influenced by the terms *'sophos'* and
'sophia' (3[18 and 19]).

This suggestion is supported by what follows (3[21]): no one must
boast by relying on *men* (not: on the wise). By a skilful detour, this
verse leads us back to the scandal of the schisms, in which the various
groups of Corinthians puffed themselves up by thinking they had to
choose one or other of the apostles as their head. (Notice that it was
not the apostles who vaunted themselves, but their supporters.)

Paul reminds his readers that it is not to the apostles that they
belong—to Paul, Apollos or Peter—as they said, according to
1[12] ('*egō Paulou*'), but that the opposite is the truth: '*Paulos humōn*'
= 'Paul is yours', etc. . . . (exact inversion of the formula in 1[12]!):
the apostles are the servants of the Church. More than that, the
entire creation, visible and invisible, including the powers of life and
death, of the present world and the future world (Bengel: '*in terra*
et in caelo'), operate for the wellbeing of Christians (cf. Rom 8[28, 38–9]),
who one day will 'judge the world' (6[2–3]).

[7] Attested by a number of minuscules, the Armenian version, as well as by
MARCION (according to EPIPHANIUS, *Haer.* 42, *MPG* XLI, col. 724 B, etc., 781 A).

On the other hand, the Christian is subject to Christ (not to men), and this directly, without the mediation of any apostle; and Christ Himself is subject to God (subordinationism, notwithstanding the uncreated and eternal nature of the Son of God).

This conception is extremely characteristic for the Pauline conception of salvation: submission to Christ is the secret of the liberation of the human being in the face of all human and cosmic powers.

3^{21-3} are written in rhythmical prose and end in a combined antithesis (*'panta humōn, humeis de Christou'* = 'all is yours, but you are Christ's') and gradation (*'humeis de Christou, Christos de Theou'* = 'you are Christ's, and Christ is God's') which are most impressive.

CHAPTER IV

(1) *Because these things are so, let us be regarded as ministers of Christ and administrators of the divine mysteries. (2) Hence, moreover, seek nothing else of administrators than that they are faithful. (3) It is of very little consequence to me to be judged by you or by any human tribunal whatever. I do not even pretend to judge myself. (4) For although I am unaware of any fault, it is not that which justifies me; but the one who will judge me is the Lord.*

(5) *Consequently, do not judge prematurely, I mean, before the Lord comes, who will bring to light what is hidden in the darkness, and reveal the thoughts of the heart; and then each will receive his praise from God.*

(6) *These truths, brothers, I have represented in a figurative form which applies to myself and to Appollos, and I have done so for your sake, that you may learn from our example not to be puffed-up by taking sides for one against the other.*

4¹. In spite of the '*hōs*' which follows, '*houtōs*' has a consecutive not a comparative sense—'because these things are so, then . . .'.—For the expression 'administrators of the divine mysteries' see above on **2¹**.

4² presents several difficulties of detail: (*a*) the meaning of '*hōde*' is the same as '*houtōs*' in the preceding verse = '*cum eo statu res nostrae sint*' (in agreement with J.W. who cites in this connection four texts from Revelation: 13¹⁰,¹⁸, 14¹², 17⁹). (*b*) What does '*loipon*' mean? It can only be an ellipsis for 'there is only one more thing to do, namely . . .'. (*c*) Should we read '*zēteitai*' with Nestlé, Bachmann and the Textus Receptus, or '*zēteite*' with the majority of good manuscripts and in particular P 46, ℵ, A, C, D, E, and P? We see no reason against reading '*zēteite*', on condition that it is read as an imperative (F and G give the subjunctive *zētēte*, which comes to the same): 'You have no right to judge us according to any other standard than our faithfulness. This is the only thing to be taken into account, and not the eloquence of the apostles, or their compliance with the Church members.' Nevertheless, the Apostle does not intend to submit to the judgement of the Corinthians. He does not even judge himself—not because he fears the voice of his conscience, which indeed does not reproach him (2 Cor 1¹², Rom 9¹), but to reserve the judgement for the Lord, i.e. Jesus Christ, who in the Day of Judgement will bring to light all that is hidden and who alone will be able to justify the Apostle.—The word '*kairos*', like '*hēmera*', denotes here the appointed time when the affair will be brought to

judgement; any judgement at the present time would be premature. '*Tou skotous*' is a subjective genitive, as in **14²⁵** and Rom 2¹⁶: 'the hidden things of the domain of darkness.'¹

Paul clearly appears here as under accusation. But what is he accused of? Up to this point we can only have suspected that his critics have turned to account his lack of eloquence; but in what follows the criticisms become a little more definite (4¹⁰). The end of 4⁵ leads us back to the end of the parable in 3¹⁰⁻¹⁵. '*Metaschēmatizein*' means 'to change the form of someone or something'. Here the verb reminds us that the author has 'clothed' certain truths which were a little abstract when he presented them in figurative form. Other interpretations are unacceptable.² But the real difficulty occurs in the few words from the first '*hina*' to '*gegraptai*'. Let us confess at once that it is untranslatable, even if with the Textus Receptus we add '*phronein*' after '*gegraptai*', a reading which is extremely ill-attested. The phrase must have suffered textual alteration. The attempt is made to translate: 'in order that by your example you may learn (to observe?) the saying: nothing beyond what is written.' But we do not know in what way conformity with Scripture is supposed to sum up the good relationship between Paul and Apollos, still less so because he has neither referred to a definite text nor to a general scriptural principle.

Furthermore, the repetition of '*hina*' is odd, while by suppressing these questionable few words the sentence becomes clear and comprehensible. The Apostle, perhaps after a pause in the dictation of the letter, comes back to the central idea of the parable about building (3¹⁰⁻¹⁵). But he now removes a possible misunderstanding. He had not insisted on his relations with Apollos in order to sermonize to Apollos, but to exhort the Corinthians themselves to observe rules of modesty and not to judge either of them, by taking sides for or against, and hence by thinking themselves superior Christians who can judge apostles. The term '*phusiousthe*' ('*phusioumai*' = 'be puffed up') taken up later perhaps alludes already to arrogant gnostics who scorned other Christians, and against the false wisdom of whom true wisdom has already been ranged.

It remains to explain how the unfortunate phrase '*hina . . . gegraptai*' came into being. The only explanation at all satisfactory has been proposed by the Dutch scholar Baljon;³ somewhat simplified it is as follows. The original text was the one we have translated. But a copyist, who had at first omitted the word '*mē*' between '*hina*' and '*heis*', inserted it above the line, or to be exact, above the

---

¹ With J.W., we might suspect that the parenthesis '*hos kai . . . tōn kardiōn*'' which is characterized by the parallelism of its members, could be a quotation from some unknown Jewish writing which spoke in this way of God. In the thought of the Apostle, it is Christ who judges, but God who rewards.

² Usually, '*meteschēmatisa*' is translated by 'I have applied', which is never the meaning of the verb.

³ In his dissertation, *De tekst der brieven van Paulus aan de Romeinen, de Corinthiers*, . . . (Utrecht, 1884), pp. 49–51.

(7) For who concedes you any distinction? And what have you got that you have not received? But if it is true that you have received it, why do you boast as though you had not received it? (8) Are you already surfeited? Have you become rich? Have you already entered into possession of the kingdom without us? In truth, I could wish that it were so, so that we also might be able to reign with you! (9) For I think God has set forth us, the apostles, last of all, and exhibited us like those condemned to death, so that we might be a spectacle to the world, to angels and to men.

(10) We are fools for Christ's sake, but you are wise in Christ. We are weak, but you are strong. You are honoured, but we are despised. (11) Up to the present hour we suffer hunger, thirst, and destitution, we are beaten and are homeless, (12) and toil at work with our own hands. Insulted, we bless; persecuted, we endure; (13) calumniated, we comfort. We have become like the scum of the world, the refuse of the universe, and so we remain.

letter '*a*' of the word '*hina*'. A highly conscientious second copyist re-inserted the '*mē*' in the text, but noted in the margin: 'the "*mē*" was written over the alpha' ('*to mē huper a gegraptai*'). Then a third one unfortunately put in the text the marginal gloss which he did not understand.—Some scholars have found this explanation too ingenious (J.W.: 'too clever'). But a better one has not been found. It may be noted that it is not the two words, '*heis*', or more exactly the '*heis*' and the '*huper tou henos*', which depend on one another, but the '*huper tou henos*' and '*kata tou heterou*', since each Corinthian had the bad habit of taking the side of one apostle against another.

But the dispute is not over. The Apostle, having already moved over to the attack, now follows up his advantage by speaking ironically and with much sarcasm of the alleged superiority of the Corinthians, or at least of those who are 'puffed up'.

4[7-9] reminds the Corinthians, proud of the powers of the Spirit, that these powers are a gift of God—that they would never have received anything unless they had been converted by the Apostle's preaching. It is therefore doubly presumptuous on their part to boast that they are within the Kingdom and even in its government, while the apostles sacrifice their existence and risk their lives for them. (Cf. **15**[30-2] and 2 Cor 11[23-33].) They surrender themselves as a spectacle to the world like gladiators condemned to death ('*epithanatioi*') in the arena.[4]

[4] The same figure is used also by the Stoics, but not in quite the same sense; v. SENECA, *On Providence* 2[9], where Cato, standing in the middle of ruins, is admired by God. In the Apostle's usage the idea of the spectators' contempt is dominant. This shade of difference is very characteristic of the distinction between the Stoic and the Christian attitude to trials.—In Christian literature, it is interesting to notice the passage in Ignatius, *Epistle to the Trallians* 9[1], according to which the angels ('*hoi epouranioi*') contemplated the death of Christ.

4[10] summarizes this situation in three vigorous antitheses: 'We are fools for Christ's sake, but you, . . .' What gives these their pungency is the fact that the first term of each (the weakness and folly of the apostles and the contempt heaped upon them) expresses a cruel truth, whilst the second term (the wisdom, strength and honour of the Corinthians) only expresses an illusion. All the misfortunes mentioned in 4[9-13] belong in reality to a martyr's situation, except for the manual work which the Apostle Paul (and he alone, together with Barnabas, according to Chapter 9) has voluntarily imposed upon himself, so as not to be a burden upon the Church members. While 4[11] illustrates the tragic lot of the Apostle, and to a degree that of all true witnesses, the verses which follow (4[12,13a]) throw a vivid light on the attitude with which the Christian should react to his misfortunes. 'Insulted, we bless . . .', etc. The lack of any conjunction between the antitheses, even the simple '*de*' of 4[10], makes still more striking the paradox of the uniquely Christian reaction, which is summarized with incomparable terseness.[5]

4[13b] doubtless contains an allusion to a rite known in certain cities of Asia Minor and Greece. Not only were contemptible people in general called '*perikatharmata*' = 'sweepings', but in particular, men sacrificed to the gods to ward off some calamity. The principal texts about this have been given by Wettstein and are found in two scholia relating respectively to (*a*) the *Equites* and (*b*) to Aristophanes' *Plutus*.[6]

They read: (*a*) 'The Athenians maintained some utterly ignoble ("*lian ageneis*") and good-for-nothing men ("*achrēstous*"), and when the city was attacked by a calamity, for example by an epidemic or something of that sort, they killed them in order to remove the defilement ("*heneka tou miasmatos*"); and these men were also called "*katharmata*".'

(*b*) 'Men sacrificed to the gods for expiation in times of pestilence or other epidemics, were called "*katharmata*", and this custom has also grown up among the Romans.'

An analogous text is given by Photius[7] on the subject of '*peripsēma*'. This Byzantine scholar relates that it was a sacrifice to Poseidon and that the victim was addressed with the words: '*Peripsēma hēmōn genou, ētoi sōtēria kia apolutrōsis.*'

---

[5] We prefer the reading '*dusphēmoumetha*', with P 46, A, C, CLEMENT of Alexandria, *Stromateis*, Ch. 7, § 51.3 (STAEHLIN, II.272), ORIGEN, *Contra Celsum*, V.63 (KOETSCHAU II.66), rather than '*blasphēmoumetha*', a more conventional term. The meaning is the same ('calumniate').

[6] The modern editions of the scholia by RUTHERFORD and by DÜBNER-DIDOT do not give them, but they are to be found in the beautiful edition of the *Works* of ARISTOPHANES published by Frobenius of Bâle in 1547, pp. 249 and 24 respectively.

[7] *Lexicon* (pub. G. Hermann, Leipzig, 1808). The precise meaning of '*perikatharma*' is 'rinsing' (of vessels), while '*peripsēma*' signifies the 'scraping' of the same.

(14) *I do not write these lines to shame you, but to admonish you as children of mine whom I love.* (15) *For though you might have ten thousand guardians in Christ, nevertheless you have not many fathers. For it is I who, in Christ Jesus and by the Gospel, brought you to birth.* (16) *Therefore I beg you to become imitators of me.* (17) *For the same reason I am sending you Timothy, who is my beloved and faithful child in the Lord. He will remind you of my Christian principles, such as I teach everywhere in each Church.*

Since the sacrifice had to be voluntary only the most wretched of beggars offered themselves as victims, attracted by a period without care, which was offered to them until the moment when there was need of them (it goes without saying that at this point the parallel to the apostles breaks down).

These strongly emotional lines are the more moving because the Apostle was really conscious of sacrificing himself for the Church. We know that if he wished to boast himself (as 2 Cor 11[16–33]), he would do so precisely on the grounds of this weakness, and that he was not far from accepting the name of 'vagabond' as a title of nobility. But he leaves the privilege of boasting to the Corinthians, to use in their own way!

4[14–16]. Is the Apostle afraid that he has wounded his readers, or is this return of affectionate feelings explicable by a natural psychological reaction? Whatever the reason, he reminds them that these exhortations spring from a paternal love which no one can share with him. For he alone has founded the Church of Corinth, the other apostles are only *'paidagōgoi'*, that is, less than schoolmasters—a term used for the slaves who took care of children and escorted them to school. The figure of spiritual paternity does not go back to Numbers 11[12], where Moses asks if he is the mother of the people, rejecting the very idea. But it was widely current in Judaism; the Babylonian Talmud (Sanhedrin)[8] expresses it thus: 'If a man teach the Torah to his neighbour's son, Scripture puts it to his account, as if he had begotten him.'[9] In some of the mystery religions the initiator was called the 'father' of the initiated. It was the same, as we know, in the Christian monasteries from ancient times. Note further that *'tekna mou'* lacks the article: Paul evidently has other spiritual children.

The first *'en Christō'* (4[15a]) certainly has no mystical sense, but indicates merely the Christian quality of the *'paidagōgoi'*. On the other hand, *'en Christō Iēsou'*, in 4[15b], is a reminder that the birth of the Corinthians is a new birth in Christ, engendered, moreover, by Paul's preaching (*'dia tou euanggeliou'*).

[8] Fol. 19 B (GOLDSCHMIDT, VIII.531), (cf. 91 B).
[9] Compare the numerous texts of the Old Testament where the disciples of the prophets are called their sons, e.g. 2 Kings 2 *passim*; 4[1, 38], 5[22], 9[1], Amos 7[11], etc.; and also Acts 3[25].

(18) Now, there are some who are puffed-up with pride, as though I were not coming to you. (19) But I will come to you swiftly, if the Lord permits, and then I will know not the eloquence of the proud, but their

His paternal love allows him exhortations such as those of 4¹⁶; for children should imitate their parents (cf. 11¹, Gal 4¹², 2 Thess 3⁷,⁹, Phil 3¹⁷). In what ought the Corinthians to imitate the Apostle? Evidently in his humility, thrown into relief in the preceding passage (against J.W.).

4¹⁷. For the same reason, that is because a father has the right to exhort his children, he has sent Timothy. According to this passage, he was converted by Paul himself, which is not what we should gather from Acts (14⁶ff, 16¹). We know that he was the faithful companion and collaborator of Paul, from the time of what is usually called the Second Missionary Journey (Acts 16ff), to the end. According to 2 Corinthians 1¹⁹ he may even have assisted the Apostle, along with Silvanus, in the foundation of the Corinthian Church. He is associated sometimes in the writing of some of Paul's letters: 1, 2 Thessalonians, Colossians, 2 Corinthians. Sometimes he was entrusted with important missions, as this one. However, he was not the bearer of this letter (nor of the first part of the letter, if our division of it into two is accepted); for Chapter 16 should reach Corinth before Timothy himself. Therefore, in agreement with Acts 19²², we must conclude that Timothy is going or has gone via Macedonia, while the letter or letters will take the shorter route by sea, as is quite natural. For this reason the aorist '*epempsa*' can well be attributed to the ancient epistolary style, which treated the moment of the receipt of the letter as the present. We cannot therefore conclude that Timothy had already departed. In modern speech in a case like this the verb would be used in the present tense: 'I am sending you.'

The words '*en kuriō*' = 'in the Lord', before '*hos humas*', might also be linked with '*piston*' = 'faithful in the Lord', i.e. Christian. But after the reference to the conversion of Timothy by Paul this would be a pleonasm; so it would be better to connect them with '*teknon*' = 'my spiritual child'. '*Hē hodos*' in the singular or '*hodos kuriou*', '*hodos Theou*' or '*hodos sotērias*' are all possible synonyms for 'Christianity'.[10] The plural '*hai hodoi*' means moral principles, rather like the word '*halacha*' in Hebrew (cf. Acts 14¹⁶, Jas 1⁸, Rev 15³). Up to a point, these principles are personal to Paul; in fact, the Apostle does not hold the same opinion as the others on the value of the Jewish Law. But they are catholic in the sense that he teaches them everywhere.

4¹⁸⁻²¹. Those who are 'puffed up' are without doubt the same as in 4⁶ff. They seem to have insinuated that the Apostle was too much afraid of them to dare to face them openly, and the sending of

---

[10] Acts 16¹⁷, 18²⁵,²⁶, 19⁹,²³, 22⁴,¹⁴, 24¹⁴,²², 25³, 2 Peter 2² ²¹, Hebrews 9⁸.

power. (20) *For the kingdom of God does not consist of eloquence but of power.* (21) *Which do you prefer? Shall I come to you with a rod, or with love and a spirit of meekness?*

Timothy could be interpreted in this sense. Paul would undeceive them; and he will give them the opportunity of showing their spiritual power, which is alone of consequence (cf. 1 Thess 1[5]). However, he adds: *'ean ho kurios thelēsē'* = 'if the Lord permits' (cf. Jas 4[15]). 4[21] even announces that he will administer correction, if the Church should follow his adversaries. *'En rhabdō'* is synonymous for *'meta rhabdou'* = 'with a rod'; and the same for *'en agapē'* and *'en pneumati'* = 'with love', 'with a spirit'. This use of *'en'* is attested by the papyri.[11] But on the other hand, it is also a Semitism common in the LXX, where *'en'* is often equivalent to the dative of the instrument, or to *'meta'* with the genitive.[12]

[11] See PREISIGKE, *Griechisches Wörterbuch der Papyrus-Urkunden* I.480: *'ho deina en machairē.'* KUHRING, *De Praepositionum Graecorum in Chartis Aegyptiis usu quaestiones selectae* (Diss., Bonn, 1906) thinks that originally *'en'* could mean the clothes one was wearing, then any object carried (pp. 43-4).

[12] For example, Psalm 73(74)[13], 77(78)[6, 15, 36, 45]. This usage goes back to the ambiguous use of the Hebrew preposition ב and in some cases of כ.—According to P. SPICQ, *'Une réminiscence de Job* 37.13 in 1 Corinthians 4[21]?' (*RB*, LX [1953].309-12) our passage alludes to the passage in Job, which teaches that God accomplished his will whether for chastisement (*'eis paideian'*, שׁבט) or through mercy (*'eis eleos autou'*, חסד). But the context is obscure because of the mention of *'eis tēn gēn autou'.*

CHAPTER V

(1) *Everywhere a case of misconduct in your midst is being talked about, and misconduct of such a sort that it is not even found among pagans: one of you is actually living with his father's wife. (2) Yet you are puffed-up with pride! And you have not rather gone into mourning so that the one who has committed this crime might be separated from your community!*

(3) *As for me, I am absent in body, but present in spirit; so I have already decided this, as though I were personally present: (4) when, in the name of the Lord, my spirit and yours are united together, accompanied by the power of our Lord Jesus, (5) then I shall deliver this malefactor to Satan for the destruction of his flesh, that he may be saved spiritually in the day of the Lord Jesus.*

(6) *You certainly have no grounds for boasting! Do you not know that a little leaven leavens the whole lump? (7) Sweep out the old leaven, that you may be fresh dough, in conformity with the fact that you are 'unleavened'!—For Christ has been sacrificed as our Paschal lamb. (8) Therefore let us keep the feast, not with the old leaven, nor with the leaven of malice and evil, but with the unleavened bread of sincerity and truth.*

5^{1-8}. The verse of the Torah which condemns this kind of union is found in Leviticus 18^8: 'The nakedness of thy father's wife shalt thou not uncover.' The previous verse (18^7) forbids the uncovering of 'the nakedness of thy mother'. The difference between the two cases lies in the fact that 5^8 is referring to a second wife (step-mother). It is to 5^8 (union with the step-mother, regarded as incestuous) that the Apostle alludes when he speaks of the '*gunē tou patros*' (5^1). Naturally there is no question of any legitimacy in the union, for Roman law forbade such unions even after the death of the father, as the Institutes of Gaius affirm.[1]

If the father were still living, adultery was added to incest, and this considerably aggravated the case; but the stress is laid here on the incestuous nature of the union, which even pagan customs forbade.

The word '*holōs*' can only have a local sense = 'everywhere'. There is no doubt about the meaning of '*akouesthai*' = 'to speak of someone'. The affair has gained notoriety in several Churches. 5^2 points out the attitude the Corinthians should have taken: they should

---

[1] '*Item amitam*' (paternal aunt), '*et materteram*' (maternal aunt), '*uxorem ducere non licet, item eam quae mihi quondam socrus*' (mother-in-law, i.e. wife's mother), '*aut nurus*' (daughter-in-law), '*aut privigna*' (step-daughter, i.e. wife's daughter), '*aut noverca*' (second mother) *fuit*. (*Institutiones*, I.63, TEUBNER, pp. 17–18.)

have gone into mourning in order to provoke the death of the guilty. '*Airesthai*' cannot signify voluntary separation. The Vulgate translates it well by '*de medio tollatur*'. There is no ground at all for questioning the final sense of '*hina*'. What is implied is a rite of exorcism having the same aim as the curse mentioned in 5⁵. Externally the rite must have resembled that observed after a person's death. Now the essential feature of mourning customs amongst the Hebrews was the sacrifice of the hair. This was also an element in certain vows according to Acts 18¹⁸, 21²³ᶠᶠ. No doubt merry-making and the wearing of finery were also shunned. In the Old Testament, belief in the efficacy of mourning and fasting for warding off public misfortune is well attested by 1 Kings 21⁹, Amos 5¹⁶, 8¹⁰. Here the scourge to be removed is the presence of a guilty party within the Church, which he defiles.

According to Jewish tradition, the malefactor should have been stoned.[2] It goes without saying that the Christian Church neither could nor would claim such a right. But the Apostle may have wished that the Corinthians should use the method he mentions. As that was not so, he promises that he will be spiritually present with them when they meet again together. The Church will be united in prayer, which explains the reference to the power of Christ ('*sun tē dunamei*', etc.).

Absent ones can be present, by uniting themselves with the rest on a spiritual plane. It is then that the Apostle will put forward his judgement, which he seems sure will prevail: he wishes to deliver the wrongdoer to Satan. This gives us an insight into the way in which such an excommunication might operate. By removing the wicked person from the Church his physical existence is abandoned to the powers of destruction. The excommunication is therefore akin to that practised by the synagogue, with the difference that amongst the Jews it was the elders alone who formed the tribunal.

If this Jewish excommunication already involved, at the beginning of our era, curses such as are attested for a later period,[3] it is probable that the Christian Church also used formulae of this kind.

But why is Satan and not the wrath of God the agent of destruction? In this connection we must remember that according to the Gospels also scourges were brought about by the powers of evil. Nevertheless, there is no ground for thinking of an invocation of Satan; such an hypothesis is entirely excluded. But it was thought, as we have just said, that exclusion from the Church would *ipso facto* deliver the guilty party to the forces of destruction.

[2] Mishnah, Sanhedrin, VII.4, GOLDSCHMIDT, VIII.674.
[3] A sample of Jewish excommunication is: 'May grave and terrible sicknesses fall upon him. . . . May he be swallowed up like Korah and his tribe.' See SCHÜRER, *Geschichte des jüdischen Volkes*, II.506 (4th edn). More complete formulae are found in Deuteronomy 28¹⁵ᶠᶠ. Cf. also SCHENKEL, *Bibellexikon*, I.351ff. (Leipzig, 1869).

His '*pneuma*', however, would survive the destruction of his '*sarx*'. The terms used might make us think of the Platonic view of the immortality of the soul. But that is by no means correct. For '*sarx*' is material only in so far as it is contaminated by sin, and '*pneuma*' denotes the human spirit in so far as it is already regenerated by the Spirit of God and contains in germ in the inner man the resurrection body, which will survive the Day of Judgement.[4]

This proceeding may seem to have little compatibility with the spirit of the incident in John 8[1-11]. But it must be remembered that we have here an unrepentant sinner (cf. Mt 18[17]).

5[6]. '*Ou*' is omitted by Lucifer of Calaris[5] and Ambrosiaster.[6] If these authors have preserved the best reading, then the Apostle would have been expressing himself with biting irony: 'This mania of boasting about yourselves suits you!'

For the comprehension of 5[6-8] it is important to remember certain details of the Jewish Passover: (1) In the night of the 13th/14th Nisan and in the morning of the 14th, the house had to be cleaned out carefully to remove every trace of leavened bread, which in this instance was regarded as containing a principle of contagious impurity.[7] (2) The Passover bread had to be '*azumos*', i.e. without leaven. Likewise, the Christians must remove all leaven, that is to say, every trace of the spirit of impurity and wickedness, which brings the danger of contaminating the entire Church, and they must keep the true Passover, by making real the ideal of purity which is symbolized by the unleavened bread.

Up to this point the development is perfectly clear. But two questions remain to be solved: (1) Why is it said, at the end of 5[7], that the Corinthians *are* already without leaven, if they still have to be exhorted to become so? The Jewish rite also explains this detail. The Passover bread, as we have seen, was unleavened; but there was the fear that any remainder of old (leavened) dough might defile the new mixture, which is no doubt the sense in which we must take 5[6b]; the Christians are like a new organism which runs the risk of being infected by 'microbes' surviving from an earlier epidemic. (2) What is the exact part played by Christ in all this? It seems to us that His identification with the Paschal lamb must justify the fact of the renewal of the Christians who are '*azumoi*'.

It may be asked, furthermore, whether this verse exhorting Christians to celebrate their Passover, does not contain, in addition to an exhortation about the Christian life, an allusion to the Eucharist.

---

[4] The opposition between body and soul in an anthropological sense, as the Jews conceived them, is usually given by '*sōma*' and '*psuchē*'. Either of these elements can be destroyed by Satan, according to Matthew 10[28].
[5] '*Bona gloriatio vestra*', *MPL* XIII, col. 785 A; *CSEL* XIV.23.
[6] Item, *MPL* XVII, col. 209 A.
[7] Exodus 12[15], Mishnah Pesahim, I and II, *passim*; GOLDSCHMIDT II.313ff; cf. Jn 18[28].

(9) *I wrote to you in my letter to have no relations with immoral
people;* (10) *by that I was not wanting to forbid you in a general way
from having contact with the immoral people of this age, or with rogues
or brigands or idolaters, for in that case you would have to leave the
world entirely.* (11) *But now I write to you to have no relation with a
so-called Christian who may be immoral, a rogue, an idolater, a
slanderer, a drunkard, or a brigand, and not to eat with such.*

(12) *For why should it be my job to judge outsiders? Is it not those
who are inside whom you judge,* (13) *while God will judge the outsiders?
'Clear away the evil from your midst!'*

For Christians are the body of Christ; and moreover the Apostle is
aware of the equation: 'Eucharistic bread' = 'body of Christ'.
Hence Christians are, in a cultic sense, the bread without leaven;
there would then be more here than a simple analogy. And the
sacrificed Christ plays a real part in the drama which makes possible
the celebration of the Christian Passover. Without His atoning death,
no resurrection, and no glorious body present at the Lord's
Supper.

The expression *'thusai to pascha'* = 'sacrifice the Passover' was the
technical term, according to Deuteronomy 16[5], for killing the Passover lamb.[8]

5[9–12]. This is the first time that the Apostle makes reference to an
earlier letter. It is commonly regarded as lost; but some modern
scholars believe that it can be traced, in whole or part, in certain
parts of our canonical epistles. This is purely an hypothesis. A statement in the earlier letter must have been misunderstood. That is why
the Apostle clearly states here[9] that it is not a matter of breaking off
all connections with pagan wrongdoers, but only with Christians
guilty of great crimes. The remark has important bearings in two
ways. On the one hand, it authorizes the Christian to continue in his
commercial or social relationships with pagans. In particular, we
may suppose from the first chapter that many members of the
Church were workers or slaves in pagan businesses or houses. They
would have had to leave the world altogether—the world, that is, in
its natural sense—if they were to avoid these contacts; and this was
impossible. But on the other hand, the Apostle recommends an even
greater severity with respect to 'those inside', i.e. Christians. What is
difficult to explain is that 5[12b] speaks of the Church as exercising this
judgement, whilst previously it was only recommended. Apparently
'krinete' (5[12b]) has the sense: 'You are judges, you therefore have the
duty to judge.' It is nonetheless awkward that 5[12a] and 5[12b] suggest a
distinction between the functions of the Apostle and those of the

[8] Cf. O. CULLMANN, *Christology of the N.T.* (E.Tr.1959), pp. 71, 76.
[9] It is true that *'nun de'* can be used to express simple opposition (J.W.); but
the expression cannot apply to an event in the past. That is why 5[11] can only
mean the present letter.

Church, whereas in reality the distinction is between the functions of the Apostle and those of God (5¹³). We must therefore suppose that the writer originally intended simply to oppose 5¹²ᵃ and 5¹³ᵃ (it is not I but God who judges the pagans), but that his preoccupation with recalling the Corinthians to their duty interrupted the natural course of his thought.

'*Hoi exō*', as in 1 Thessalonians 4¹², Colossians 4⁵ (cf. 1 Tim 3⁷, Mk 4¹¹) means the pagans.[10]

5¹³ᵇ is a quotation from Deuteronomy 13⁵.

Naturally, the catalogue of vices makes no pretension to completeness. Other lists are found in 6⁹⁻¹⁰, Galatians 5¹⁹ᶠᶠ, Romans 13¹³, 2 Corinthians 12²⁰, Colossians 3⁸; cf. Ephesians 4³¹, 1 Timothy 1⁹⁻¹⁰, 2 Timothy 3²⁻⁵.

If some of these vices had not been found in the Church, the Apostle would not have mentioned them. But it is not said that they were all represented at that moment. Further, the '*onomazomenoi*' (5¹¹) are not pagans who may have wrongfully passed themselves off as members of the Church. They are actual (or possible) unworthy Christians.

The substantives designating the various categories of wrongdoers are clear enough, except perhaps for '*pleonektēs*'. This word can be used in a vague way for egoism and cupidity. According to 2 Corinthians 7² and 12¹⁸, '*pleonektēs*' is one who has wronged another. But since in this passage the Apostle lists in detail specific and grave sins, it must be remembered that the word is sometimes a synonym for '*kleptēs*' and even for '*harpax*'. Then it means one who uses brute force to enrich himself at the expense of his neighbour. In Ezekiel 22²⁷ wicked leaders are compared with wolves and are called '*pleonektai*'.[11]

---

[10] This terminology is found already amongst the Jews: *v.* Ecclus., Prologue 5: '*hoi ektos*' (RAHLFS, II.377); JOSEPHUS, *Antiquities*, XV.ɪx.2 (§ 316): '*hoi exōthen*' (pub. NIESE, III.388). The corresponding Hebrew words involve the root חצנ.

[11] In the *Memorabilia* of XENOPHON (I.ɪɪ.12) Critias is called '*pleonektistatos kai biaitatos*' (TEUBNER, p. 8). In the *Cyropaedia* (I.vɪ.27) it is said that in the face of enemies one must be '*kleptēn kai harpaga kai en panti pleonektēn*' (pub. Hachette, 1889, p. 89).

CHAPTER VI

(1) How is it that any of you who has a difference with a brother has the audacity to have the case tried by unbelievers, and not by Christians? (2) Do you not then know that the Christians will judge the world? And if it is by you that the world will be judged, are you unworthy of settling such little differences? (3) Do you not know that we shall judge the angels, and with how much greater reason earthly matters? (4) Yet when you have differences of this kind you set up as judges people despised by the Church! (5) I say this to make you ashamed. So no one is found among you intelligent enough to be able to judge between a man and his brother? (6) But one Christian goes to law against another, and that before pagans! (7) To begin with, it is a mark of defect for you to have lawsuits between yourselves. Why not rather suffer injustice? Why not rather let yourselves be defrauded? (8) But you yourselves practise injustice and theft, and that against brothers!

6¹⁻⁸. The expression '*tolma*' (6¹) is a very strong one ('have the audacity') and marks the indignation and pained astonishment of the Apostle in face of the incredible fact to which he calls attention: Christians have their disputes judged before pagan tribunals. Bengel says: '*Grandi verbo notatur laesa majestas christianorum.*' The Apostle is not casting any doubt on the fundamental impartiality of Roman law-courts.[1] He believes (Rom 13¹⁻⁸) that the Roman state really received from God the mission of maintaining peace and justice in the Mediterranean basin, and there is no indication either in his own letters or in the Acts of the Apostles of any experiences which disillusioned the Apostle in this matter.

But it is a question of Christian dignity. As the Jews, careful not to display their disharmonies before the public, had their affairs judged by their own wise men, i.e. by their rabbis (playing the part of חֲכָמִים), so Christians should have the decency to settle their differences among themselves. And at a time when they were vaunting their 'wisdom' it is doubly tragic to proclaim the apparent lack of men of 'judgement' in the Church, who should no doubt have been found among the '*didaskaloi*' = 'teachers' or the '*kubernētai*' = 'guides' mentioned in 12²⁸. The Apostle's amazement implies that in other Churches things took a more normal course, and it may be that these Christian arbitrators were the prototype of what later became the ecclesiastical courts.

[1] The expression '*adikoi*' here simply means unbelievers or pagans, without any wish to insist that they have no competent legal organization. Furthermore, it is recognized that '*adikos*' is often a synonym for '*asebēs*'; *v. TWNT*, I.150ff.

6^2. What exactly does '*kosmos*' mean in the phrase '*hoi hagioi ton kosmon krinousin*' = 'The Christians shall judge the world?' Here the word really seems to have cosmic implications. It means the angelic world, the mention of which in 6^3 only repeats and clarifies the idea of 6^2, somewhat in the way of the well-known parallelism of members in Hebrew aphorisms, which Paul so often imitates. Furthermore, it is hard to see who, apart from these cosmic powers, could be the object of a judgement exercised by Christians in the future, that is, of what is commonly called the Last Judgement. For men unattached to Christ are *ipso facto* '*apollumenoi*', i.e. destined to perish. Even if a resurrection of unbelievers is admitted—which Paul does not (*v.* infra, Ch. 15)—their fate is settled in advance; while Christians themselves will be judged by the Lord, as Chapter 3 indicates.

Nevertheless, this judgement over angels requires some further explanation. We do not think that the only ones meant are Satan or Beliar and their subordinates, or even the fallen angels of Genesis 6 mentioned in the Book of Enoch as chained until the judgement. In none of these cases can their ultimate fate be seriously in question, except in so far as saints like Enoch might if necessary intercede for them. But we have already seen that careful examination of the Pauline texts leads us to recognize the existence of an order of spiritual beings in some sense intermediary between the unfallen angels and the demons. In particular we have the '*stoicheia*' = 'the elements', the '*archai*' = 'the rulers', as well as other ranks of angels who, without having been wicked in times past, are opposed to Christianity in that they crucified the Lord or proclaimed another Gospel. In addition to these we must doubtless add the angels who represent the nations. They are not expressly mentioned by the Apostle, though perhaps included among the '*exousiai*' = 'authorities' of Colossians 1^{16} (Eph 1^{21}). But they are well-known in Jewish literature.[2] Since they have not always fulfilled their tasks properly, and in particular have often opposed the people of God, their greater or lesser faults will require to be judged and punished. Thus, in the Jewish Christian book called the *Ascension of Isaiah*, the angels of the nations are rebuked for their quarrelsome spirit.[3]

Already, according to Daniel (7^{22}), the Wisdom of Solomon (3^8), and Ethiopic Enoch (1^{38}), the saints will be associated with God in the Last Judgement. The idea is taken up by the Apostle, who places them (or at least, some of them?) alongside Christ. 'With how much more reason—note the author's reasoning—are you not debarred from judging petty earthly matters among yourselves.'

[2] Notably in Psalm 149 (*v.* especially verse 6), Daniel 10^{13-21}, Eth. Enoch 89^{59} (KAUTZSCH, *Pseudepigr.*, p. 294 and note c); cf. *Test of Naphtali* (Hebrew) 8 (KAUTZSCH, ibid., p. 491); *Bab. Talmud*, SUKKA, fol. 29a (GOLDSCHMIDT, III.338), Midrash Rabba Shîr (Canticles), 8^{14} (WÜNSCHE, *Bibliotheca Rabbinica*, VI.193).

[3] Ch. 10.28ff, ed. HENNECKE, *N.T.-liche Apockryphen* (1904), I.303; ed. CHARLES (1900), pp. 74ff.

(9) *Then do you not know that the wicked will not inherit the kingdom of God? Do not deceive yourselves! Neither immoral people, nor idolaters, nor adulterers, nor effeminate, nor homosexuals, (10) nor thieves, nor rogues, drunkards, slanderers, or brigands, shall inherit the kingdom of God. (11) And such were some of you; but you have been purified, but you have been sanctified, but you have been justified in the name of our Lord Jesus Christ and by the spirit of our God.*

The future *krinoumen* only relates to **6³ᵃ** (the judgement of angels); **6³ᵇ** implies a present ('you can also judge . . .') parallel to *'este'* at the end of **6²**. The term *'biōtika'* commonly means things concerning daily life, and so it stands here as a synonym for 'profane'.

6⁴⁻⁵ develop the ideas of **6¹⁻³**, but they contain a serious difficulty of style. For the phrase *'ana meson tou adelphou autou'* is a quite incorrect abbreviation for *'ana meson tinos kai tou adelphou autou'* = 'between a man and his brother man'. As we have no divergent reading to support this, we have to suppose an oversight by the author or Sosthenes.

6⁶ introduces a new point. The very existence of disputes between Christians is in itself already a moral defeat (this is what *'hēttēma'* means),[4] and it is stressed in **6⁷**. 'Would it not be better among Christians to practise non-resistance to evil?' So the Apostle echoes the recommendation of Jesus in the Sermon on the Mount (Mt 5³⁹ᶠ; cf. 1 Pet 2²³).[5] It was on these verses that some Reformation divines rested the case for rejecting all use of force, even by the state—wrongly, in view of the fact that the Apostle expressly recognized the right that the authorities have to the sword, according to Romans 13¹⁻⁷.[6]

6⁸. But the situation is even worse: 'Not only do you resist evil, you even perform it.' This verse makes the transition to **6⁹⁻¹¹**, which gives a list of vices incompatible with any claim to enter the Kingdom of God. It is curious that along with the spirit of greed and the contempt of propriety, which figure prominently in this passage, the Apostle mentions a series of indecencies, no doubt echoing the remonstrances made a little higher up (Ch. 5).

6⁹⁻¹¹. The *'harpages'* are distinguished from the *'kleptai'* by their violence. They are not content with robbery, but commit violence on

[4] The *'men'* of **6⁷ᵇ** has no *'de'* to follow. Did the author mean to continue, 'and so much the more because you bring your cases before pagans'? But this thought, already developed, is broken off.
[5] It is only fair to say that Greek moral philosophy was not unaware either that it was better to suffer evil than to do it. See in particular, Plato, *Gorgias* 509 (*meizon men phamen kakon to adikein, elatton de to adikeisthai*).
[6] See on this subject the classic writing of LUTHER, *Von weltlicher Obrigkeit* (Erlangen, Vol. XXII), extracts from which in French are given by M. STROHL in his book, *La substance de l'Evangile d'après Luther* (Paris, pub. de la Cause, undated), p. 338ff.

(12) *I well know that 'everything is permissible for me', but not everything is profitable. I well know that 'everything is permissible for me', but I will not be enslaved by anything.* (13) *It will be said: 'food is intended for the belly, and the belly is intended for food, and God will destroy both the one and the other'. At the same time, the body is not intended for immorality, but it belongs to the Lord, just as the Lord belongs to the body.*

their fellow men in their acts of brigandage. It is more difficult to distinguish them from the '*pleonektai*' (*v.* Ch. **5**), except that this term stresses more particularly the greed of these criminals. Here again it is not expressly said that all the crimes listed were in fact committed by Church members, but Chapter **5** induces rather pessimistic suppositions in this respect. We can only be led to the conclusion that there were some black sheep at Corinth who had fallen back into their old vices.

How then can the Apostle go on to assert that the Christians are purified, sanctified, justified? The whole problem of ethics in the Pauline (and indeed also Johannine) Epistles is raised by this.

How can the Christian be at the same time purified and be a sinner? And how can the assertion of his purity be compatible with the exhortation to make it real? We know from the Epistle to the Romans that God is willing to treat the man of faith (whose prototype is Abraham) as though he were righteous, so that Luther was able to characterize the ambiguous status of the Christian in his famous dictum: '*Semper justus, semper peccator.*' But that only partially solves the problem; for the Christian is not only justified, he is also sanctified and purified. These terms certainly in the first instance have a religious meaning. The Holy Spirit removes the guilt of the Christian, and also links him with the body of Christ, so creating the inner man, the germ of a new man. In order that this may develop and bring forth the fruits of righteousness (as the Baptist said) or the fruits of the Holy Spirit[7] (as the Apostle said), the man must yield himself completely to the Spirit's influence. He can, in fact, refuse to 'walk according to the Spirit' and so be lost in spite of his baptism by the Spirit (*v.* infra, Ch.10). The goodness of God —who affords man the greatest imaginable benefit in the world, namely His Spirit as the earnest of redemption—must be a stimulant, not for the attempt to acquire merit, but to let God act freely in His will to redeem and sanctify.—Note that in 6[11] the three verbs do not seem to denote three stages but three aspects of the Holy Spirit's action: rupture with sin ('*apelousasthe*'), attachment to the body of Christ ('*hēgiasthēte*'), justification ('*edikaiōthēte*'). Cf. supra, 1[30].

6[12-17] offer considerable textual difficulties. Let us deal with the purely philological ones first.

---

[7] See the list of the fruits of the Spirit in Galatians 5[22-3].

(14) *Now God not only raised the Lord, he will also raise up us by his power.*

(15) *Do you not know that your bodies are members of Christ? Therefore shall we make the members of Christ members of a prostitute? Never!* (16) *Or do you not know that a man who is united with a prostitute forms one body (with her)?* (17) *For the Scripture says, 'one fleshly creature shall be formed from the two'. But the man who is united with the Lord forms one spiritual being (with him).*

(18) *Flee, then, from fornication! Every other sin a man commits is outside the body. But the fornicator sins against his own body.* (19) *Or do you not know that your body is the temple of the Holy Spirit within you, which you have from God, and that you do not belong to yourselves?* (20) *You have been bought with a ransom. Therefore glorify God by your body!*

The word '*aras*' 6[15b] hardly gives acceptable sense. Grammatically it should be the aorist participle active of '*airō*', which would mean 'to lift something up in order to remove it', or even 'to abolish'. But the context would require 'detach' ('detach the members of Christ'). It is true that the isolated text of Mark 2[21] (reproduced by Mt 9[16]) might give the verb the meaning of 'tear out' (although many scholars give it an intransitive sense here). But then we should have to read '*apo Christou*'. And that is not the greatest difficulty. The singular '*aras*', like the singular '*poiēsō*', is most surprising. The rest of the passage uses the plural. Our conclusion is that we must read, with P and Didymus of Alexandria (*MPG* XXXIX, col. 828 A), '*poiēsomen*'. In the light of this '*aras*' becomes utterly unacceptable. We would replace it by the conjunction '*ara*', which frequently occurs before '*oun*' ('*ara oun*' = 'therefore'), and is attested by some manuscripts.[8] The alteration of '*ara*' into '*aras*' (the alpha never being elided in this case), then involved the changing of '*poiēsomen*' (or *poiēsōmen*') into '*poiēsō*'. This conjecture of J.W. seems eminently reasonable. It would also be possible to read '*ara oun*', which could equally well introduce a question. But in that case elision ('*ar' oun*') would have been obligatory, and this would make the corruption into '*aras*' more difficult to explain.

The genitive '*timēs*' without an adjective presented difficulty even at the time of the Vulgate, where it is boldly translated '*magno pretio*'. The majority of translators have followed this, although the interpretation cannot be justified, for '*timē*' can mean a price of any magnitude. If the Apostle had wished to stress the size of the price paid he would have said so, as does the First Epistle of Peter (1[19]) by speaking of the '*timion haima Christou*'. Lietzmann seems to be on the right track by translating 'against cash', i.e. against a cash payment. So then we should translate 'with a ransom' or 'for the

---

[8] Unfortunately not clearly indicated by TISCHENDORF (according to J.W. it occurs primarily in P and certain minuscules).

payment of a ransom'. The idea presupposed, as in Romans 7[23] where it is more clearly expressed, is that man has fallen into bondage to Satan, but that God has paid a ransom to liberate him, as a father might do for a son who had fallen into the hands of brigands.[9]

To understand this passage, we must recognize the existence at Corinth of a group of gnostic freethinkers, akin to those later combatted by heresy hunters like Clement of Alexandria, Irenaeus and others.[10] Two features of their teaching stand out:

(a) Nothing concerning corporeal life is of any importance for the spiritual life and for the destiny of the soul. This is why even debauchery and other carnal excesses cannot defile the spirit, which alone inherits the Kingdom of God. (b) The body, like all material things, was created by an inferior deity. For this reason there can be no bodily resurrection.[11] These are precisely the two doctrines professed respectively by the adversaries of Paul envisaged in Chapters 6 and 8 (libertinism) on the one hand, and on the other in Chapter 15 (denial of resurrection). These could be held by the same people, for the two attitudes were often associated. We have already seen that some scholars, for example, Allo preceded by Zahn, Jülicher, Lütgert and Lietzmann, have sought to identify these libertines with the mysterious Christ party of Chapter 1. But even supposing such a party really existed, which is very doubtful (v. supra, Ch. 1), it is not in fact said that the boundaries of these personal cliques were also the boundaries of theological groups.

The refutation by the Apostle is inspired by two considerations:
(a) the Bible doctrine of the creation of the body, and
(b) the Christian view of the Eucharist.

According to the Bible, God not only created souls and spirits, but also bodies and, in fact, all material creatures. It is true that these have had their natures perverted by the Fall, according to the teaching of both Jewish apocalyptic and Paul. The body has become fleshly (the '*sōma*' has become '*sarkinos*'). But 'material' is not the equivalent of 'fleshly' (carnal). The body as a material entity has its proper place in creation. This is why it too will enter the Kingdom of Heaven in the form of a body free from corruption, realizing the ideal of a restored material substance such as can be at the service of the Holy Spirit, instead of rebelling against God's law in the

---

[9] For those who like hypotheses we might suggest another way of explaining this text. It consists in replacing the genitive '*timēs*' by the dative '*timē*', which is synonymous with '*eis timēn*': 'you have been redeemed to live in honour and not in shame'. (Cf. Rom 1[26], 9[21], 2 Tim 2[20].) But the parallel of Romans 7[23] leads us to prefer the genitive.

[10] See EUGÈNE DE FAYE, *Gnostiques et gnosticisme* (2nd edn, Paris, 1925; pub. Geuthner), pp. 413–28.

[11] This second trait was common to all 'gnostics'. The former is peculiar to the licentious gnostics. To these were opposed gnostics with ascetic tendencies, who practised mortification of the flesh in order to liberate the spirit, and who sometimes forbade marriage (see Ch. 7 and 1 Tim 4[3]).

manner of Romans 7⁷⁻²⁵.[12] Thus every sin against the body is also
a sin against the will of God and may involve the risk of losing the
inheritance of the Kingdom.

These considerations are reinforced by a reminder of the unique
condition of Christians, namely their belonging to the body of
Christ. Here some modern commentators feel themselves a little
embarrassed because they try, in spite of themselves, to spiritualize
or, better, to transpose into the world of 'ideas', what Paul says
about the body of Christ. This passage clearly shows the error of
such an interpretation. For the Apostle the body of Christ is a metaphysical reality which, because of the Eucharist (as we shall realize
better from Chapter **11**) already extends its empire over the physical
sphere, in which the future resurrection body is being prepared.[13]
This is why conduct which loses sight of the noble destiny of the
body may endanger the action of the Holy Spirit and our belonging
to Christ. Man is a unity, and the body of the Christian cannot at
the same time be orientated towards Christ and also away from Him.

One objection may even so have been raised, on this occasion by
ascetic gnostics. If fleshly communion with a '*pornē*' = 'harlot'
breaks the union with Christ, why is the same not true of the fleshly
communion in marriage? The reply will be given by implication in
Chapter 7.

Perhaps we should remember that '*pornai*' were in general sacred
prostitutes, slaves attached to the service of a pagan temple (notably
to a temple of Venus-Aphrodite), who were supposed to put those
who worshipped there in communion with the deity they served[14]—
a further reason for looking upon union with such as having a
strongly negative religious value.

These remarks will perhaps facilitate the detailed understanding
of our passage. It may be subdivided into three parts: (*a*) 6¹²⁻¹⁴—
refutation of the libertine doctrine of the body; (*b*) 6¹⁵⁻¹⁸ᵃ (as far as
'*tēn porneian*')—the irreligious and anti-Christian character of
unchastity; and (*c*) 6¹⁸ᵇ⁻²⁰—the body regarded as the temple of the
Holy Spirit. Let us take these in turn.

(*a*) 6¹²⁻¹⁴. This passage is written in two strophes constructed
somewhat according to the rules of Hebrew poetry. The first strophe
is 6¹². The parallelism of its members is clear: 6¹²ᵃ ('*panta moi exestin*')
is repeated word for word in 6¹²ᶜ; to '*all*' *ou panta*' etc. of 6¹²ᵇ there
corresponds '*all*' *ouk ego*' etc. of 6¹²ᵈ. It goes without saying that
'*panta moi exestin*' = 'everything is permissible for me', is at each
occurrence the rallying cry of the libertines, who could with some

---

[12] See Chapter **15** below, where it is explained that the body which is spiritual
and not carnal is by no means lacking in substantiality.

[13] 'Observe, that the spiritual connection which we have with Christ belongs
not merely to the soul, but also to the body, so that we are flesh of his flesh, . . .
(Eph 5³⁰). Otherwise the hope of a resurrection were weak, if our connection were
not of that nature—full and complete' (CALVIN, *Commentary*, I.217).

[14] This was one reason why many of the prophets of the Old Covenant used to
call pagan cults a form of '*porneia*', of adultery with respect to Yahweh.

show of reason appeal to the Pauline thesis on the liberty of the Christian (see especially Gal 5). The Apostle, who is replying by the two statements which commence with '*all' ou*', makes the point that not all is profitable for the Christian life, and, on the other hand, this liberty must not lead to enslavement by the flesh. In germ these two assertions contain a complete Christian ethic, which would be anti-libertine without being legalistic.

The second strophe, which is considerably longer, comprises 6^{13} and 6^{14}. 6^{13a} (up to '*katargēsei*') cites a principle of the libertines which again has been borrowed from Pauline preaching wrongly understood: the Apostle indeed teaches that the Kingdom of God does not consist in eating and drinking (nor in abstinence from certain foods or certain drinks). The gnostics drew from this licentious conclusions, affirming that carnal things were of no consequence and that the body was destined to perish, thereby twisting the true sense of the Apostle's teaching according to which flesh and blood (as principles of corruption) would not inherit the Kingdom.

Paul replies in 6^{13b} and 6^{14} that it does not follow that licentiousness is compatible with the plans God has for our body. Our body belongs to the Lord, i.e. to Christ, as He also belongs to our body (an allusion to the Eucharist). Its destiny is a resurrection like Christ's. We can notice here again a parallelism which is obvious between 6^{13a} ('*ta brōmata . . . tois brōmasin*') and 6^{13c} ('*to de sōma . . . tō sōmati*'). Similarly 6^{13b} ('*ho de Theos . . . katargēsei*') corresponds exactly to 6^{14} ('*ho de Theos . . . dunameōs autou*').

(*b*) 6^{15-18a}. Belonging to Christ precludes union with a prostitute; for by such a union the Christian would form one body with the person concerned, and it is impossible to belong at the same time to two bodies. Yet obviously this impossibility is not merely a numerical one, but of a moral and religious order. Christ on the one hand, and the '*pornē*' on the other (behind whom we see the shadow of the goddess of carnal love), represent two opposed worlds. Hence the author strikes here the impressive antithesis between '*mia sarx*' = 'one flesh'[15] (the result of union with the '*pornē*') (6^{16}) and '*hen pneuma*' = 'one spirit' (unity with Christ) (6^{18a}).

(*c*) 6^{18b-20}. The Apostle's statement that '*porneia*' = 'fornication' is the only sin committed against one's own body is surprising. Many readers will ask: Has he forgotten gluttony, drunkenness, suicide? No doubt for the reasons we have mentioned he attributes to '*porneia*' a destructive quality with metaphysical repercussions. We have seen that two worlds stand in combat, and this gives the discussion an ontological and even cosmological significance.

The figure of the temple of the Holy Spirit has been met already in 3^{16}, but then it was applied to the Church. Here it is the body of

---

[15] It goes without saying that Genesis 2^{24}, which the Apostle cites in 6^{16}, does not use '*sarx*' in a pejorative sense. It simply expresses there the complete unity of the two creatures. But in the particular case discussed by the Apostle he is not wrong to give the word a more definite meaning.

the individual which is to become the dwelling place of the Holy Spirit—not in His fullness, but in the measure in which He can reside there. (Hence we read '*naos tou en humin hagiou pneumatos*' and not simply '*naos hagiou pneumatos*'.) This ideal will only be made visibly real in the future aeon, that is in the resurrection world. But the Holy Spirit must now already gain a footing within the person of the Christian and prepare his future state. The Apostle concludes by recalling that the body also has been redeemed by Christ and must in its turn glorify God so far as it can.

These concluding statements have been criticized as somewhat disjointed and obscure, but we hope we have shown they have their inner logic in spite of appearances. If all questions or objections are not treated in a satisfactory way, it is because the practical purpose of the exhortations prevented too long a digression into theology. Yet it must not be forgotten that we are probably witnessing here the first attempt in the history of moral thought to refute libertinism in some other way than by the arguments of an ascetic, legalistic or utilitarian type which are so common in Greek philosophy. Hence the unfinished and spontaneous nature of these passages.

Philo often uses the term 'house of God' for the soul of man, but never for his body.[16]

What Stoicism has to say about God dwelling in the interior of the soul ('*ho Theos endon estin kai ho humeteros daimōn estin*') is still farther away from Christian thought. For the Stoic is thinking of a natural kinship between human reason and God.[17]

[16] This point is not sufficiently stressed by J.W., who refers to several important texts of Philo (e.g. *de Somnio*, I.§149: '*spoudaze oun, o psuchē, Theou oikos genesthai, hieron hagion*' (ed. min. COHN and WENDLAND, III.220). But this scholar has clearly seen that for Philo the divine indwelling is the result of ascetic mysticism, whilst for the Apostle it is the effect of grace.

[17] See EPICTETUS, *Discourses*, I.XIV.14 (Teubner, p. 52), the source of the above quotation.

CHAPTER VII

(1) *To come to the questions raised in your letter, I declare that it is good for a man not to approach a woman. (2) Yet I counsel each one to have his own wife, to avoid the danger of misconduct, and likewise each woman to have her own husband. (3) Let the husband fulfil his conjugal duties towards his wife, and similarly the wife towards her husband. (4) It is not the woman who disposes of her own body, but the husband. Similarly, the husband does not dispose of his own body, but his wife. (5) So do not refuse each other, unless it is by mutual consent for a limited time, that you may be occupied in prayer. Then come together again, for fear that Satan may lead you into temptation by counting upon your want of self-control. (6) But this is only a concession I make to you and not an order I give to you. (7) What I would wish is that all men were like myself. But each has received his own endowment from God, to one this, to another that. (8) Therefore I say to the celibate and to widows that it is good for them to remain in their condition, as I myself. (9) But if they cannot exercise self-control, let them marry. For it is better to marry than to be consumed by desire.*

This chapter is the most important in the entire Bible for the question of marriage and related subjects, and it is strange to notice that in some Protestant discussions of marriage it is thought possible to ignore it almost entirely.[1]

On the other hand, the Anglican Church has long followed the practice of reading the whole chapter at the blessing of a marriage.

It is difficult to subdivide the passage into paragraphs, since the Apostle repeats himself several times, by returning to questions which he has already discussed. *Grosso modo*, it may be asserted that 7$^{1-9}$ speaks of marriage in general, 7$^{10-16}$ of divorce and mixed marriages, 7$^{17-24}$ insists on the importance of the idea of vocation, 7$^{25-38}$ deals with spiritual marriage and celibacy, and 7$^{39-40}$ with second marriages.

What exactly were the questions on the subject of marriage which the letter from the Corinthians posed? The Apostle's argument shows that some Christians (probably of a gnostic tendency, but at the opposite pole from the libertines) were asking whether complete continence was not required by the nearness of the Parousia, or from the general circumstance of belonging to the body of Christ. In addition, certain special cases, as those of widows, of mixed marriages, as well as of spiritual marriages, must have been referred

---

[1] Examples of this in *Foi et Vie* (Nov.-Dec. 1936).

to the Apostle by the Church. It is conceivable that even the argument of 6¹²⁻²⁰ could have been interpreted as an encouragment given to these ascetic tendencies. If Chapter 6 is attributed to a previous letter (which is not our view) misunderstanding may genuinely have been produced. In any case, 6¹²⁻²⁰ required supplementation.

7¹⁻⁹. '*Kalon*' in 7¹ cannot here mean 'good' or 'admirable' in a moral sense. That is shown by the sequel, which makes celibacy a gift of grace and not a matter of effort or merit. Therefore we must choose for the translation 'good' in the sense of 'valuable', 'profitable' or 'it is fortunate for', and this agrees very well with what follows. It is true that secular Greek lexicography affords little support for this translation. But such a meaning for '*kalos*' is perfectly familiar to the LXX.[2] Moreover, it seems that our verse may be an echo of Genesis 2¹⁸, using it with different overtones: for the Christian, the member of the Church, the loneliness of the first Adam no longer exists.[3]

7². '*Echetō*' = 'let him have' is not in the strict sense an imperative; if it were, 7¹, which proposes celibacy as an ideal, would be invalidated. Yet it is something more than a simple concession: it is a recommendation addressed to all those who lack the grace-gift of celibacy. Such people are beset by incontinence and would fall into debauchery if they tried to abstain from marriage.

It may surprise us that the Apostle says nothing about the part which the Christian home was destined to play in the Church, nor of the beauty of the task of bringing up children as Christians. It is true to say that primitive Christianity, no doubt under the influence of lively eschatological hopes, had not yet developed detailed moral teaching about Christian family life.[4] But we must bear in mind the author's aim. He is not here attempting to describe Christian family life, but simply to show the impossibility of generalizing the ideal enunciated in 7¹. For that he goes straight to the point and considers the tendencies within human nature which are opposed to such an ideal. At the same time he makes it clear that only marriage which is strictly monogamous can be contemplated for a Christian; bigamy or debauchery were regarded as contrary to the will of God (in spite of the opposite examples afforded by the patriarchs and kings of Israel). We must also notice that there is no question of justifying

[2] We may notice Jonah 4³, ⁸: '*kalon to apothanein moi ē zēn*' ('it is better for me to die than to live'), and especially the famous verse Genesis 2¹⁸: '*ou kalon einai ton anthrōpon monon*' ('it is not good—i.e. advantageous, happy—for man to be alone).—The *TWNT* lets us choose between 'right, good, praiseworthy, valuable'. —G. DELLING, *Paulus' Stellung zur Frau und Ehe* (*Beiträge zur Wissenschaft vom Alten und Neuen Testament* [4th series, Vol. V, Kohlhammer, Stuttgart, 1931], p. 69 and note 93), translates it by 'valuable', and this strikes us as very apt.

[3] The viewpoint of official Judaism is well expressed in the Talmudic treatise Yebamoth, fol. 63b (GOLDSCHMIDT, IV.536). 'A man who takes no part in procreation, must be regarded as one who sheds human blood.' There is no comparable statement in the New Testament.

[4] But see traces of it in Colossians 3¹⁸⁻4¹, Ephesians 5²²⁻6⁹.

marriage by procreation. Conjugal love has its own particular value.
Again on this point, the Apostle separates himself from a view widespread amongst the rabbis, who only permitted marriage with procreation as its aim.[5]

But furthermore, natural conjugal love must be sanctified by
'*agapē*': this is why elsewhere husbands are exhorted to love their
wives with (it is understood) Christian love (Col 3[19], Eph 5[25]).[6]

7[3] and 7[5] dot the i's, as the saying goes. The Apostle will not admit
asceticism within marriage, unless it is exceptional and for a period
of spiritual retreat.[7] For any ascetic exaggeration could only play into
the hands of Satan, whose spectre looms on the horizon, and who,
knowing human nature, urges towards misconduct married couples
who regard conjugal life simply as a 'spiritual union'. It is well-
known how the Reformers, notably Luther, stressed this aspect of
the question.

7[4], which is the heart of this short pericope, makes a most tactful
assertion ('*elegans paradoxon*', Bengel) bearing upon the ultimate
nature of Christian marriage, and which naturally has a greater
value than the implications of 7[3] and 7[5].[8]

7[6]. '*Sunggnōmē*' indicates a *concession*. But to what does '*touto*' =
'this' point? J.W. thinks that the Apostle 'allows' a return to married
life after the period of abstention. But, on the contrary, this return
seems to us to be required as the normal thing, according to what has
already been said. What he allows without ordering is precisely
these periods of '*engkrateia*' = 'continence'. This alone agrees with
what follows: while the Apostle recognizes abstention as the ideal
('be as I am', 7[7]) in conformity with 7[1], he will not admit that it
should be imposed, even temporarily, on those who have not the gift.[9]

What is the other gift to which the author alludes in 7[7]? To answer
this question would show an over-zealous wish to give the exact
meaning of the text. '*Houtōs—houtōs*' certainly does not set out an
alternative, but refers to the multiplicity of grace-gifts in the Church
—as might be said in Latin: '*alius aliud habet.*' For indeed, according
to the teaching of Chapter 11, the Holy Spirit is not given to believers

[5] See Tobit 8[7], as over against 7[2].
[6] This recommendation is incomprehensible if conjugal love in itself were
nothing but a form of '*agapē*', as some moralists have thought fit to suppose.
[7] Later Judaism likewise admitted such exceptions. In particular, see the
Testament of Naphtali 8 (CHARLES, *Pseudepigrapha*, II.338).—The opinions of
the rabbis on the duration of this period varied between a week and a month. See
Tractate *Ketuboth* of the Mishnah, V.6 (Danby, p. 252).—Calvin well translates
7[5]: 'Do not defraud each other.'
[8] Thus, the wife should have regard for the health of her husband, who ought
not to neglect himself because he no longer belongs to himself alone—and *vice
versa*.
[9] For IGNATIUS of Antioch chastity is similarly a '*charisma*'. See the Epistle to
Polycarp 5[2] ('*ei tis dunatai en hagneia menein*').

(10) *In the case of married people, I charge—no, not I but the Lord
—that the wife does not separate from her husband,* (11) *and if she is
already separated, I prescribe that she lives without remarrying or that
she be reconciled to her husband, and likewise I charge a husband not
to repudiate his wife.* (12) *In the case of others, I declare (I myself and
not the Lord): if a Christian has a pagan wife and she agrees to go on
living with him, let him not repudiate her.* (13) *And if a [Christian]
woman has a pagan husband and he agrees to go on living with her, let
her not repudiate him.* (14) *In fact, the pagan husband is sanctified by
his wife, and similarly the pagan wife by her Christian husband. For
otherwise your children too would be impure, while in reality they are
sanctified. But if the pagan partner separates, let that partner remain separated.* (15) *A Christian man or woman is not bound in these
circumstances, but God has called us to live in peace.* (16) *Now, how
do you know, wife, whether you will save your husband? Or how do
you know, husband, whether you will save your wife?*

in an abstract or general manner, but under the form of definite and
very varied grace-gifts. It would not distort the Apostle's fundamental teaching to include also among these gifts the endowment of being
a good father to a family.

7^8 and 7^9, which depend directly on what precedes, only repeat in
different words the recommendation of 7^1, to which 7^7 has recalled
us; but now '*chērais*', 'widows', are expressly mentioned. Since they
are again expressly referred to in 7^{39ff}, some[10] have sought to delete
mention of them here, only that would do violence to the text. A
subject to be treated later at greater length may well be touched upon
lightly first. It has also been suggested that '*chērois*' be read because
of the masculine '*autois*' and the active '*gamēsatōsan* = 'let them
marry' (used for men). But these words also relate to the '*agamois* =
'the unmarried' (men or women). Moreover, it could be that widows
already at this time formed a distinct group, the status of which had
given rise to discussions (Acts 6^1 and particularly 1 Timothy 5^{3-16}).

7^{10-16}. In this passage orders given by the Lord, introduced by the
imperative '*paranggellō* = 'I charge', are carefully distinguished
from the Apostle's own recommendations; thus, he refutes in advance
the attempts of those literal interpretations of Scripture which
regard all the words of the apostles as on the same level as those of
the Master. We may conclude for the recommendations in the
preceding pericope that they also come from the Apostle himself,
since the Lord is not mentioned.

The commandment of the Lord (7^{11}) applies to Christian marriages,
as the opposition between '*hoi gegamēkotes* = 'the married' (7^{10})
and '*hoi loipoi* = 'the others' (7^{12}) shows. The latter are the partners

---

[10] HOLSTEN, *Das Evangelium des Paulus*, I (Berlin, 1880)298, note 1.

of a mixed marriage.[11] The indissolubility of Christian marriage is affirmed, as well as the prohibition of a second marriage for the wife who even so may have been divorced. The word of the Lord to which reference is made is not actually quoted. It is idle to ask whether the author already knew a written collection of *Logia* (the Sermon on the Mount?)[12] or was depending upon an oral tradition; we have no means of answering. By and large, the text of Mark 10^9 and 10^{12} corresponds best to the prohibitions pronounced here. But the forbidding of a second marriage for the divorced husband (Mk 10^{11}) is lacking in our Epistle, although in a general way this chapter maintains a strict balance between the rights and responsibilities of the two partners. It may be concluded that Paul did not know the commandment of Jesus in the form given by Mark 10 (and Mt 19). But he may have known Matthew 5^{31-2} or a similar *logion*, which also only envisaged the case of the remarriage of the divorced *wife*.

Since mixed marriages were not envisaged by any word of the Lord, the Apostle himself will legislate on this question. Naturally, the marriage of a man or woman already a Christian with a pagan partner was regarded as so undesirable that the author does not even consider such a case. He is treating of pre-Christian marriages, one of the partners to which was subsequently converted. Contrary to the case of '*porneia*' (Ch. 5), he thinks that the non-Christian partner is indirectly consecrated by the other who belongs to the body of Christ. This liberal view is in harmony with the idea which the Lord deliberately stressed (Mk $10^{6\pi}$ and par.), that monogamous marriage had been instituted by God at the beginning of human history. This is why a regular, though pre-Christian, marriage cannot contravene the dispensation of salvation. Mixed marriages even allow a hope of the conversion of the pagan partner. Hence the union should continue, without any restraint and in conformity with the recommendations of 7^3.

What is harder to understand is the argument drawn from the idea of 'sanctification', namely of the state of consecration of children. Is it a general observation concerning all Christian children? Or is the author thinking of the children of mixed marriages, as J.W. assumes? It would truly be surprising if the Churches had regarded these latter as Christian without further question—as the *reductio ad absurdum* from this verse would however suppose. So then the observation certainly applies to the children of a Christian marriage or to children born before the conversion of both parents ('your children', Paul says, and not 'their children'). On the other hand, the analogy between the situation of the pagan partner and that of the children

[11] It is interesting and has hardly been noted by commentators, that the word marriage is here kept for Christian marriage. Nevertheless, in what follows, pagan marriages are equally thought of as valid.
[12] Our opinion is that the Sermon on the Mount in fact antedated the composition of the Gospel according to St Matthew. For this, see our article '*Dieu, Moïse, et les anciens*', *RHPR* (1941), p. 201, note 15.

would break down if the children had in some way been baptized. For in that case their position would have been as different as possible from that of the pagan partner.[13] But in fact, says the Apostle, you must regard these children, though unbaptized, as attached in an indirect way to the Church, through the intermediary of their parents. The same will be true of the non-Christian partner in mixed marriages.

However, the rule formulated by the Apostle allows of an exception ($7^{15, 16}$): if the pagan leaves the Christian partner the marriage is regarded as having been nullified,[14] and the Christian can marry again—that is, of course, with a member of the Christian Church ('*en kuriō*', 7^{39}).[15] But what exactly is meant by '*kalein en eirēnē*' (7^{15b})? In the first place, notice that the reading '*hēmas*', according to P 46, B, D, E, F, G, L and the majority of ancient versions, though it is rejected by Nestlé, seems to us better attested than '*humas*'. The use of '*en*' for '*eis*' is in no way surprising in Koiné or in New Testament Greek.[16] As for the substantive '*eirēnē*', it corresponds in general to the Hebrew שָׁלוֹם = 'complete peace', *outward and inward*. This meaning suits admirably here. God wishes to grant not only spiritual peace, that subsists even in the midst of tribulation, but He would also spare us needless scruples. Now, the feeling of being tied to a pagan partner in the circumstances indicated here would belong precisely amongst such scruples as God does not approve.

It would only be in the case where there was the certainty of leading to the Christian faith a partner who had forsaken one, that an attempt to find again and lead back this partner at any cost would really be justified (7^{16}). But who could have this certainty?

[13] This observation, which is purely historical, does not indeed suffice to settle the question of the legitimacy of child baptism, the discussion of which should take account, amongst other matters, of a revelation which is normally neglected in contemporary discussions. The reader may gather that we refer to Matthew 18^{10}. For this see our article '*Un texte oublié: Matthew 18:10*', in *Aux sources de la tradition chrétienne* (*Mélanges Goguel*, Neuchâtel, 1950). Cf. also O. CULLMANN, *Le baptême des enfants et la doctrine biblique du baptême* (Neuchâtel, 1949); *Baptism in the New Testament*, E.Tr. J. K. S. Reid (S.C.M., London, 1950).

[14] LUTHER thought that 'what is true of a pagan partner applies also to the case of a bad Christian' (Erlangen edn, LI.43). CALVIN was more cautious: '*Hodie tametsi nobis fere similem rationem cum Papistis esse volunt, prudenter tamen considerandum, quid intersit, ne quid temere tentetur* (Opera, Vol. XLIX, col. 413). In another connection CALVIN (*Consilia*, Opera, X.239, a text kindly pointed out by François Wendel) allows a woman to leave a husband guilty of persecuting her for religious reasons. But he seems to have been thinking of a separation only and not of divorce.

[15] From the philological viewpoint we do not insist on the reading *autē* (v.12) given by the Textus Receptus, nor on the corresponding reading *autos*, equally ill-attested. With Nestlé and the best MSS we read *houtos* and *hautē*.—In v. 13 one may hesitate between *ētis* (NESTLÉ, following, A, B, C, D, K, L, syr., coptic) and *eitis* (P 46, D, F, G, P, lat. vulg.), though the sense would be the same.

[16] See MOULTON and HOWARD, *A Grammar of N.T. Greek*, 1.62f, 103ff. Cf. PREISIGKE, *Wörterbuch zu den griechischen Papyri*, I.481, who gives the following examples: '*en Alexandreia apantō*' and '*anelthein en tē polei*'.

(17) *Very well, let each live in conformity with the state allotted him by the Lord, and in which God has called him. This is what I lay down in all the Churches.* (18) *Was someone called when already circumcised? Let him stay circumcised. Was someone called when uncircumcised? Let him not be circumcised.* (19) *Circumcision is nothing, and uncircumcision is nothing, but the keeping of God's commandments (is everything).* (20) *Let each remain in the state in which he was when he was called.* (21) *Were you a slave when you were called? Let that not trouble you; on the contrary, even if you are able to become free, remain rather in slavery.* (22) *For the slave who has been called by the Lord is the Lord's freedman. Similarly, the free man who has been called is Christ's slave.* (23) *You have been redeemed with a ransom. Do not become slaves of men.* (24) *Let each one, brothers, remain in the condition he was when called—in God's presence.*

7^{17-24}. This passage enlarges the theme by expounding the relativity of human conditions with respect to the coming of the Kingdom. The Apostle's point of view can be summarized by: make the least possible change in the human conditions of existence, so long as they do not hinder the realization of the Christian vocation. To impose circumcision on pagan converts would be as senseless as recommending its abolition to Jewish Christians. Even human slavery is of so little importance in relation to the liberation from another slavery which Christ has obtained for us, that it would be better to make no change.

But if the thought of the author is clear in broad outline, the explanation of the details of this pericope yet present some real difficulties.

(1) What does '*ei mē*' mean in 7^{17a}? The analogy with Galatians 1^7 suggests an adversative sense. But then, how does 7^{17} link with 7^{16}, which has already expressed a closely parallel idea: make no change in the existing situation? It must, then, be remembered that in 7^{16} the Apostle uses two rhetorical questions ('*ti oidas . . .*'), which logically demand a negative reply. With respect to this implied answer 'No', he continues: 'Very well, in that case it would be better on the contrary "*quieta non movere*".'

(2) What is the meaning of the verbs '*memeriken*'[17] and *keklēken?*[18] '*Merizō*' means 'to give a share in', and it could simply refer to the earthly lot of a man regardless of his vocation. This would agree with the general tenor of the passage. But a further comment must be added: it is not God, but the '*kurios*', i.e. Jesus Christ, who is the subject of '*memeriken*'. So it is the vocation of a Christian which is in question. This interpretation is confirmed by the parallelism

---

[17] Constructed with the dative through attraction of the relative: *hekastō hōs = hekastos hōs autō.*
[18] With the accusative, because *hekaston hōs = hekastos hōs auton.*

between '*memeriken*' and '*keklēken*'. For '*kalein*' has a religious force, namely 'to call to be a Christian in such-or-such a way'. It is therefore a matter of accepting, as a way of realizing our individual Christian vocation, the social situation (celibate or married, slave or freeman) in which we find ourselves at the time of our conversion.

7[19] presents this in a striking statement, akin to Romans 14[17] (and to 10[31]). We can now understand better the condensed expression in 7[20]. Accordingly, '*klēsis*' there does not mean the *calling* which makes us Christians, but that which we have to actualize by accepting our situation in life. This somewhat unexpected use of the word '*klēsis*' may have been influenced by its use in the popular philosophic literature of the time.[19]

There is little need to remark that this term employed in our Epistle has passed into extensive use in Christian ethics, notably in Protestant ethics, in which 'vocation' is frequently employed for the work committed to Christians. In German, '*Beruf*', 'business, profession', seems to derive directly from '*Berufung*' = 'vocation'.

Furthermore, it is noteworthy that the Apostle makes no reference here to any commandment of the Lord; so, once again, we have his own counsel. Of necessity its importance will decrease for later generations of Christians. For on the one hand belief in the *nearness* of the Parousia will weaken, and on the other, conversions will normally take place in Christian families at an age when the choice between marriage and celibacy has not yet been finally made. In addition, as the Church, under the influence of Christian education in moral sensibility, becomes progressively aware of the dignity of the human person, the state of slavery will appear intolerable to it, even though it is not an obstacle to salvation.

(3) What is the force of '*mallon chrēsai*' (7[21b])? Luther, followed by Calvin amongst others, and also by Godet, translates: '*then rather make use of it*' (i.e. of the possibility of liberating yourself from slavery).[20] This then would be an exception to the Apostle's ruling of which we have just been speaking. But '*ei kai*' always has a concessive sense—'*Even though . . .*'. We, therefore, agree with the interpretation of John Chrysostom: '*mallon chrēsai, tout' estin mallon douleue*';[21] of Peter Lombard: '*magis utere servitute*';[22] and of Bengel: '*servitute utere*'. This makes the adverb '*mallon*' more intelligible: 'Even if you are able to become free, remain *rather* in the state of slavery.' Admittedly, the use of the verb '*chraomai*' is rather surprising. But it can be

---

[19] See EPICTETUS, *Discourses*, I.xxix.33–49, e.g. 49 (Teubner, p. 96), where the philosopher forbids '*kataischunein tēn klēsin hēn keklēken [ho Theos]*', i.e. falling short of the vocation imposed upon us by God.

[20] S. EPHREM, *Commentarius in epistulas Divi Pauli* (Venice, 1892), p. 61: '*Si potes etiam fieri liber, et exire ad predicare evangelium, et pati persecutionem pro illo; id tibi expediet, liber esto.*'

[21] 19th Homily on 1 Corinthians §4, *MPG* LXI, col. 156.

[22] *MPL* CLXLI, col. 1595 B.

(25) On the subject of virgins, I have no command of the Lord, but I give my own opinion in my capacity as a believer, which the mercy of the Lord has granted me. (26) I think that because of the approaching calamity it is advisable not to change the state in which one finds oneself. (27) Are you bound to a wife? Do not seek separation. Are you free from any tie with a woman? Do not seek a wife. (28) Nonetheless, if you do marry you commit no sin; and if a virgin marries she commits no sin; but those who marry will suffer affliction in their outward life, which I would spare you. (29) This then, brothers, is what I would say to you: the time has been shortened. Henceforward let those with a wife live as though they had none; (30) those who weep as though they wept not; those who rejoice as though they rejoiced not; those who buy, as though they possessed not, (31) and those who use this world's (goods), as though they used them not. For the world is a form which passes away. (32) Now I would have you free from all cares. An unmarried person cares for the things of the Lord, seeking to please the Lord; (33) but a married man, cares for the things of the world, seeking to please his wife, (34) and he is divided. Similarly, the unmarried woman, and the virgin, are occupied with the Lord's affairs, so as to be consecrated in body and spirit. But the married woman is occupied with worldly affairs, seeking to please her husband. (35) I say this for your benefit, not in order to set a trap for you. On the contrary, my desire is that you may live becomingly and with unwavering attachment to the Lord.

(36) But if any man thinks that the integrity of his virgin is endangered because he overflows with vitality, and that he ought to let things

explained on analogy with expressions like 'tois nomois chrēsthai'[23] = 'live under the Law's commands'. Moreover, the interpretation which we support agrees very well with what follows. 'These matters are of small importance, for the converted slave will console himself by remembering that he is Christ's freeman (which is the essential thing). Conversely, the free man will remember his obligations which arise from the fact that he is Christ's slave.' This entire way of looking at things is inspired by the doctrine of man's deliverance by means of a ransom, which is the death of Christ ('timēs ēgorasthēte', 6[20]), a redemption from the power of darkness (cf. Rom 6[18,22], 1 Pet 1[19]).

The end of 7[23], 'mē ginesthe douloi anthrōpōn' = 'do not become slaves of men', of course does not contradict what has preceded. For here 'doulos' has religious force, 'become victims of human preoccupations' which should no longer have a place in the heart of believers. 7[24] concludes the pericope by repeating almost verbally 7[20].[24]

7[25-38]. The preposition 'peri' = 'on the subject of' (7[25]), which introduces the heading of this pericope, may show that we have here

[23] Hermas, *Sim.* I.§§3, 4.
[24] Notice that the later Stoics such as EPICTETUS (who himself was a slave) laid similar stress on the freedom of the wise man. Diogenes had said (according

*take their course, let him do as he desires; he will not sin; then let them
be married.* (37) *But suppose that a man does not allow himself to be
moved in his heart, having his desire under control, and that he is free
to make his own decisions: if such a man has decided in his innermost
heart to keep her as his virgin, he will do well.* (38) *Thus, one who
married his virgin does well, and one who refrains from marrying her
does even better.*

the reply to a question asked by the Corinthians. Once again the
Apostle regrets that he knows no word of the Lord amongst those
which, preserved orally or in writing and resistant to any arbitrary
additions, were authoritatively used in the Christian Churches. He
gives his own opinion (*'gnōmēn didonai'*) as that of a thoughtful
Christian, without making any appeal to his particular apostolic
authority. This latter concerned only the proclamation of the
Gospel and eschatological mysteries, not the development of ethics
or of ecclesiastical law.

If we translate *'pistos'* (7[25]) by 'believer' or 'Christian' we are not
unmindful that many commentators prefer the meaning 'worthy of
trust', on analogy with *'pisteuthēnai'* (1 Thess 2[4]). But since it is not
the faithful transmission of a message entrusted to him or infor-
mative teaching which is in question, we do not think this sense is
suitable here.

'Parthenoi' = 'virgins', in the same verse, could also be used of
men, as in Revelation 14[4]. But the sequel, from 7[28b], seems to exclude
this application. The construction of 7[26] is problematical. Does the
pronoun *'touto'* announce the phrase with *'hoti'*, the latter giving the
content of the *'touto'* ('this—namely')? But in that case the repetition
of *'kalon'* would be difficult to understand. Hence, we prefer to
regard the *'touto'* as linked with the advice already given, doubtless
that of 7[20]. But since the maxim of 7[20] may have been lost sight of
the author repeats it: 'I mean, that it is advisable not to change the

to EPICTETUS, *Discourses*, III.XXIV.67–8, Teubner, p. 297): 'Since Antisthenes
freed me I have no longer been a slave. How did he free me? Listen to what he
said: He showed me how to distinguish between what depended on myself and
what did not depend on myself.'

The same EPICTETUS exclaims elsewhere (*Discourses*. IV.VII.16–17, Teubner,
p. 369): 'No one has power over me. I have been freed by God.'—Here the
liberation is not the result of knowledge, but of divine intervention. This is the
text which perhaps approaches closest to a Christian viewpoint. Yet we hardly
need say that the God of Epictetus is far removed from the Christian God, and
that the idea of a new aeon contrasted with the present aeon is wholly unknown
to him.—Generally speaking, the Stoics, like the Declaration of the Rights of
Man in 1789, attributed their freedom to the fact that man is born free. See
SENECA, *De vita beata*, 15 (Teubner, I.I.213): *'Deo parere libertas est.'* But he has
previously said (ibid.): *'In regno nati sumus.'* The commentator ADOLF BON-
HOEFFER, in his book, *Epictet und das N.T.* (*Religionsgeschichtliche Versuche und
Vorarbeiten*, X [Giessen, 1911], p. 376), quotes it, indeed, with approval. See
ARNIM (*Die europäische Philosophie des Altertums*, p. 249): 'It cannot be denied
that the Christian idea of the Kingdom of God, of a Christian world-order, had
its origin in Stoic cosmopolitanism.' But the statement seems most hazardous.

state in which one finds oneself.'[25] The expression in 7[26], '*dia tēn enestōsan anangkēn*' = 'because of the approaching calamity', will be explained by what follows (7[29]).[26]

7[27] applies the quoted maxim to marriage: the best solution is that the married man should not separate from his wife. Since the divorce of Christians is forbidden by a word of the Lord (7[10,11]), this can only refer to mixed marriages (treated already in 7[12–15]), or to separation by mutual consent, against which also the author advises, in harmony with what may be gathered from 7[2] and 7[5]. On the other hand, 'unengaged' men ('*lelusai*'), that is, bachelors and widowers (in conformity with 7[8], although there only widows and not widowers were mentioned) would do well not to tie themselves down. But the Apostle hastens to add that this is not a law; and this is so, not only because he has no wish to be a lawgiver, but also because marriage is no sin, as was thought, even at this time, by the rigorist elements we have already encountered (precursors of the Marcionites).

In 7[28b] the author mentions the case of virgins, and with this seems to arrive at the principal subject of the passage. But again he defers it in order to intercalate a passage giving a new argument in favour of celibacy. It is briefly stated in 7[28b] and developed at length in 7[29–35]. Without this expansion the expression '*thlipsis tē sarki*' = 'affliction in the flesh' would be obscure; from it we gather that what is meant is tribulation caused by earthly cares. These will be particularly severe in the short period separating us from the Parousia, and will be most grievous for those who have founded a family. With this consideration is associated, once again, the idea that during this lapse of time too much importance must not be attached in a general way to earthly affairs. The statement '*kairos sunestalmenos*' = 'the time has been shortened', introduced by '*touto phēmi*' = 'notice what I say' (no doubt implying that it is a new revelation), is explicable in the light of Mark 13[20]: God has shortened the period of time which separates us from the end. The last days will be full of distresses, and it is to these that the expression '*dia tēn enestōsan anangkēn*' alludes, for '*anangkē*' is synonymous with '*thlipsis*', and '*enestōs*' refers to an imminent future which is already in a certain way operative in the present (generally '*enestōs*' = 'present', in opposition to '*mellōn*' = 'future').

From this particular situation are drawn first some general conclusions that lead us away from the actual problem of marriage; they are introduced by '*to loipon*' = 'for this remainder of time';

[25] In theory, '*hoti*' might have causal force ('because . . .'); but in that case '*touto*' would have to be given more precise meaning in order to avoid a truism, and of that there is no hint.

[26] Certainly, '*enestōs*' could also mean 'present'. But the meaning 'imminent', which suits it here, is equally well attested (just as with '*instare*' in Latin). Cf. J.W., p. 190, and PREUSCHEN-BAUER, *Wörterbuch*.

but it is strange that the recommendations of **7**[30] and **7**[31] have a much wider bearing and are independent of the date of the Parousia. They refer to an aspect of the moral position of the Christian: he has the right to use wordly possessions, without fixing his heart upon them. In this the Christian spirit breaks new ground in relation to the world and its goods, equally remote from pagan hedonism and Ebionite shrinking from the world. At first glance it seems to resemble that of the Stoa. But there is a perceptible difference. The Stoic forbade emotion. The Apostle suppresses neither joy nor sorrow, but he knows that the Christian must not become once again a slave to the world, its possessions and its passions, which absorb the pagan. This Christian liberty is expressed in a magnificent paradox. Nothing is changed outwardly: the married Christian will continue to have his wife (and **7**[2] and **7**[5] show what this means), he will continue with his occupations, such as his business; but his inward situation will be changed by the fact that his wellbeing no longer depends upon his success in this world.

7[31b] can be regarded as a résumé of this attitude. But what is the precise significance of '*katachrōmenoi*'? If the Apostle had wanted to give this verb the same force as '*chrōmenoi*' = 'using', he would simply have repeated it as a participle ('*chrōmenoi hōs mē chrōmenoi*'), on the analogy of the other verses. On the other hand, the sense of 'abuse' is too remote from '*chrēsthai*', because it would denote a way of behaving outwardly different from a simple using of the word. Once again we therefore think that Bengel has hit the nail on the head when he says: '*utendum, non fruendum.*' It is the hedonistic attitude which is condemned.

7[31]. Finally, the formula of this verse, which avoids the simple expression 'end of the world', can be interpreted in two different ways, although the verb '*paragein*' is not ambiguous. 1 John 2[17] uses it with the same meaning ('pass away'), though in the middle voice. It is the force of the genitive which needs clarifying, '*tou kosmou toutou*' = 'of this world'. If, as is usually thought, this were a subjective genitive, the Apostle would be implying that the world will not be absolutely and simply destroyed, but trans-'formed'. '*Praeterit figura mundi, non natura, ut in aliam speciem mundus vertatur.*'[27]

But objection can be raised to that translation, because if that were the meaning one would expect to read: '*to schēma tou kosmou*' (without '*toutou*') = 'the form of the world.' When 'this world' is mentioned, what is always meant is our present world as something which must perish, over against '*ho kosmos ho mellōn*' = 'the world to come' or '*ho aiōn ho mellōn*' = 'the aeon to come'. Hence, we prefer to take *tou kosmou toutou* as an objective genitive: the figure which

---

[27] HERVÉ DE BOURG-DIEU, *MPL* CLXXXI, col. 885 D.

passes like an actor leaving the stage, is our world. It happens that
'*schēma*' can bear the sense of a 'part played in a theatre' (*v*. Wettstein), and '*paragein*' means 'to pass across the stage' (to disappear
again, of course).[28] Thus the meaning would be: the world will soon
have played its part—a statement which might particularly scandalize
any Greek intellectuals imbued with Stoicism.

This passage has shown us, besides the relativity of all earthly
things, the imminence of the tribulations of the end time. It now
remains to show why married people will be especially subject to
them. Yet the verses which follow only give an indirect indication,
insisting on the fact that in a general way they will have more worldly
anxieties.

7[32], '*thelō*' = 'I would', expresses a desire which is regarded as
somewhat unrealizable. To understand what follows it must be
noted that there is no pejorative force here in the use of '*merimna*'
and its derivatives, such as we find in the Sermon on the Mount
(Mt 6[25ff]). The 'cares' here are not caused by lack of faith, but by
entirely legitimate preoccupations, whether in the religious domain
('*merimnan ta tou kuriou*' = 'to care for those things which concern
the Lord') or in the secular realm ('*merimnan ta tou kosmou*' = 'to
care for those things which concern the world'). So there is no
question of condemning the preoccupations of married people with
their legitimate family affairs; neither is it a simple statement of fact
(the Apostle was not unaware that, unhappily, many husbands take
no trouble to please their wives). But he is establishing a norm: it is
just and right that the husband should seek to 'please his wife';[29] and
to understand this expression we must remember that in the LXX
'*areskō*' usually means 'to gain the approbation of someone by
giving satisfaction.'[30] So '*areskein tō kuriō*' here means 'to fulfil the
demands of the Lord'. Similarly, '*areskein tē gunaiki*' or '*tō andri*' =
'to submit to the demands of family life'.

Such cares are therefore legitimate.[31] Yet it is nonetheless true
that they partly deflect a man from concerns which the service of the
Lord should inspire. He becomes 'divided' (notice the play on the
words '*merimna—memeristai*'). Has celibacy moral superiority?

---

[28] In an analogous sense '*paragein*' is used for an army marching past (see
POLYBIUS, V.XVIII.4. = Teubner, II.129).

[29] The problem of the relationship in Paul's language between the indicative
and the imperative is touched upon by WINDISCH, '*Das Problem des paulinischen
Imperativs*', *ZNW*(1924), pp. 265ff.—Cf. Romans 13[1-7], where the Apostle uses
the indicative when dealing with the duties of governing powers.

[30] Cf. the frequent expression: '*areskon enōpion tou Theou*' = 'that which
receives the approbation of God.'

[31] If the Apostle were even slightly a mysogynist, as preachers sometimes
childishly suggest, how then are we to understand this precise parallelism between
the statements relating respectively to man and wife?

The opposite rather, for it is easier to remain faithful to the Lord when one is not 'divided'.[32]

This little dissertation can be divided into two strophes, in strict parallelism except for the words '*kai memeristai*' = 'he is divided', in 7[34a], which are not repeated at the end of the verse. The first strophe opens with '*ho agamos merimna*' and goes to '*memeristai*'. The second opens with '*kai hē gunē*' and ends with '*tō andri*'. Each strophe devotes one line to the unmarried person and one to the married. Again we observe the Apostle's concern that there should be perfect equality between the position of the man and of the woman.

We have now to justify the attachment of '*kai memeristai*' to the preceding verse. For some manuscripts, namely D, E, F, G, K, L, attach '*memeristai*' (preceded or followed by '*kai*'), on the contrary, to the words which follow, '*hē gunē kai hē parthenos*', and then commence a new sentence with '*hē agamos merimna*'. Some manuscripts of the Old Latin as well as several of the Latin Fathers also presuppose this reading, and translate by '*discrimen est inter mulierem et virginem*', or similar words. Such a reading should mean: 'there is also a difference between the woman and the girl. The unmarried woman is occupied with the Lord's affairs', etc. But '*merizo*' = 'to divide' never has this meaning. Still more impossible is the reading of א and A: '*memeristai hē gunē hē agamos kai hē parthenos. Hē agamos merimna*', etc. For between the unmarried woman and the virgin there is no difference whatever in this connection.

The only good reading is that given by P 15, B, P, the group 37, 73, 137, the Vulgate ('*et divisus est*') and the Coptic versions: '*memeristai*' (±'*kai*') '*hē gunē hē agamos*', etc. It need be no embarrassment to us if the Apostle forgets to repeat the phrase at the end of the second strophe, for the argument, once grasped, will apply automatically to the married woman.

Nevertheless, the author introduces one variation into the second strophe. In place of '*pōs aresē tō kuriō*' he writes '*hina ē hagia kai tō sōmati kai tō pneumati*'. '*Hagia*', here as always, means 'consecrated'. This has been clearly seen by Godet, who explains (I.384) that the unmarried woman is 'entirely devoted in body and spirit to the service of the Lord'; and he adds: 'As to the words, "*in her body*", one must compare verse 4, where it is said of the married woman that she has not power over her own body. As to *the spirit*, compare what follows.'

In 7[35] we encounter a real difficulty of construction. Does the phrase '*ouch hina . . . epibalō*' (35[b]) belong to what precedes or what

---

[32] This is why Clement of Alexandria particularly admired the married man who, in spite of all his cares, remains faithful to the Lord. The Apostle himself does not draw this conclusion, because he does not wish to pass moral judgements. See CLEMENT OF ALEXANDRIA, *Stromateis*, VII.XII.§70.7 (STAEHLIN, III.51) and our Memoir '*Etude sur la doctrine de la chute et de la préexistence des âmes chez Clément d'Alexandrie*' (*Bibliothèque de l'Ecole des Hautes études, sciences religieuses*, Vol. XXXVIII, Paris, Leroux, 1923), pp. 10–16.

follows? Either connection can be justified. We prefer the second, because '*alla pros to*', etc. (35ᶜ) stands in natural opposition to '*ouch hina . . .*' (35ᵇ). 35ᵇ and 35ᶜ taken together express in a more detailed way the intention underlying 35ᵃ ('*touto de legō*'). '*Brochon epiballein*' = 'set a trap' is an expression from hunting. But why should the Apostle be reproached for wanting to snare his flock in a net? The complaint would be justifiable if he wished to enslave them to an ideal beyond their ability to achieve. In actual fact, he is only giving advice which is governed by two desires, namely that each individual should be consecrated to the Lord, and yet should remain within the limits of his own charismatic endowment. To wish to go farther might run the risk of involving them in situations which would endanger seemly behaviour. This twofold concern is shown on the one hand by '*euschēmon*', which is a reminder of the requirement of 'decency', and on the other by '*euparedros*' = 'one who is eagerly attached to something', supported by the adverb '*aperispastōs*' = 'without allowing oneself to be diverted', which indicates unswerving attachment to the Lord. This double ideal some will best achieve in the unmarried state, others within marriage.

This is why 7³⁵ forms the transition to the following pericope (7³⁶⁻⁸), which rounds off the chapter by dealing fully with the question of '*parthenoi*' = 'virgins'. From the very beginning of the chapter it might be asked whether the term '*parthenoi*' does not refer to a group of young people who had taken a vow of celibacy. We shall see that this is the interpretation which becomes necessary in the explanation of 7³⁶⁻⁸. But first we give below the traditional explanation of the verses—which is different from our own—in order to go on to show that it faces insuperable difficulties: 'But if anyone thinks that he behaves in an unseemly way towards his daughter (who is a virgin), when she begins to pass the flower of her age, and that things should follow their natural course, let him do what he wishes (i.e. allow his daughter to marry). He will not sin. Let them marry. Yet if one remains resolute in his heart, without being constrained by necessity, and if he has power to act according to his own will, and if he has decided in his heart to keep his daughter a virgin, he will do well. Thus, a man who gives his daughter in marriage does well, while he who does not give her does better.'

This interpretation was already supported in antiquity by John Chrysostom.[33] Saint Ephraim did not know of it. Ambrosiaster does not mention the father,[34] and Atto contemplates the possibility that affianced persons are meant.[35] Hervé de Bourg-Dieu[36] accepts Chrysostom's explanation, but particularly stresses its allegorical significance: the father represents the Christian; the daughter, the flesh ('*virgo*' = '*caro*').

[33] *De virginitate* (*MPG* XLVIII, especially §73 = col. 586ff.)
[34] *MPL* XVII, col. 225 A, B.
[35] *MPL* CXXXIV, col. 359 B to 360 A
[36] *MPL* CLXXXI, col. 888 A.

These are our objections to John Chrysostom's interpretation. (1) The first difficulty lies in the unusual use of *'parthenos autou'* (or *'heautou'*) as meaning 'his daughter'. Such a usage might have been just intelligible if we had previously been warned that this was a discussion of the rights of a father. As that is not the case, the interpretation becomes highly improbable.

(2) *'Huperakmos'* naturally derives from *'akmē'*, which could mean 'maturity' though it usually means 'vigour'. The translation 'past maturity' is therefore possible philologically. But it is impossible to see why the rules of decorum should be endangered or violated (*aschēmonein*) from the time when the young woman passes the flower of her age, or why the father who might desire to impose perpetual virginity on his daughter should have scruples only at this late hour.

(3) The plural of the imperative *'gameitōsan'* = 'let them marry' (plural as dual) would be unintelligible if father and daughter alone were in question. The verb can only refer to *them*, i.e. *the virgin and her fiancé*. But nothing has been said of the latter up to this point according to the interpretation we are criticizing, simply because bethrothal has not been envisaged.

(4) The idea that the father might commit a sin is just as strange. It could, however, be explained if need be by his having made a vow to offer his daughter to the Lord. Nevertheless, such vows are unknown in the early Church.

(5) On the other hand, is it not grotesque to praise the unswerving constancy of the father in a decision which costs him nothing, and in which it is his daughter, who is not consulted, who bears the full weight of the sacrifice?

(6) Then the extent of paternal authority over children who have reached maturity is hardly in accord with passages such as Colossians 3[21] (Eph 6[4]) 'fathers, do not irritate your children, so as not to discourage them', or with the many declarations of the Apostle in this chapter about not wishing to impose a constraint on anyone but to desire for each and all a life 'in peace'.

So far as we are aware, the first to give the right explanation was Grafe[37] followed by Achelis[38] and Lietzmann.[39] Paul here presupposes the existence of an institution which we might call spiritual marriage: a young man and woman would pledge their permanent mutual affection and would agree to cohabit occasionally, but without breaking the vows of virginity which they have made one to the other. This dangerous way of living seems to have been known to Hermas,[40] who gave it positive approval. Eventually the Church forbade it because of the increasing abuses to which it gave rise.

---

[37] *Theologische Arbeiten des rheinischen wissenschaftlichen Prediger-Vereins* N.F. III (1899).575ff.
[38] *Virgines subintroductae* (Leipzig, 1902).
[39] Commentary *ad locum*.
[40] Sim IX.11.

(39) *A wife is bound to her husband only as long as he lives. If the husband dies, she is free to marry whom she will, providing it is a Christian marriage.* (40) *Nevertheless she will be happier by staying as she is—at least in my opinion; and I think I have the spirit of God.*

It is true that we have no text definitely attesting this arrangement for the first century; but it is *a priori* most probable that it goes back to the time of great eschatological enthusiasm, that is, to the earliest days. Indeed, this is the only plausible explanation of our passage. The Apostle's attitude towards these spiritual marriages may be summarized in a phrase: he does not condemn them, but he allows (and in some cases even counsels) the affianced couple to marry. Thus, he does not recognize the validity of their vows of virginity.

We can now understand the terms which are left obscure by the traditional interpretation.

(1) The expression '*hē parthenos heautou*', most strange for 'his daughter', is entirely suitable for 'the fiancée'.

(2) The adjective '*huperakmos*' readily refers to the fiancé who is overflowing with vitality and zest for life,[41] who for this reason might behave inconsiderately ('*aschēmonein*') towards his fiancée. These expressions would then be entirely in place, and the connection of the thought is perfectly clear.

(3) The plural or dual '*gameitōsan*' is no longer incomprehensible, because in all that preceded, the relation of the affianced couple is under consideration.

(4) The supposition, contested by the Apostle, that the fiancé might be committing a sin in marrying 'his virgin' is quite intelligible, as well as the praise he might receive for his firmness of purpose.

(5) Finally, no question now arises about excessive paternal authority, which for the reasons stated would be hard to understand in the realm of Paul's ethics.

The fact that in classical Greek '*gamizō*' used in 7[38] means '*to give in marriage*' and not '*to marry*' need not trouble us. For the confusion in the Koiné between verbs in '*-eō*' and those in '*-izō*' has long been known. It could have been facilitated by the same pronunciation of the two aorists (like '*egamēsa* and '*egamisa*')[42] and by the common use of the passive '*gamizomai*' in the sense of 'to be married', as in Mark 12[25] and parallels and Luke 17[27].[43]

7[39-40] expressly permit remarriage. Remarriage can take place after the death of the partner. It is true that explicit mention is made only

[41] In general use '*akmē*' meant 'vigour'. (See the *Thesaurus* of HENRY ESTIENNE.)
[42] For this see the BLASS-DEBRUNNER *Grammar*, §101.
[43] It is noteworthy that BALJON (*De tekst der brieven van Paulus aan de Romeinen, de Corinthiers, . . .* [Utrecht, 1884], pp. 65, 66) had already seen that there was no reference to a father in this passage and that '*parthenos*' could only mean 'virgin' ('*ongehuwd meisje*'). But since he knew nothing of spiritual marriages he did not arrive at a satisfactory solution.

of widows and not of widowers. It might be said that widowers are mentioned in 7^8. But in that case '*chēroi*' would have to be read in 7^8, and this has no textual support. It seems to us that the Pastoral Epistles, which on the whole are non-Pauline and which depict the condition of the Pauline Churches after the death of the Apostle, afford the best explanation: in them we see that the '*chērai*' formed a kind of order, endowed with special duties and privileges. The members should not, on principle, remarry. Our author advises young widows not to enter this sort of 'convent arrangement'—they would do better to remarry (1 Tim 5^{14}). There is nothing that prevents us thinking that this could go back in origin to the very early days. The Apostle Paul, more categorically than his successors, expressly allowed the remarriage of widows and thereby set himself against a prejudice which was tending to implant itself in the Churches.

7^{40} re-echoes motifs developed above. '*En Christō*' = 'remaining within the body of Christ', i.e. in the Church: a Christian marriage. '*Gnōmē*' is a personal opinion, as elsewhere. The Apostle does not speak in the name of Christ, nor in virtue of his being an apostle, but because he has the Holy Spirit.

To summarize, we have seen that the Apostle regards both marriage and celibacy as legitimate. If he shows a preference for celibacy it is largely for the reasons stated in 7^{26} and 7^{32-4}. It is not possible, on balance, to speak of the moral superiority of one of these solutions over the other. What the Apostle does repudiate are hybrid solutions: celibacy as a pretext for a life of debauchery, or a married life which is not fully lived. We may note particularly that what is condemned by the Apostle is the type of 'married bachelor' who avoids family obligations even for the best of reasons (for example, for the entire devotion of his time to learning or to the Church).

CHAPTER VIII

(1) Concerning meat offered to idols, we know we all have knowledge —knowledge puffs up, but love builds up. (2) Yet if someone claims to possess complete knowledge, he has not even begun to know as he ought. (3) But if anyone loves God, he has been known by him.

(4) Now on the subject of eating meat sacrificed to idols, we well know that there are no idols in the world, and that there is no God but the One. (5) For even if so-called gods should exist in heaven or on earth—and there really are many gods and lords—(6) it would none the less be true that for us there is but one God, the Father, who is the source of the universe and the goal of our existence, and there is but one Lord, Jesus Christ, the mediator of all creation and of our existence.

8^{1-6}. The substantive *'eidōlothuta'* = 'meat sacrificed to idols' is of Jewish origin.[1] The pagan term was *'hierothuta'*. The problem under discussion here has been well summarized by Godet: 'The believers of Corinth and the other Greek cities found themselves in a difficult position in regard to the heathen society around them. On the one hand, they could not absolutely give up their family and friendly relations; the interests of the gospel did not allow them to do so. On the other hand, these relations were full of temptations and might easily draw them into unfaithfulness, which would make them the scandal of the Church and the derision of the heathen. Among the most thorny points in this order of questions were invitations to take part in idolatrous banquets. The centre of ancient worship was the sacrifice; it was in this religious act that all the important events of domestic and social life culminated. As in Judaism (cf. Deut 27^7, the peace offering), these sacrifices were followed by a feast. All that remained of the victim's flesh came back to the family which offered the sacrifice, and these consecrated meats were eaten either in the apartments or sacred wood belonging to the temple, or in the worshipper's house; sometimes, also, they were sold in the market. . . .

'Now various questions might be raised on this subject. And first of all: Is it allowable for a Christian to be present at a feast offered in the temple of an idol? Some, in the name of Christian liberty, answered: Yes! They boldly took advantage of the adage: All things are lawful for me (6^{12}, 10^{23}). Others said: No! for in such a region one subjects himself to the danger of malign and even diabolical influences. The scruples of the more timorous went farther: Even in a private house, even in one's own house, is it not dangerous to eat of that meat which has figured on the idol's altar? Has it not con-

[1] See 4 Maccabees 5^2 (RAHLFS, I.1163), Revelation $2^{14, 20}$.

tracted a defilement which may contaminate him who eats it? Not at
all, answered others. For the gods of the heathen are only imaginary
beings; meat offered on their altar is neither more nor less than
ordinary meat.'[2]

Sometimes, with reference to this question, the famous Apostolic
Decree of Acts 15 is mentioned, wherein it is forbidden to eat blood
and things strangled, that is to say, meat derived from animals not
killed ritually. But in that case the stress is different from Chapter 8,
where the scruples arise from the consecration of the food to demons.
Moreover, the date and provenance of the decree are debatable.[3]

In 8[1], '*peri tōn eidōlothutōn*' = 'concerning meat offered to idols'
could at a pinch depend on '*gnōsin echomen*' = 'we all have knowledge'. But parallelism with 8[4] implies its attachment to '*oidamen*' =
'we know'.

But why does the thought of the Apostle, instead of reaching out
at once to the question of '*eidōlothuta*', occupy itself with a digression
about gnosis? Apparently because those who were 'strong' at Corinth,
'the gnostics' we have already encountered in 5[2], boasted that they
had a superior knowledge which dispensed them from all scruples
in this matter. The Apostle takes up their catch-phrase in order to
let them understand, first of all, that they are not the only ones to
'have knowledge'. 'We also ourselves have it.'

Then he gives them the shrewd reminder that their pride ('*dokein*'
= 'to vaunt oneself', cf. 3[18]) itself proclaims that they are devoid
of true knowledge.

8[2] would best follow on from 8[1a], after '*echomen*'. But unfortunately
this close linkage is broken by 8[1b], which mentions '*gnōsis*' without
any restriction (that is, or so it would seem, both good and bad
'*gnosis*'): it swells with pride. This is a quite unfitting remark at the
very moment when a distinction between true and false gnosis is to
be drawn. Moreover, the asyndetic construction of 8[1b] is more than
striking. We should certainly expect to have the phrase 8[1b] introduced by '*de*' or, better still, by '*alla*'. We cannot rid ourselves of the
impression that we are here in the presence of a parenthesis added
either by Sosthenes or by a reader who remembered the phrase about
'puffed-up' gnostics, in 5[2].

To return to 8[2], commentators have not sufficiently attended to the
deliberate opposition between the perfect '*egnōkenai*' and the aorist
'*egnō*'. This aorist is inceptive (or ingressive): 'You who claim to be
already in possession of complete gnosis' [this is the force of the
perfect '*egnōkenai*'], you are not even at the beginning of true
knowledge.'

---

[2] GODET, I.401–2.
[3] See the commentaries, and the book by ETIENNE TROCMÉ, *Le livre des Actes et
l'Histoire* (Paris, 1957).

8³. How is the true gnostic to be recognized? By his love for God.[4] But the pen of the author has a fresh surprise in store for us; he does not write: he who loves God 'knows Him'—but, 'is known by Him'. This twist, at first glance a surprising one, can be explained in the light of 13¹² and Galatians 4⁹, where it is explained that no one can know God unless he is already known by God.[5] In our verse there is therefore a kind of ellipsis. Furthermore, for its full understanding we must remember that 'to have been known by God' (and observe again the use of the perfect '*egnōstai*') is almost synonymous with 'to have been chosen by Him'. It is just the same in the well-known passage, Romans 8²⁸⁻³⁰, which confirms for us the close association between the two ideas. Love for God is therefore the true sign of election and the only token of true gnosis.

8⁴⁻⁶. This passage presents no difficulty of construction like the preceding one, except for noticing that **8⁵ᵇ**, '*hōsper eisin*', etc. = 'and there really are', is evidently a parenthesis and that '*ouden eidōlon*' = 'no idol' is the subject, as is shown by the parallelism with '*oudeis Theos*' = 'no God'.[6]

On the other hand, there are some very complex theological problems here, about which a commentator must give his opinion, though he cannot hope, however, to convince all his readers. The first is the opposition between the distinct monotheism of **8⁴** and the concession (theoretical, of course) to polytheism in the parenthesis **8⁵ᵇ**. On one side, the existence of idols, that is, of the gods represented by idols, is denied, and the oneness of God is affirmed ('*heis*' = 'one only'!); however, it is conceded that a multitude of gods and lords really exist. Thus, it is not **8⁵ᵃ** which creates difficulty; for the phrase introduced by '*eiper*' is purely hypothetical, introducing an imaginary or perhaps even impossible case ('even if there were . . .'). Moreover, it leads on very well to the idea of **8⁶**, that only one God ('*Theos*') must be worshipped, and only one Lord ('*kurios*') is the Saviour. It is **8⁵ᵇ** ('*hōsper . . .*') which requires explanation.

Since the terminology of **8⁵ᵇ**, which gives the name '*theoi*' = 'gods' (without '*legomenoi*' = 'so-called') to other beings than the Creator, is foreign to the general thought of early Christianity, it is scarcely possible to fall back on a gloss. But indeed, basically the thought is truly Pauline and can be explained by Jewish angelology. For if pagan gods such as Zeus, Hermes (cf. Acts 14¹²) or Artemis (cf. Acts 19²⁶ᶠᶠ) do not exist, there were nevertheless, according to Jewish

---

[4] A theme extensively developed by CLEMENT OF ALEXANDRIA in Books IV and VII of his *Stromateis* (*v.* DE FAYE, *Clément d'Alexandrie* [2nd edn, 1906, Leroux], pp. 301ff).

[5] The antithesis 'know—be known' in biblical and Hellenistic texts has recently been studied by HUGEDÉ (*La métaphore du miroir*, pp. 164–76). His researches confirm our opinion of the relation between 'to know' and 'to elect'.

[6] LUTHER's translation, 'that an idol is nothing' ('*dass ein Götze ein Unding ist*'), ingenious as it is, is untenable. It is, indeed, found already in the Middle Ages, e.g. ATTO DE VERCEIL has 'nihil est' (*MPL* CXXXIV, col. 361 C).

theology, which Paul follows, a number of angelic beings of great power which men might be tempted to worship and which are sometimes called 'gods'. The chief Old Testament texts relating to this are Psalms 81[1] (82[1]), 97[7] (Hebrew), and 138[1] (Hebrew). Further, Clement of Alexandria also admitted that some powerful angels may be called gods and lords: in *Stromateis* V.xi.§77 [7] the '(apocryphal) prophecy of Zephaniah' is cited, at the point where the prophet attains in spirit the fifth heaven and says: '*kai etheōroun anggelous kaloumenous kurious*'[8] = 'and I beheld the angels called Lords.' The title '*kurios*' = 'lord', or more precisely '*kuriotēs*' = 'overlordship', is one which Paul has also given to certain categories of angels, *v*. Colossians 1[16] (cf. Eph 1[21]); this is in contradiction with Philippians 2[11], but in accord with the terminology of Psalm 135[3] (136[3]), and Deuteronomy 10[17].[9]

Is it possible to go farther and show wherein the exact distinction lies between '*Theoi*' and '*kurioi*'? We can rule out that the Apostle might have used the term '*kurios*', even hypothetically, for the Emperor. In passages like this there is rather a concealed polemic against such a usage, just as there is in a general way in the Christian confession: '*Christos kurios*' = 'the Christ is Lord.'

We could better suppose that '*kurioi*' referred to the angels of the nations, concealed behind political powers (cf. the comments on 6[2–3]), although in Romans 13 where these are expressly mentioned the title given them is '*exousiai*' = 'authorities'.[10]

The one true God receives in 8[6] the name of '*ho patēr*' = 'the Father', which is fully in the gospel tradition. On the other hand, the expression '*heis Theos*' = 'one God alone' reminds us of the famous 'Shema Israel' (cf. Deut 6[4]). The term אֶחָד‎ יְהֹוָה‎, translated by '*kurios*', was kept by the Christians for the glorified Christ (*v*. Phil 2[11]).

In short, the Apostle denies the existence of pagan gods, but admits that there are angelic powers, though they must not be worshipped whatever the name that is given to them.

The second major difficulty resides in the phrase in 8[6b]: '*ex hou ta panta*' = 'from whom are all things.' Certainly, if this expression were encountered in a pagan philosopher it would be taken by

---

[7] STAEHLIN II.377.

[8] On the other hand, *Str.*, VII.ii.§5.6 (STAEHLIN, III.6) reads: '*toutō* (*scil.* '*tō huiō tou Theou*') '*pasa hupotetaktai stratia anggelōn te kai Theōn.*' THEODORET (*MPG* LXXXVII, col. 288 D) thinks that Paul has simply made a concession to pagan terminology: '*kata tēn Hellēnōn philosophian legei.*'

[9] Cf. Slav. Enoch 20[1] (CHARLES *Apoc. and Pseudepigrapha*, II.441) and Eth. Enoch 61[10] (KAUTZSCH, p. 271) where terms equivalent to '*kuriotētes*' denote groups of angels.

[10] We might notice, out of curiosity, that some ancient writers like JEROME (*MPL* XXX, col. 741 C) followed by ATTO DE VERCEIL (*MPL* CXXXIV, col. 363 A) think that '*theoi*' means the angels of Heaven, and '*kurioi*' the elect upon earth. Observe also that the Seer in the Apocalypse of John almost yielded to the temptation to worship an angel (Rev 19[10], 22[8–9]).

readers in the sense of emanation, and translated: 'It is from Him
that the Universe proceeds'. But the Apostle Paul, in harmony with
the religious thought of the Old Testament, is a creationist (v.
Colossians 1[16], already mentioned). An attempt might be made to
resolve the difficulty by supposing that Paul had borrowed the
formula from the current speech of the Hellenistic world. But apart
from the fact that it is not easy to find expressions akin to this,[11]
it would then have to be asked in what sense the Apostle was using
it, and so the problem would only be pushed farther back.

To reach clarity it must be remembered that the doctrine of
creation can take various forms. According to Genesis 1, God
created the world from pre-existent matter; for creation is nothing
other than the transformation of 'chaos' (the 'tohu wabohu') into a
cosmos. The Wisdom literature and probably also the prologue of
St John's Gospel (if 'egeneto' and 'gegone' are in fact used as the
passive of 'poieō' = 'to make') seem, on the contrary, to teach
'creatio ex nihilo'; and this became the official doctrine in Christianity.
Neither of these two conceptions can be reconciled with our formula
in 8[6] or analogous expressions.

But a third conception of creation is possible. It is taught in the
Kabbalah.[12] According to this, God created the universe by taking
from Himself all the elements of creation. On this basis the Pauline
formula would be comprehensible, without appealing to a much
more questionable emanation explanation. For, on the one hand,
we have active creation brought about by the wisdom and will of
God and not by some simple quasi-natural process. On the other,
creatures receive a measure of independence irreconcilable with
emanationism, but such as is presupposed by both Jewish and
Christian doctrines of the world.

Similar considerations might hold for the second part of the phrase
('eis hon ta panta' = 'unto whom are all things'). It does not necessarily mean the reabsorption of the world into God, as in the Upani-
shads or with Plotinus. It might well be a reminder that the universe
has for its aim the glorifying of God, or, more probably, that the
goal of history is the establishment of the Kingdom of God, wherein
the Creator will be present anew in the universe from which he has
been separated by the Fall (cf. 15[28]).

The Christological formula of 8[6c] is precisely parallel to the
theological one we have just analysed. It is easy to see that we are
dealing with two parallel strophes, each of three lines.

[11] An expression which approaches somewhat closely to this of ours is found
in PLUTARCH'S Quaestiones platonicae, II.II.1001 C (Teubner, VI.124), where he
deals with the creation of the soul by God: 'ap' autou kai ex autou gegonen.'
[12] The reader who disbelieves in the high antiquity of the Jewish Kabbalah is
asked to view our remark as simply pointing to an analogy, without any presup-
position about historical dependence.—We commend the following works about
the Kabbalah: FRIEDLAENDER: Der vorchristliche jüdische Gnosticismus (Göttingen,
1898), GINSBURG: The Kabbalah (2nd edn, London, 1920), SCHOLEM: Major
trends in Jewish mysticism (New York, 1941).

The affirmation that Christ was the intermediary and source of creation ('*di' hou ta panta*') raises no difficulties in the ambit of Pauline Christology, provided we observe the difference between '*ex hou*' ('author of creation') and '*di' hou*' ('intermediary').[13] For we know that Christ, the image of God, is prior to the creation (Col 1[15–16]) and that He possesses all the secrets of divine wisdom (Col 1[19], 2[3,9]). Therefore He is predestined to succeed, in some degree, to the place of '*sophia*' which in Jewish Wisdom literature had been the instrument of God in creation (Prov 8[30]).[14] Furthermore, we must not forget that the pre-existent Christ is also the heavenly Adam, and that according to some Jewish speculations '*Adam quadmôn*' veritably contained in germ the entire universe.[15] In any case, there is perfect fundamental agreement on this matter between the Christology of the Johannine prologue and that of Paul.[16]

However, the end of the verse ('*hēmeis di' autou*' = 'we through Him') is not as clear as the commentators sometimes suppose. Does the Apostle allude to the first or the second birth? Two arguments can be put forward in support of the latter: (*a*) as creatures we form part of the universe: in that case it would not be necessary to refer specially to the part played by Christ in this; (*b*) parallelism with **8[6b]** requires an allusion to redemption. The meaning of the phrase would then be: 'Christ, through whose mediation we exist as Christians.'

But the reply could be made to (*a*) that all Gnostics would not admit being placed on the same plane as the universe, and that there might be here a protest against a kind of false spiritualism which attributed a divine nature to spiritual men, excluding all idea of creation; and to (*b*) that the repetition of '*dia*' in **8[6c]** not found in **8[6b]** already disrupts the parallelism.

It is hard to decide definitely, but we are inclined to think that there is a reference to the creation of man.

---

[13] B and the Ethiopic tradition read '*di' hon*' instead of '*di' hou*'. This is very improbable, because it would imply the antecedence of the world to Christ. We could better understand an alteration of '*di' autou*' into '*di' auton*' in Romans 11[36] (where God is the subject). But that does not concern us here.—P 46 has quite clearly '*di' hou*' in our verse.

[14] Cf. *Jerus. Targum* (= Pseudo-*Jonathan*) on Genesis 1[1], which identifies חכמה and ראשׁית (ETHERIDGE, I.157) and PHILO, who establishes the following equivalences: '*patēr kosmou*' = '*logos*'; '*mētēr kosmou*' = '*sophia*' ('*quod deterius potiori insidiari soleat*, §54) (Ed. minor WENDLAND AND COHN I.250).

[15] Cf. *Encyclopaedia Judaica* I.763ff and 783ff; GINSBURG, *The Kabbalah* (London, 2nd edn, 1920), pp. 89–108; *The Jewish Encyclodaedia*, I.181ff.

[16] Nineteenth-century theology did not always reveal clearly the cosmological perspective of Pauline Christology. Yet here we have a cornerstone of the Apostle's theology. For the identity between the originator of creation and the originator of redemption is like a warning against every attempt to interpret his theology in a Marcionite or Gnostic sense, doctrines according to which the saviour God is alien to the world and creation itself can only have been a transient accident.

(7) *But not all possess the knowledge; in fact some, by being accustomed to idols until now, eat as if the meat were really a sacrifice, and their conscience, being weak, is defiled.* (8) *Now food will not commend us to God. If we abstain from eating we shall not fall behind; and if we eat we shall not advance further.* (9) *Yet beware that this liberty of yours does not become a stumbling-block to the weak.* (10) *For if anyone sees you, who have knowledge, taking part at a banquet in a pagan temple, will not his conscience, which is weak, be 'edified' to the extent that he also eats the sacrificial meat?* (11) *See how the weak will be swept away for lack of your knowledge, the brother for whom Christ died.* (12) *By thus sinning against your brothers and wounding their conscience, which is weak, you sin against Christ.* (13)

8^{7-13}. 8^7 opens with an affirmation—or, rather, with a negation—which is in flagrant contradiction with 8^1, where knowledge is attributed to everybody. We cannot avoid this by taking (contrary to our explanation) '*pantes*' = 'all' in 8^1 as no more than a gnostic slogan. For the fact is that the Apostle accepts it. We can only suppose that '*gnōsis*' in 8^7 does not mean intellectual knowledge, but in this place means a *strong faith* which does not hesitate to draw certain practical conclusions repugnant to the 'weak', i.e. to the victims of old habits. Here, as elsewhere (Rom 14), it is to be noticed that the terminology of asceticism is inverted: whilst for asceticism the weak, the less developed, are those who eat anything, it is precisely the reverse for the Apostle who means by the weak those who have scruples with regard to food sacrificed to idols or with regard to food in general. To this extent the Apostle takes sides with the 'gnostics'. We shall see later where he opposes them.

There is, however, one philological difficulty to be surmounted. Witnesses to the text of 8^7 are divided between two readings: '*sunētheia*' = 'by custom' or '*suneidēsei*' = 'by conscience'. The former is given primarily by P 46, ℵ, A, B, and the Coptic versions, that is to say, in a general way, by the Alexandrine text; the latter is no less well attested, for it is supported not only by the Textus Receptus, but also by D, the early Latin, the Latin Fathers, the Vulgate and the Peshitto, that is, by the Syro-Occidental text. But with Godet and the majority of modern commentators we prefer the former reading, because the replacement of the rare word '*sunētheia*' by '*suneidēsei*' could have been suggested by the occurrence of '*suneidēsis*' at the end of the verse. Moreover, '*heōs arti*' = 'even now' fits particularly well with '*sunētheia*'. The meaning is: a habit which continues to engender, by the association of ideas, certain superstitious attitudes.[17]

[17] It must, however, be admitted that this construction presents difficulties. First, '*sunētheia*' is separated by '*heōs arti*' from the genitive '*tou eidōlou*' which completes it; then, the verb '*esthiousin*' lacks a direct object. But there is no other way of construing it without considerable conjecture. We must, then, assume the presence of an accusative such as '*tēn sarka*', 'meat'.

*This is why if a food causes offence to my brother, I would prefer to eat
no meat for ever, so that I might not cause offence to my brother.*

The noun *'suneidēsis'* naturally has a moral force here. The
'defiled' conscience is opposed to the pure conscience, called a
'kathara suneidēsis', 1 Timothy 3[9], 2 Timothy 1[3].[18] Here, over against
the weak conscience is placed *'pistis'*, cf. Romans 14[22], where the
Apostle says to the 'strong': *'su pistin echeis'* = 'you who have
faith'. We know definitely that everything which is not done through
faith is sinful (*'pan ouk ek pisteōs, hamartia estin'*—Romans 14[23]).

This is why those who are strong lack charity and themselves
commit sin by inciting those who are weak to commit it; they place
them in a situation in which they run the risk of losing the benefits of
the work of Christ. Moreover, one who pays attention to these
scruples is no less of a Christian than the strong, and will not for that
reason have any the less standing at the Last Judgement. Godet, it is
true, prefers the present *'paristēsin'* (beginning of **8**[8]) which is given
by D. But all the other good authorities, including P 46, have the
future *'parastēsei'* = 'it will commend'. There is a clear allusion to
the Judgement, as the parallel text of Romans 14[10–12] confirms.

The passage **8**[9–13] presents no particular difficulties. Yet in order
not to misunderstand these verses it must be observed that *'oiko-
domēthēsetai'* (**8**[10]) = 'be edified' has to be taken in an ironical sense.
The strong think to edify the weak by their example. 'Fine edification', retorts the Apostle, 'which leads them to their ruin!' At the
opening of **8**[12], *'houtōs'* must certainly be attached to the participle
'hamartanontes' and not to the indicative *'hamartanete'*, otherwise
we should have something akin to a tautology. What the text means
is—the sin for which I reproach you and which is a sin committed
against your brother, under the conditions I have indicated,[19] is also
a sin against Christ.

The soteriological significance of the death of Christ is presupposed. This theme will be found developed in the Epistle to the
Romans, and to the Colossians (see the Commentaries in this series);
see also on Chapter **2**, above.

[18] See EDMOND GRIN, *Morale de la conscience et morale de la grâce* (Cahiers de
la Faculté de théologie de l'Université de Lausanne, VI, 1934), and, by the same
author: 'Le rôle de la conscience morale dans la théologie romande et dans l'évan-
gile' in *Hommage et reconnaissance, recueil de travaux publiés à l'occasion du
soixantième anniversaire de Karl Barth* (Neuchâtel and Paris, 1946); and H.
CLAVIER, ' "Suneidēsis", une pierre de touche de l'hellénisme paulinien' (in the
Volume jubilaire du 1900ᵉ anniversaire de la visite de saint Paul en Grèce (Athens,
1953). See the comment in our *Commentaire de la 2ᵉ Épître aux Corinthiens*
(Delachaux & Niestlé, Neuchâtel, 1958), p. 24. The main texts on *'suneidēsis'* in
2 Corinthians are 1[12], 4[2], 5[11].

[19] A similar thought is expressed by Rabbi Jehudah according to *Midrash
Sifre* on Deuteronomy 14[21], fol. 95b, §105: 'There are things which are permissible,
although some people regard them as forbidden. Then they must not be permitted
in the presence of those who hold the more strict view.' The text of this, together
with a Latin translation, is found in UGOLINO, *Thesaurus*, Vol. XV, col. 661
(Venice, 1753).

The pericope culminates in an impressive ejaculation, reminiscent of the still more dramatic one in Romans 9[3].

When the author's thought has been grasped, it is surprising that, according to Galatians 2[11ff], he resisted the Apostle Peter so forcefully when at Antioch Peter broke off table fellowship with the Gentile Christians out of regard to the Jewish Christians who had come from Jerusalem. Were not these latter exactly in the position of the 'weak' who should not be made to stumble? It might be said that Peter acted out of cowardice and not from love. But this reply would be inadequate, for it could then be asked why Paul did not do the same thing from the right motive. The reason was that the Jerusalemites showed the annoying desire of wanting to impose their weak faith upon the strong; they 'judged' them, which is explicitly condemned in Romans 14[3].[20] From that moment a question of principle arises over which Paul could not yield. Moreover, separation from Gentile Christians would have implied an outrageous lack of love for them, such as the Apostle of the Gentiles could not contemplate for one moment.[21]

[20] 'In the meantime, he [the Lord] hints that strong giants, who may be desirous tyrannically to subject our liberty to their humour, may safely be let alone, because we need not fear giving offence to those who are not drawn into sin through infirmity, but eagerly catch at something to find fault with.' (CALVIN, *Comm.*, E.Tr., p. 282.)

[21] An examination of the meaning of '*skandalon*' is given in the study by G. STAEHLIN, in *Beiträge zur Förderung christlicher Theologie*, II.24 (Gütersloh, 1930).

CHAPTER IX

(1) *Am I not free? Am I not an apostle? Have I not seen Jesus our Lord? Are you not my work in the Lord?* (2) *If for others I am no apostle, nevertheless I am for you. For it is you who are the seal of my Christian apostleship.*

Chapter 9 opens up a new subject without any transition. It is this which impels us to attribute Chapters 8 and 9 to different letters (*v.* Introduction), and to take Chapter 9 as the commencement of Letter B, in so far as B has been preserved. The series of rhetorical questions throughout the passage 9^{1-13} reveals the author's strong feeling in the face of the attacks which must have been made on his apostolic authority by the Corinthians, incited no doubt by people from Judaea for whom the Twelve were the only true apostles. Nevertheless, it must be remembered that this way of arguing by using questions was very widespread amongst preaching philosophers of the time.[1]

The order of the two first questions is uncertain. The Textus Receptus starts with '*ouk eimi apostolos*' = 'am I not an apostle?' supported by D, Ambrosiaster[2] and several lesser witnesses. Others[3] open with '*ouk eimi eleutheros*' = 'am I not free?'; J.W. thinks we have the gloss of an editor who wanted to contrive a transition between the two chapters; then, in some manuscripts, this slid into the second place. The hypothesis deserves favourable consideration, particularly since we have no indication at all to what kind of freedom the author is alluding (though of the freedom to eat meat there is no question here). But in any case the exclamation '*ouk eimi eleutheros*', if we wish to retain it, must precede the other, because '*ouk eimi apostolos*' links closely with '*ouchi . . . heōraka*' = 'have I not seen?'.

9^1 and 9^2 serve to introduce this apologia. The first indispensable mark of apostleship is the privilege of having seen the risen Christ and of having been called by Him. This requirement was fulfilled by the appearance on the Damascus road. But if others wished to con-

---

[1] See, for example, EPICTETUS, *Discourses*, III.XXII.48 (Teubner, 1894, pp. 270f), '*ouk eimi alupos, ouk eima aphobos, ouk eimi eleutheros; pote humōn eiden me tis en orexei apotungchanonta, pot' en ekklisei peripiptonta*'; etc.; cf. R. BULTMANN, *Der Stil der paulinischen Predigt und die kynisch-stoische Diatribe* (Göttingen, 1910).

[2] *MPL* XVII, 228 C.

[3] Especially P 46, ℵ, A, B, Vulgate, Peshitto, TERTULLIAN (*MPL* II, col. 1006 B), AMBROSE (*MPL* XVI, col. 1089 C).

*(3) Here then is my defence against those who accuse me: (4) Have
we not the right to eat and drink? (5) Have we not the right to be
accompanied on our missionary journeys by a Christian wife, as are
the other apostles and (in particular) the Lord's brothers and Cephas?
(6) or again: is it only myself and Barnabas who have no right to refrain
from working? (7) Who ever serves as a soldier at his own expense?
Who plants a vineyard and does not eat its fruit? Or who shepherds a
flock and does not partake of the milk of the flock? (8) Am I taking up
a purely human standpoint when I say these things? Does not the Law
say the same? (9) Indeed it is written in the Law of Moses 'thou shalt
not muzzle an ox which treads out the grain'. Is God concerned about
oxen, (10) or is it for our sake he always speaks? Yes, indeed, this
word was written for us. For it is in the hope of having his share that
the ploughman must till the ground and the sower must sow his seed.*

test the fact, there was the missionary work accomplished at Corinth
by Paul, or, more precisely, by the Lord working through him; this is
what '*en kuriō*' = 'in the Lord' means at the end of 9[1].[4] The second
'*en kuriō*', at the end of 9[2], seems to be superfluous and is lacking in
D and the Peshitto (P 46 is defective); it may have been added in
conformity with 9[1]. The Corinthian Church is the seal of his apostleship; yet in some sense it is God who applies the seal. For this use
of '*sphragis*' = 'seal' see 4 Maccabees 7[15].[5] The datives '*allois*' and
'*humin*' (9[2]) mean 'in the eyes of', with a suggestion also of 'for you',
'in your service'.

With his apostleship validated the Apostle starts his real apologia
('*hautē*' in 9[3] relates to what follows). We gather that his enemies,
not content with contesting the validity of his apostleship because
of its origin, have even found grounds for complaint ('*anakrinein*' =
'institute proceedings at law against someone') over the scruples he
showed by refusing to live at the expense of the Church members, as
many others did (cf. 2 Cor 11[20]!); they pretended to view it as the sign
of a bad conscience and a confession of the lack of apostolic authority.
Hence, the first step in the apologia must be to show that the Apostle
has the same prerogatives as others, secondly that he has voluntarily
renounced some of his rights in order to minister to his flock.

9[4] does not refer to the right to eat or drink this or that—a question
discussed in Chapters **8** and **10**—but of the right to live at the expense
of the Church. The right is expressly recognized in a tradition preserved in Matthew 10[7-14]. But it is unlikely Paul knew of it in that
form; it definitely forbids working for money, as Paul did. Moreover,

---

[4] See 15[10], Philippians 4[13], and naturally also Galatians 2[20]; cf. also Romans
14[20], where the life of a Christian is called '*ergon tou Theou*'.
[5] RAHLFS, I.1167, John 3[33], cited by J.W., has no relevance here, because it
refers on the contrary to the seal which a man applies to the truthfulness of God.

the right to be accompanied by a wife on one's travels, affirmed in
9[5], is unknown to the instructions preserved by Matthew.[6]

There seems no doubt about the precise meaning of '*adelphēn
gunaika*': '*adelphē*' = 'Christian woman', '*gunē*' = 'wife'. The apostles
had the right not only to be married and to be accompanied by their
wives on their journeys ('*peri-agein*', 9[5]), but also to have them supported by the Church. If '*adelphē*' meant here any Christian woman,
travelling as spiritual assistant, the substantive '*gunē*' would be quite
superfluous. Clement of Alexandria proposed a third explanation:[7]
an apostle could be accompanied by his wife without living maritally
with her, but treating her as a sister. But this over-elaborate explanation has nothing to support it. In Chapter 7 '*adelphos*' and '*adelphē*'
were used as meaning male and female Christians (7[12,14,15]).[8]

It is curious that, in 9[5], Peter should be separated from and named
after the 'other apostles' as though he did not belong to them. The
conjunction '*kai*' can mean only 'and without forgetting Peter in
particular'. But a further question arises: Are the brothers of Jesus[9]
also, like Peter, included in the group of the apostles and only mentioned separately because of their importance? John 7[5] attests that
none of them belonged to the Twelve, 'for his brothers did not believe
on him'. Thus, every attempt to discover their names—the names,
that is, of James, Joses, Simon, Jude—in the list of the apostles
(Mk 3[16–19] and pars) is foredoomed to failure. On the other hand,
we know that Paul never restricted the number of the other apostles
to the Twelve. Here, for instance, he refers to Barnabas as an apostle.
It would therefore be quite possible that he gave this title to the
brothers of Jesus, converted after His resurrection. This is certain
in the case of James (*v.* Galatians 1[19], where James is expressly called
an apostle); and this is not surprising in view of the great part he
played at Jerusalem and the particular resurrection appearance of
the Lord granted to him (*v.* Chapter **15**, below). Here we further
learn that the brothers of Jesus actually did missionary work, a
point we should have been unaware of if we had had to write our
history solely with the aid of the Acts of the Apostles.

---

[6] If Peter and other apostles had their wives with them on their travels—and
there is no reason to doubt what this verse says—this would be a serious argument
against the strict authenticity of the instructions attributed to the Lord by
Matthew 10. See also JOHANNES B. BAUER: 'Uxores circumducere' (1 Cor 9[5]) in
Bibl. Zeitschr. (Paderborn, 1959), Vol. I. He brings new arguments in favour of
our interpretation of '*adelphēn gunaika*', and observes that a rabbi would never
have been able to collaborate or travel with a woman who was not his wife.

[7] *Stromateis*, III.VI.§53 (STAEHLIN, II.220).

[8] Other instances of this usage of '*adelphos*' and '*adelphē*' in the Acts and
Epistles are too numerous to mention here (see the Concordances).

[9] Even the Gospel texts which teach the supernatural birth of Jesus know
nothing whatever of Mary's perpetual virginity. There are therefore no reasons
for arguing, with Catholic thinkers, that James, Joses, Simon and Jude were not
true sons of Joseph and Mary. And a similar remark could, of course, be made
about their sisters.

(11) *If we have sown the spiritual seed for you, is it outrageous if
we should reap material things from you?* (12) *If others have a share in
your goods, is there not yet more reason that we should? But we have
not exercised this right; on the contrary, we bear all the cost, so as to
set up no obstacle to the Gospel of Christ.*

9^{7-12} demonstrates the right of the apostles to be maintained, first
by the use of three secular examples: the soldier, the vineyard cul-
tivator, and the shepherd. All three are thought of as serving a master
who gives them pay or who allows them to be sustained from the
fruit of their toil. The same idea is found, Paul thinks, in the Law of
Moses when spiritually interpreted (9^8 and 9^9).[10] Deuteronomy 25^4
reads: 'Thou shalt not muzzle the ox when he treadeth out the
corn.'[11] This text, says the Apostle, really has 'us' in view, i.e. 'We
preachers of the Gospel, who have the right to reap some wordly
harvest when we have sown the word which represents incomparably superior benefits' (9^{11}).[12]

The '*gar*' in 9^{10} presents no difficulty, if the author's occasional
elliptical style is remembered. The meaning is: 'Yes, indeed, because
it relates to us . . .'—'*Hoti*' preceding '*opheilei*' might mean 'that', in
which case '*egraphē*' = 'it was written' would introduce a new
quotation, drawn from some unknown source (so J.W.). But this
supposition is not necessary. Following Bachmann, '*hoti*' could be
given a causal or explicative sense. The Apostle is referring to a very
sensible custom, and the fact that he does so in a Hebraic manner in
a sentence of two parallel members need cause no surprise. In con-
firmation of his statement he follows the Rabbinic manner by
arguing '*a minore ad maius*': the right of one who sows spiritual
benefits which are incomparably superior will be so much the more
beyond dispute.

Who are the '*alloi*' = 'others' in 9^{12}? Apollos? Perhaps. But the
way in which Paul speaks of the Judaizing apostles in 2 Corinthians
11^{20} makes it possible that apostles or evangelists from Judaea are
here in question, though there is no means of telling. Then who are
'*hēmeis*' = 'we', 9^{11}? In addition to Paul himself, Apollos, as well as
Titus and Timothy might be meant, although these are not apostles
in the stricter use of the word. But the plural could quite well be no
more than a plural of modesty, with a singular meaning.

The phrase '*tēs humōn exousias metechousin*' is usually translated as
if '*humōn*' were an objective genitive, and '*exousia humōn*' meant
'right over you'. But the construction, with '*humōn*' between the

[10] Some manuscripts, including F and G, read '*ei*' for '*ē*' in 9^8. But we can
agree with TISCHENDORF that '*ei*' was felt here to be equivalent to an interrogative
particle.
[11] Read '*kēmōseis*' from '*kēmos*' = 'muzzle', with B, D, G; other authorities,
including P 46, read '*phimōseis*', which means the same but is a harmonization
with the text of the LXX.
[12] Deuteronomy 20^6 or Proverbs 27^{18} could also be cited.

(13) *Do you not know that those engaged in Temple service eat the portion of the sacrifices which falls to them? And that those who serve the altar have their share of what is offered on the altar?* (14) *Likewise, the Lord ordered those who proclaim the Gospel to live by the Gospel.* (15) *But I myself have exercised none of these rights. And I do not write this in order to claim them. For I would prefer to let myself die than . . . in short no one shall deprive me of this boast.* (16) *For indeed, if I simply proclaim the Gospel, I have nothing to be proud of, because the task is laid upon me as a necessity. Woe is me, if I do not proclaim the Gospel.* (17) *Supposing I did this by my own decision, then I deserve a reward. If I do it independently of my own will, it is a charge committed to me.* (18) *But by what then do I merit a reward? It is that in preaching the Gospel I offer it without cost, so as not to take advantage of the right granted me by the Gospel.*

article and the noun, does not favour this interpretation. Further, '*metechein*' would in this case have to have the sense of 'exercise' (a right), which seems hardly possible. Hence it is more natural to take '*humōn*' as subjective genitive and to regard '*exousia*' as a synonym for '*ousia*' = 'substance, goods', leaving '*metechein*' with its one possible sense of 'to share'. It may be somewhat of a difficulty that '*exousia*' in 9^{12} does not have quite the same meaning, but this could be explained by the fact that the word was still in the author's mind. It is even quite possible that 9^{11} may originally have had '*ousia*', and that the '*exousia*' of 9^{11} was an error caused by the occurrence of the same word in 9^{12}.

The verse contains a further argument *ad maius*: Paul had worked harder than the rest (*v.* 2 Cor $11^{23\text{ff}}$), should he not then have at least the same rights that they enjoyed?—If the Apostle has not exercised these rights it is solely in order to assist the progress of the Gospel, which might have been hindered by a way of life open to malevolent criticism. '*Stegein*' = 'endure' (as in 13^7). '*Panta*' = 'all things' must allude to the material privations and the manual labour to which the Apostle had to submit.

But he is afraid that his detractors will not have been silenced, so he adds a further scriptural proof: priests also live from the sacrifices offered to God. This sends us to Numbers 18^{9-32} and Deuteronomy 18^{1-8} where the rights of the priests and Levites are fixed, both in general and in detail. This assumes that there is a parallelism between the priesthood of the Old Covenant and the ministry of the apostles. The same analogy is attested in Romans 15^{16} ('*eis to einai me leitourgon Iēsou Christou eis ta ethnē*'). It is true that the same right was granted in pagan sacrificial cults, but there is no suggestion that Paul is referring to such here, as J.W. thinks.

9^{13}. If we wish to press the distinction between '*ergazomenoi ta hiera*' = 'those engaged in Temple service', and '*paredreuontes tō thusiastēriō*' = 'those who serve the altar', then we must think of the Levites

on the one hand and the priests, who officiate at the altar, on the other. There is close parallelism between the two phrases (yet no quotation is being made!).

The '*logion*' of the Lord which the Apostle knew (9¹⁴) must have approximated to that preserved in Matthew 10¹⁰, without being verbally identical with it, or to the summary of recommendations in Matthew 10⁸⁻¹⁴.

In 9¹⁵, after denying the idea that he is seeking to claim anything for the future, the Apostle gives a further reason for the renunciation of his undoubted rights. He does it not only to minister to the Church but also in order to have something of his own to offer to the Lord. Proclaiming the Gospel might itself be meritorious if it were done as the result of a free decision ('*hekōn*'), but that is not so in his case. Evangelism is a service imposed upon him by his vocation ('*akōn*, epikeitai*'). He has nothing to boast of by following a call the refusal of which would lead to despair ('*ouai gar moi . . .*'). But—argues the Apostle—the subject of my boasting is that I have taught without cost. The antithesis '*hekōn—akōn*' must not be weakened by translating the first adjective by 'with a will', as though the Apostle did his work reluctantly. His feelings are not under discussion, but his decision which he was not free to shirk.¹³

It should not trouble us that the Apostle is in fact speaking of what might be called works of supererogation. Granted the Apostle's right to be supported by the Church, it cannot be denied that he was practising voluntary renunciation. Moreover, the idea of '*misthos*' is by no means absent from the Gospels.¹⁴ What must be maintained, with the Gospels and Paul, is that the reward is always a favour, since in the last resort we are never more than 'unprofitable servants'.

Furthermore, in some passages in the Sermon on the Mount it is to be observed that '*misthos*' does not necessarily mean '*reward*'; by metonomy it is used as a synonym for 'something which is meritorious or in some way extraordinary'. In Matthew 5⁴⁶ it is asked 'Where is your *misthos*?', and the parallel phrase in the next verse ('*ti perisson . . .*') shows that this is equivalent to 'What have you done out of the ordinary?' Luke 6³²⁻⁵ uses '*misthos*' as a synonym for '*charis*'!

So the Apostle is not anxious to *claim* some reward in the manner of the Pharisees. Rather, he would insist on the fact that he has made a sacrifice of which he can be proud. And it must always be remembered that *salvation* is never regarded as a reward. Such a thing could

¹³ In order to remove the anacoluthon in 9¹⁵ᵇ, BALJON (*De tekst der brieven van Paulus aan de Romeinen, de Corinthiers, . . .* [Utrecht, 1884]), on 4⁶ proposes to read '*nē to kauchēma mou, ho oudeis kenōsei*' ('it is as true as the fact that I have something to boast of, which no one shall take away from me'). The parallel in 15³¹ ('*nē tēn humeteran kauchēsin*') shows that such a manner of speaking would be Pauline. But two emendations would be required: '*ne*' for '*ē*' and '*ho*' added before '*kauchēsin*'. In favour of these it could be said that the letter '*n*' of '*nē*' might have disappeared by haplography with the final '*n*' of '*apothanein*', and that the '*o*' might have been omitted because of the initial '*o*' of '*oudeis*' which follows.

¹⁴ Matthew 5¹², ⁴⁶, 6¹, ², ⁵,¹⁶, 10⁴¹, ⁴², Mark 9⁴¹, Luke 6²³, ³⁵, 10⁷, John 4³⁶.

never arise; for salvation is acquired by accepting in faith the work of Christ, and never from the works of men. What the Apostle does presuppose here, as he has in Chapter 3, is the idea that—salvation apart—Christians will be subject to a kind of grading. In this realm of ideas, and here only, human achievements and sacrifices have their place. Such an attitude must be accepted, even at the risk of suggesting an over-simplified view of Pauline ethics. G. DIDIER correctly observes [15] that in 9^{14-27} Paul makes no reference whatever to a supernatural reward. The subject of his boasting is that he is able to proclaim the Gospel free of charge. Didier would then read 9^{17-18} in this way: 'If in fact I do this of my own volition, then I have a reward. If I do it regardless of my own will, then it is a charge committed to me. In that case of what does my reward consist?
. . .' This interpretation, equally remote from the traditional translation and from ours, has the advantage of giving '*misthos*' its natural sense of 'reward' and not 'right of reward'. But it is then still more difficult to understand why the Apostle nevertheless raises the question of reward again in 9^{18}.

One further misunderstanding must be removed. It has been thought that 9^{18} means that preaching the Gospel without cost would itself be the reward. Such exegesis could be justified by the letter of the text, but it would distort the Apostle's argument, according to which he represents his sacrifice as worthy of a '*misthos*'.

9^{19-23}. This passage gives expression to a general principle which dominated Paul's missionary work, namely, the renunciation of certain liberties in order to gain the greatest number of converts. It is one of the reasons for the renunciation explained in the preceding section, and so establishes the logical connection between the two passages. A further consequence follows from it: the Apostle lived in conformity with the Law of Moses when he was doing missionary work among Jews, although he regarded himself as freed from it by the Gospel. He will observe the Law again when he arrives in Jerusalem, as we are clearly told in Acts 21^{24}. But when evangelizing Gentiles there was naturally no reason for submission to Mosaic requirements.

It follows that this passage has considerable historical importance, for it answers a question the historian cannot help asking: did the Apostle continue to observe the Law as a personal discipline after his conversion to the Gospel? He could have done so as a Jewish Christian and in accordance with the strict application of the principle enunciated in 7^{17ff} of not changing one's manner of life from that followed at the time the Christian call was received. We learn from our passage that this was not quite his position. He felt himself to be genuinely freed from Mosaic obligations, and if nevertheless he sometimes observed the commandments of the Law it was for the

[15] In '*Le salaire du désintéressement*' (*Recherches de sciences religieuses et historiques* [June 1955], XLIII.228–51).

(19) *For while being free in respect of all men, I subjected myself to all, that I may gain the greatest number.* (20) *That is why to the Jews I was like a Jew, to gain the Jews. To those who live under the Law, as if I were under the Law—although I am not myself under the Law—to gain those who live under the Law.* (21) *To those who are without the Law, as one who lives without the Law—to gain those who live without the Law, —although I am not without law with respect to God, being in subjection to the law of Christ.* (22) *To the weak I was weak, to gain the weak. I have been all things to all men, that by all means I might save some.* (23) *And all that I do, is for the sake of the Gospel, so that I may share in it with others.*

particular purpose of not offending Jews who were likely to become Christians, in conformity with the principle stated in 8^{13}. The question of what attitude exactly he recommended to Jewish converts is of little importance, since a time came after which he regarded himself as entirely an apostle to the Gentiles.[16] If the point arose again when this letter was written, he must have left Jewish converts to make their own free decision.

9^{19-23}: '*Tous pleionas*' (9^{19}) = 'the larger part', essentially equivalent to '*hōs pleistous*' = 'the largest number' possible. The particle '*hōs*' (9^{20}) before '*Ioudaios*' is lacking in some manuscripts, but is demanded by parallelism with '*hōs anomos*' in 9^{21}. The presence of '*mē ōn autos hupo nomon*' = 'although I myself am not under the Law' (9^{20}) is necessary for the sense, and it is hard to see how the Textus Receptus came to omit it. The first '*anomos*' in 9^{21} naturally means 'free from the Law of Moses' which Gentiles do not know. But then the writer is careful to distinguish between the Gentile and the Christian lack of a law: the Christian is not without a religious law, because he accepts the law of Christ. This law is not stated. It might be the law of love (8^{13}?; 13?). But it is more likely that Paul is thinking of the dependence on Christ in which the redeemed Christian places himself.[17]

9^{22} is reminiscent of the principle stated in Chapter 8, although it is not necessary to identify the 'weak' in the present passage with Jews. 9^{23} links this attitude with the way in which the Apostle views his dependence with regard to the Gospel.

[16] On this question see the work by ANTON FRIDRICHSEN, cited on 1^1.

[17] Must we follow TISCHENDORF and NESTLÉ and read '*kerdēsō*' (weak aorist subjunctive of the present '*kerdainō*') in 9^{20}, and '*kerdanō*' (subjunctive from the strong aorist '*ekerdana*' of the same verb) in 9^{21}? The alternation of two forms syntactically and semantically equivalent is quite contrary to the custom of this writer. It may be that the more archaic '*kerdanō*' was originally read in both places; but in 9^{20} all the ancient manuscripts known have adopted the correction '*kerdēsō*', while in 9^{21} many texts have preserved the earlier reading, and in particular A, B, C, F, G.—In 9^{21} GRIESBACH suggested reading the future indicative '*kerdanō*', and in that case '*kerdēsō*' would naturally also be future. It would make no change in the sense.—P 46 has '*kerdēsō*' in both places.

(24) *Do you not know that, in a race, all run but only one gains the prize? Run therefore that you may carry off the prize.* (25) *And every athlete places restrictions upon himself in many ways; but they do it to win a perishable crown, but we an imperishable.* (26) *I too run, and in no aimless way. I deliver punches, but not to hit into the air.* (27) *On the contrary, I pommel my body and hold it in subjection, in fear that after having preached to others I myself might be rejected.*

9²⁴⁻⁷. A series of tiny parables drawn from sport. It need hardly be said that they do not imply praise for physical culture as such, any more than the passage 3¹⁰⁻¹⁵ is in praise of architecture, or 3⁶⁻⁹ of horticulture (or the comparison of the Church to a spouse in Ephesians 5²³⁻⁵ is a eulogy on earthly marriage). Nevertheless, the author would not have made this comparison if he had been strongly averse to sport. Godet even thinks, and not without reason, that Paul must sometimes have been present at the games.

(1) The runner, 9²⁴,²⁶ᵃ (cf. Phil 3¹⁴). '*Brabeion*' = 'the prize for victory', usually a crown. '*Houtōs—hina*' (not so correct as '*houtōs— hōste*') 'brings out better the aspiration of the runner after victory'.[18] '*Egō toinun*' (9²⁶) is a little stronger than '*egōge*' (Latin '*equidem*') = 'as for me'.—'*Adēlōs*' (cf. 14⁸) = 'uncertainly', here 'without clear aim'.

(2) 9²⁶ᵇ: the boxer. '*Pukteuō*' appears to be derived from '*pux*' = 'with the fist'. '*Ouk aera derōn*' = 'not hitting into the air', a phrase parallel to '*ouk adēlōs*'. If in 9²⁷ we follow Nestlé and the majority of texts in reading '*hupōpiazō* we then have a further reference to boxing. Dissecting '*hup-ōpiazō*' we have the verbal root, '*op*', meaning either eye or face; hence, 'to hit in the eye', or perhaps 'to hit in the face'. The '*hupo*' element is then more difficult to explain. It might imply a blow from below upwards, or a blow under the eye. But if, with P 46, F, G, Eth., and some other texts, '*hupo-piazō*' is read we then have

(3) a reference to wrestling. The word would mean 'to crush against the ground'. But the first reading is the better attested.

In 9²⁵ the general term '*agōnizomenoi*' is used, which would cover all kinds of '*athletes*', but it could equally well denote a wrestler, in a metaphorical sense (cf. Col 4¹², Lk 13²⁴). The points of comparison between an athlete and a Christian which are being stressed are (*a*) the effort needed to gain the prize, (*b*) the restrictions imposed by the moral training of the Christian, which are akin to those of the physical training of the athlete.

In 9²⁷ the figure changes somewhat. The Christian's adversary is named—his own body, which he must treat firmly, not out of contempt, but in order to subdue it ('*doulagōgō*'). In 9²⁷ᵇ the Apostle alludes to the possibility of losing the crown, which he has spoken about to other people. He recalls the general principle that one who does not practice what he preaches will have no permanent success.

[18] GODET, II.44.

CHAPTER X

(1) *For I do not wish, brothers, to leave you in ignorance that our fathers all passed under the cloud and that all passed through the sea;* (2) *and thus all were baptized into Moses, in the cloud and in the sea.* (3) *Further, all ate of the same supernatural food,* (4) *and all drank of the same supernatural drink. For they drank at the spring of the supernatural rock which followed them; and the rock was—Christ.* (5) *Nevertheless the majority of them did not find acceptance with God, for their corpses 'were strewn in the wilderness'.*

10¹⁻⁵. The formula *'ou gar thelō humas agnoein'* = 'I do not wish to leave you in ignorance' introduces an important communication, as in **12¹**, Romans 1¹³, 11²⁵, 2 Corinthians 1⁸, 1 Thessalonians 4¹³. Chapter **10** seems to be linked with what goes before in the following way: the greatest moral effort is necessary; for the sacraments do not guarantee salvation, as some of the Corinthians think—the spiritual-minded undoubtedly, who were over-confident of their superiority and who, through analogy with the mystery religions, interpreted the Christian sacraments in a magical way. This statement is proved by a typological interpretation of certain scenes from the migration of Israel through the sea and over the desert, after the flight from Egypt.

To understand this short midrashic treatise several presupposed ideas must be borne in mind:

(1) The Israelites were the spiritual ancestors of the Christians. (2) Many events of olden times were 'shadows' of what happens to Christians. We are here in the full stream of the spiritual exegesis of the Old Testament, so dear to the rabbis and notably to Philo (who passed this method and his results on to the Christians in Alexandria). It comprises two different procedures which must not be confused:

(*a*) *Allegorical interpretation:* this sets aside the historical sense of the texts, the soundness of which indeed is sometimes denied. Instead a hidden meaning is substituted. This was the Apostle's method in the ninth chapter (9⁹), in interpreting Deuteronomy 25⁴ (oxen as such are not meant, but the preachers of the Gospel).

(*b*) *Typological interpretation.* In this, the historical sense is accepted. But in the facts and events of Israel's history foreshadowings of future things are seen; for Christians, these things have already partially become real. It is evidently the second procedure which is used here. The Apostle, far from denying the historicity of the facts, takes them for granted; but crossing the sea and passing through the cloud on the one hand, the miraculous food and drink in the desert

on the other, are considered as kinds of sacraments which fore-
shadow respectively baptism and the Eucharist of Christians. However, there is here something more than a simple typology, at least,
so far as the Eucharist is concerned. The rock in the desert is not
merely a type of the future Messiah, it is the Messiah Himself, that
is to say the pre-existent Christ. Perhaps baptism is similarly thought
of, if it is admitted as in Exodus 13²¹ that God was in the
cloud.

Let us examine the two sacraments separately:

(1) *Baptism* (10²). Passing through the cloud, which is taken as a
representation of baptism, is not taught in the Book of Exodus
(*v.* Ch. 13), which speaks only of a cloud preceding or following the
Israelites.[1]

But fortunately we can draw on another tradition found in Psalm
104³⁹ (105³⁹) and expressed in these words: 'He stretched out a cloud
to cover them' (*'diepetase nephelēn eis skepēn autois'*) and undoubtedly also in Wisdom 10¹⁷ which says: 'He (God) became a covering
for them by day' (*'kai egeneto autois eis skepēn hēmeras . . .'*), as
well as Wisdom 19⁷ which says:'the cloud which overshadowed the
camp', i.e. which hid the Israelite camp from the eyes of the Egyp-
tians (*'hē tēn parembolēn skiazousa nephelē'*). It can then be understood that the cloud, which covered and enveloped the Israelites,
could be considered as a baptism.

It is much more difficult to explain the words *'dia thalassēs'* =
'through the sea'. For Exodus clearly states that the Israelites crossed
the sea dryshod. How can there be baptism without contact with the
water, which God expressly drew aside? J.W., who at least had the
merit of pointing out the difficulty, believes that the Israelites 'being
surrounded by water on all sides' can be considered as baptized (i.e.
immersed in water),[2] provided that the exegete shows 'a good deal of
boldness'. We are not so bold and prefer the view that the Apostle is

---

[1] Is this a reference to Exodus 14¹⁹? But this rather ambiguous text simply says
that the angel of God who went in front of the camp moved his position (*'exēre'*)
and stationed himself at the rear (*'kai eporeuthē ek tōn opisthen'*). Similarly the
pillar of cloud moved from in front to behind (*'exēre kai ho stulos tēs nephelēs
apo prosōpou autōn kai estē ek tōn opisō autōn'*). As the text describing the move-
ment of the cloud uses the same verbs as that dealing with the angel, and as the
angel must have gone round the camp (or disappeared only to reappear), the
same things must have applied in the case of the cloud. Nevertheless Jewish
exegetes were able to infer from this text that the cloud must have crossed the
camp.

[2] AMBROSIASTER gets round the difficulty: the passage is a foreshadowing of
baptism, because by it the Israelites are saved from death. *'Illis enim id est Aegyptiis in mari mortuis, dum hi duce Moyse feliciter transeunt, erepti sunt a morte':
quod prestat baptismum'* (*MPL* XVII, col. 233 D).—This interpretation is far too
clever. As for the cloud, he thinks as does Wisdom 19⁷ that it hid the people from
the eyes of their enemies. This also allows him to insist again on deliverance
from death: *'Contecti enim nube et ab adversariis suis tuti praestiti, dum a mari
liberati sunt baptizati dicuntur'* (ibid.).

drawing on an apocryphal tradition which gave the account in a way different from Exodus 13.[3]

In 10^2 the reading '*ebaptisanto*' = 'they baptized themselves' of the Textus Receptus, and B, as well as of P 46 ('*ebaptisonto*' emended to '*ebaptisanto*') and of Origen,[4] is certainly preferable to '*ebaptisthēsan*'. For the Jewish neophyte baptized himself.[5] The passive form is therefore probably a correction made by a pagano-Christian reader who was unacquainted with Jewish custom. On the other hand, the expression '*eis Mōüsēn*' = 'into Moses' cannot be explained by Judaism; the Apostle coined it by analogy with '*eis Christon*' (for the meaning of this formula, see Rom 6^3).

(2) *Eucharist* (10^{3-4}). The adjective '*pneumatikon*' obviously refers, not to anything immaterial, but to something supernatural and heavenly.[6] '*Brōma pneumatikon*' = 'supernatural food', that is the manna of the wilderness (cf. Ex 16^{15}), which Psalm 77^{24-5} (78^{24-5}) calls '*artos ouranou*' = 'bread of heaven' and '*artos anggelōn*'[7] = bread of angels,' just as Wisdom 16^{20} speaks of '*anggelōn trophē*' = 'food of angels' and of '*artos ap' ouranou*' = 'bread from heaven'. About the water from the rock, the Apostle will be more explicit, as we shall see. But why does the pronoun '*to auto*' = 'the same' (absent moreover from P 46, ℵ and A) precede both '*brōma*' = 'food' and '*poma*' = 'drink'? Undoubtedly because the sacrament of the Eucharist requires exactly the same food for all partakers, perhaps also to emphasize that the rejected majority received the same privileges as the small minority of the saved.[8]

The spring which Moses caused to flow miraculously from a rock is naturally that of Exodus 17^6. But the Old Testament does not speak of a moving rock ('*petra akolouthousa*') which followed the camp like the cloud. St Thomas Aquinas,[9] quoting Isaiah 48^{21}, and Calvin[10] think that by metonomy 'rock' means the water which trickled from

---

[3] Perhaps Wisdom 10^{18} alludes to this tradition in these words: '*diebibasen autous thalassan eruthran kai diēgagen autous di' hudatos pollou.*' But strictly speaking '*dia*' could be used to mean the passing between two walls of water.— Notice for the sake of analogy the well-known verse 1 Peter 3^{20}, which recalls that Noah and his family had to pass through the waters (miraculously or in some other way) to reach the Ark. This tradition is also unknown in the Old Testament.

[4] *Contra Celsum*, IV.XLIX (KOETSCHAU, I.322) and *Commentary on John 4*, Ch. 44, §227 (KOETSCHAU, IV.153).

[5] See MERX, *Die vier kanonischen Evangelien nach ihrem ältesten Text* (Berlin, 1897), II.I.38.

[6] As '*sōma pneumatikon*' in Chapter 15.

[7] BENGEL: '*Manna spiritualis cibus erat non per se, nec solum ratione prefigurationis; sed quia Israelitis una cum cibo corporis alimentum animarum ex Christo datum est.*'

[8] BENGEL: '*Eundum, respectu Patrum cadentium vel non cadentium; non respectu illorum ac nostri*' (against Calvin).

[9] *Commentarius in Epistolam ad Cor. I*, in *Opera* (Paris, pub. Vivès, 1876), XX.705.

[10] *Comm.*, E.Tr., p. 319.

the rock and followed the people. This seems difficult to support.
Godet looks on the idea of the moving rock as puerile too. The idea
was, probably, that the invisible Christ followed the caravan, like
the angel of the Lord in the Jewish conception. This was the opinion
of Theodore of Mopsuestia who states: 'It was not the rock itself
that followed them, but only the power emanating from Christ' ('*hē
petra tou Christou dunamis*').[11]

But in our passage Christ and the rock are inseparable. Elsewhere[12]
in the Tosephta Sukka 3[11], we read: 'Thus the spring which was with
Israel in the desert, was like a rock . . . which travelled up mountains
with them and accompanied them into the valleys; wherever Israel
was, it was opposite them.'[13] Another text is cited by Hans Vollmer,[14]
who does not give its exact source. According to him the Midrash
Bamidbar rabba reads: '*Quomodo comparatus erat ille puteus*? *Fuit
sicut petra et ivit cum ipsis in itineribus ipsorum.*' In both texts there is
a straightforward allusion to a rock which followed the Israelites
during their march. But it can refer only to the same tradition.

In the matter of identifying the rock with the Messiah, it is not
enough to cite Exodus 17[6], where God seems to say that He is standing on the rock. For there is no question of the Messiah in that context.[15] Still less can a conclusion be drawn from the fact that the Old
Testament often compares God to a rock. But Philo has no hesitation
in identifying our rock with the Wisdom of God: '*Hē gar akrotomos
petra sophia Theou estin*'[16] and '*petran tēn sterean kai adiakopon
emphainōn sophian Theou*'.[17]

We are already aware of Paul's tendency to replace Wisdom by
Christ. So there is here, as has already been stated, more than a simple

[11] Quoted after STAAB, *Paulus-Kommentare aus der griechischen Kirche* (Munster,
1933), p. 185. This work brings together the fragments of lost Commentaries,
preserved in the Catenas. It appeared as Vol. XV of *Neutestamentliche Abhandlungen* (ed. MEINERTZ).

[12] Ed. ZUCKERMANDEL (Pasewalk, 1880), p. 196, line 25, to p. 197, line 1.

[13] כן היתה הבאר שהיתה עם ישראל במדבר דזמה לסלע עולה עמהן
להרים ויורד לגיאיות במקום שישראל שרויין היא שורה כנגדן.

The masculine participle יורד can only refer to סלע (the rock); for באר (the
well) is feminine. The texts of the Onkelos and Jerusalem Targums (the latter also
called the Targum Pseudo-Jonathan), which are sometimes quoted in this connection, prove nothing. There is certainly reference to something which accompanied the Israelites up hill and down dale, but it is only the spring. This would
at a pinch permit an interpretation similar to Calvin's. These texts will be found
respectively on pp. 300 and 413, Vol. II, of the translation by J. W. ETHERIDGE,
The Targums of the Pentateuch (London, 1865).

[14] *Alttestamentliche Zitate bei Paulus* (Freibourg and Leipzig, 1895), p. 87.

[15] Again we must resort to the Hebrew text. For the LXX is not clear on this
point: '*egō hestēka ekei pro tou se epi tēs petras.*' If the words '*pro tou se*' are
authentic—and it is difficult to see who could have interpolated them—they give
the impression that an infinitive has been dropped and that the sentence should
be translated: 'I [God] will place myself thereupon, before you [Moses] come
to the rock', a text given by א ('*pro tou se elthein*'). The link between God and
the rock is weakened still further.

[16] *Legum Allegoriae*, II.§86, Ed. minor Cohn and Wendland, I.97.

[17] *Quod deterius potiori insidiari soleat*, § 115, ibid. I.265.

(6) *But these events took place to serve as indications of our destiny,
to prevent us from coveting evil, as they coveted it.* (7) *Do not become
idolaters, as did some of them, according to the Scripture which says:
'The people sat down to eat and drink, then they arose to dance'.* (8)
*Neither let us be fornicators, as were some of them, after which in a
single day they died to the number of twenty-three thousand.* (9) *Nor
let us tempt the Lord, as did some of them, after which they perished
by the serpents.* (10) *And do not murmur against the Lord, as did some
of them, after which they perished by the Destroyer.*

(11) *Now, all these misfortunes which happened to them, had a
typological meaning, and they were handed down by the Scriptures to
be a warning for us, who are at the meeting-point of the (two) ages.* (12)
*Consequently, let him who boasts that he stands beware he does not
fall.* (13) *No test has overtaken you which was not within human
endurance. And God is faithful and will not allow you to be tested beyond
your strength. On the contrary, he will, along with the test, provide a
happy escape by making you capable of bearing it.*

analogy with the Christian Eucharist, because Christ Himself distributed the supernatural water.[18] *'Ouk eudokein'* is synonymous with
'to reject'.[19]

10⁶⁻¹³. *'Tupos'* means 'an imprint', hence the sense of 'sign' or
'pattern'. Thus events in Israel's history, while being taken as his-
torically correct—and precisely because they were real—are interpreted as signs of certain events in the new order, that is in the history of the Christian Church, the spiritual heir of Israel.

But what is curious in our case is that the signs selected from the
Old Testament are only hypothetical types in some degree. It is not
said that the Christians will perish like the Israelites in the desert.
The 'types' indicate only the possibility of such disasters. They will
only take place in actual fact if the Christians are disobedient and
commit certain serious sins as their spiritual ancestors did. That is
why the *'tupoi'* here play the part of warnings (*'nouthesia'*, **10¹¹**). That
the punishments of Israel in the wilderness should have carried
their purpose and justification in themselves is evidently not excluded
by this. On the contrary the whole argument takes it for granted.

On points of detail, the expression *'ta telē tōn aiōnōn'* in **10¹¹** must
first be fully understood. Usually it is translated by 'the ends of the
ages', and at first sight this interpretation seems excellent. Do not

---

[18] There is much discussion these days over the timeliness of reintroducing into
Protestant preaching reflections of an allegorical or typological nature. It cannot
be denied that such methods are in principle legitimate through their use by the
Apostle Paul. But on the other hand there is good reason for taking notice of the
warnings of our reformers who feared like the plague the allegorical extravagances
of the Alexandrines.

[19] Cf. Habakkuk 2⁴, *'ouk eudokei hē psuchē mou en autō'*, cited in Hebrews
10³⁸.

Christians live at the end of time?[20] But why speak of '*ta telē*' in the plural, if the end of time or of the present times is meant? Further, the plural '*aiōnes*' should then mean the present *age* which is approaching its end. Now, there is no example in the Pauline Epistles for such a use of the plural.[21] When the present world is envisaged as coming to its end, it is counted as a single age, as is the new world when it is mentioned in contrast.

'*Aiōnes*' in the plural can only have the sense of the dual number and mean the well-known two ages. This conclusion causes us to give favourable consideration to the interpretation of J.W. which removes the two difficulties. What is meant are the two ages (the old and the new) which touch end to end, in the sense that the close of the old coincides with the beginning of the new. At once the plural '*ta telē*' is explained, as well as the plural '*aiōnes*'. But this interpretation raises a further difficulty which J.W. did not even point out. According to the usual translation, the words '*eis hous*' should mean the purpose of the meeting made by the 'ends of the ages'; the Apostle was probably speaking of the future (now a reality) as having come effectively upon Christians. But with rare exceptions, the preposition '*eis*' after the verb '*antaō*' and its compounds means the place of a meeting, and not its purpose, which is expressed by the dative (sometimes by the accusative or genitive).[22] Further, '*antaō*' in the active may very well have the middle sense of 'meet one another'.[23] The Apostle means, therefore, according to our view: 'The two ages meet one another at their extremities at the point where we Christians stand. We are at the point of intersection of the two worlds.' This idea is in perfect harmony with that other, current in the New Testament, that the Christians live on the one hand in the last days of the former age, and on the other, in the Kingdom of Christ, which is an anticipation of the future age.

But why do the events in the wilderness assume such importance at the beginning of the new age? If there is any link between the old and the new world-order, should we not rather search for signs of the new order in the Creation narratives? We think that the Apostle is less interested here in the relation between the two worlds than

---

[20] '*ep' eschatou tōn chronōn*', says 1 Peter 1[20], using a very similar turn of phrase.

[21] The plural '*aiōnes*' is used only to express eternity which has no '*telos*'! (Thus in the expression '*eulogētos eis tous aiōnas*', Romans 1[25], 9[5], or '*doxa eis tous aiōnas*', Romans 11[36], 16[27] [doubtful], Galatians 1[5], Philippians 4[20]); or again to mean something which precedes all the ages, that is which precedes the creation of the world: '*pro tōn aiōnōn*', 2[7], or '*apo tōn aiōnōn*', Colossians 1[26]. The Epistle to the Ephesians does not come into the picture here, because the drift of the text is probably not of Pauline origin.

[22] '*Eis tēn Aigupton tois pasin ethnesin apantēsantes*' ('they met all the Gentiles in Egypt'), says 3 Maccabees 3[20] (RAHLFS, II.1145).—'*Tous presbeis apantan eis Kuzikon*' ('to meet the messengers at Cyzicus'), (*Xenophon, Hellenica*, I.3[13] Teubner, p. 14). Many other examples in HENRY ESTIENNE, *Thesaurus*.

[23] '*Sunetithento rhētēn hēmeran, en hē pros Rhion apantēsousin*' ('they agreed on a particular day, when they were to meet at the place called Rhion'); POLYBIUS IV.xxvi.5, Teubner, II.35).

in the parallelism between the two peoples: the Jews and the Christians. For life in the desert represents the childhood of Israel, and typologically, in consequence, the beginnings of the Christian Church.

What were the sins of the people in the wilderness? The Apostle lists four, which however partially overlap:

(1) *Covetousness*, **10⁶** ('*epithumia*' always has a bad sense). As, in Numbers 11³⁴, the noun '*epithumētēs*' can be found and also (Num 11⁴) the phrase '*epethumēsan epithumian*', it is reasonable to suppose that events in that chapter are referred to, that is the discontent of the people who sighed for the fleshpots of Egypt. The mention of this sin is quite in place since it is through desire for gastronomical pleasure that the Corinthians might be led astray to pagan feasts. (There is a further allusion to banquets in **10⁷**, but from another point of view.)

(2) *Idolatry*. Here the cult of the Golden Calf recorded in Exodus 32 is referred to; indeed the quotation in **10⁷** '*ekathisan . . . paizein*' is taken from that chapter.²⁴ '*Paizein*' can mean 'to play'; but Exodus 32¹⁹ speaks of '*choroi*' = 'dances'. Perhaps the dances in honour of the idol also had a licentious character, as was the case in many Semitic cults and as Tertullian supposes in *Jejunium* 6: '*intellege sanctae scripturae verecundiam: lusum nisi impudicum non denotasset.*'²⁵ In any event for the Old Testament prophets, idolatry and fornication were closely linked, a point which explains the transition to

(3) *Sin of misconduct* ('*porneia*') (**10⁷·⁸**), the punishment of which is told in Numbers 25⁹. However the LXX and the Massoretic text speak of 24,000, as does Philo.²⁶ Does this mean a lapse of memory when the Apostle speaks of 23,000 or was he reading another text? Or again could a copyist have taken the letters '*trs*' (abbrev. for '*tettares*') for '*treis*'? It is difficult to say. In any case, the reading 24,000 given in the text of **10⁸** by the Armenian version and some Syrian manuscripts must be considered as an emendation of our text by that of the LXX, and is therefore valueless.²⁷

(4) The fourth *sin* (**10⁹**) is the most difficult to be precise about. What is the meaning of 'tempt the Lord'? Notice first that the reading '*ton Theon*' = '(the) God', which has almost no support except in A, should be rejected in favour of '*ton kurion*' = 'the Lord' or

---

²⁴ If the warning is applicable to the Corinthians, it must be admitted that taking part in pagan banquets must be avoided because of the danger of idolatry, and not merely out of consideration for the weak. This point of view is different from that of Chapter 8, but recurs in 10¹⁴⁻²². On this point see our Introduction and the remark at the end of this chapter.

²⁵ *CSEL* 20, p. 280.

²⁶ *Vita Mosis*, I.§304, COHN AND WENDLAND, ed. minor IV.160.

²⁷ The strangest point is that the Ethiopian reads 22,000. Could it have known a third reading? Calvin (*Comm.*, E.Tr., p. 325) admits that the real number was between 23,000 and 24,000. Paul would have preferred to take the least number. But how did Paul know that the number given in the Bible was a maximum?

'*ton Christon*' = 'the Christ', both being well attested and moreover
synonymous (for Paul '*kurios*' = '*Christos*'). Further, as serpents are
mentioned in Numbers 21[6], the sin spoken of in that passage must be
considered: the people lacked confidence in the promises—'*ōligo-
psuchēsen*', 'they lacked fortitude' and patience and they despaired
because of the absence of resources in the desert.[28] Thus they began
to 'impeach God' ('*katelalei pros ton Theon*', Num 21[5]), a sin expressly set down later as

(5) (**10**[10]): '*mēde gongguzete*' = 'do not murmur', where with
Godet we prefer this reading to '*gongguzōmen*',[29] because it was the
Corinthians, not all Christians, who were in danger of committing
this sin. Which text is alluded to here? Undoubtedly the revolt of the
Korah clan and that of Dathan and Abiram (Num 16), perhaps also
Numbers 14; each of these narratives ends with an account of a great
extermination, although the '*olothreutēs*' = 'the destroyer'[30] of
10[10] is not expressly mentioned.

Let us pause for a moment longer on **10**[9], as we render it. It constitutes not only the transition to **10**[10] as has just been seen, but also
prepares for **10**[13]. 'Do not commit the sin of tempting God, that is
of straining the divine patience, by your lack of fortitude; this despondency and these murmurings are all the more stupid since God
will not allow you to be tested beyond your strength.' Other interpretations of **10**[9] have, however, been proposed. J.W. thinks that the
Apostle, allowing himself to be guided by Psalm 77 (78) may have
found there (77[18]) the expression '*kai exepeirasan ton Theon*' = 'and
they tempted God', which the Psalmist then explains in the following
way: the Israelites tempted God by asking Him for another miracle
to provide them with food in the desert. In this case the Corinthians
may have asked for miracles. But this is unlikely; for according to
1[22], it was the Jews who made such demands.

A third fairly widespread interpretation of **10**[9] (*v.* Godet), which
we also reject, makes it say this in effect: 'You gnostics, do not put
too much trust in yourselves. Avoid putting yourselves in unsavoury
situations. It would be tempting God, who might punish you.' It
must be admitted that this interpretation is quite in harmony with
10[12]. Indeed the gnostics boasted that they were strong ('*dokein*' =
'to boast, to glorify oneself', *v.* 8[2]). On the other hand, it is incompatible with the assurances given in **10**[13]. For the idea of the text is
very close to that of temptation, and is expressed by the same Greek
word ('*peirasmos*'). If **10**[9] did indeed condemn their over-confidence,
would not the gnostics have seen in **10**[13] the express annulment of
this warning? For what does this verse state but God's promise to
bring them victorious out of trials and temptations? However, our
interpretation removes the contradiction between **10**[9] and **10**[13].

---

[28] Calvin: 'for tempting is opposed to patience', *Comm.*, E.Tr., p. 325.
[29] Both readings are well attested by first-class texts. A, B, C, read '*gongguzete*'
whilst ℵ and D give '*gongguzōmen*' (P 46 is defective).
[30] Probably a destroying angel as in 2 Samuel 24[16], 1 Chronicles 21[15].

'Do not sin by despondency, for God will uphold you in your trials.' 'For my part, I am of the opinion that it was intended for their consolation', Calvin very fittingly says in connection with **10**¹³.[31] We do not know to what trials the Apostle refers. But all Christians seriously living according to the Gospel were exposed to persecution, first by the Jews, then by pagans in proportion to their refusal to take part in pagan ceremonies, such as the banquets mentioned here.[32]

A further word about the sense of '*peirasmos*'. As we have just recalled, this noun can mean either 'test' or 'temptation'. As Godet points out, the same event (*v.* the story of Job) can be considered as a temptation if looked at from the point of view of Satan who seeks to cause man's downfall, or as a test, if considered in terms of the divine order, which seeks to offer to the believer the opportunity of showing his mettle ('*dokimazesthai*').[33] As the point here concerns God (who according to the Christian conception does not tempt, *v.* James 1¹³), we prefer to translate by 'test'. Further it would be curious if the author who has just used in **10**⁹ the verb 'peirazein' for 'tempting God', should use the same word to speak of God tempting man.

10¹³ contains a further serious difficulty of construction. What is the exact sense of the genitive '*tou dunasthai*'? Obviously it depends on the noun '*ekbasis*' = 'the way out'. We might be tempted to take this genitive as epexegetical: 'The way out (happy issue), which is made possible by the fact that the test does not exceed human resources.' But this interpretation may seem tortured. That is why other commentators like Godet view this genitive as the indication of a consequence or a purpose (Godet: 'in order that you may . . .'). We should then be faced with a Semitic influence not unknown in the New Testament, in which the genitive sometimes behaves like the

Hebrew infinitive preceded by the particle ל. But once on this road,

why not recognize that this construction inspired by Hebrew is often the equivalent of a gerundive?[34] The phrase would then mean: 'He will provide for you a happy outcome by the fact that it will not go beyond the limits of your strength.' Our interpretation more closely

---

[31] *Comm.*, E.Tr., p. 331.

[32] If this verse has the gnostics in mind, their contempt for martyrdom may be recalled; they considered it quite openly as the sad privilege of 'simple believers'. Concerning this see the very characteristic theory of the higher 'karma' of the gnostics held by Basilides, a theory mentioned by CLEMENT OF ALEXANDRIA in his *Stromateis*, IV.XII.§81 (STAEHLIN, II.284).

[33] Luther sometimes uses the word '*Anfechtung*', which has both shades of '*peirasmos*'.

[34] See Matthew 5²⁸, where '*pros to epithumēsai autēn*' is certainly a clumsy translation of an Aramaic infinitive preceded by ל, which should have the sense of the gerundive ('by coveting her').—We owe this rendering of Matthew 5²⁸, like many other suggestions in this field, to the encyclopaedic knowledge of M. CHARLES JAEGER.

(14) *Because of that, my brothers, flee from idolatry.* (15) *I speak to you as reasonable people. Form your own judgment of what I tell you.* (16) *The cup of blessing which we bless, is it not fellowship in the blood of Christ? Is not the bread which we break fellowship in the body of Christ?* (17) *For we are one loaf, one body, while remaining a multitude. For we all share together in the single loaf.* (18) *Look at Israel according to the flesh: Are those who eat the sacrifices not participants of the altar?* (19) *What then do I mean by that? That the sacrifice is something? Or that the idol is something?* (20) *No! But that the sacrifices offered by pagans, are offered to demons and not to God. Now, I do not want you to enter into communion with demons.* (21) *You cannot drink from the cup of the Lord and from the cup of demons. You cannot sit at the table of the Lord and at the table of demons.* (22) *Or do we wish to provoke the wrath of the Lord? Are we stronger than he?*

approximates to the first analysis (explicative genitive), while perhaps improving upon it.

10¹⁴⁻²². In **10¹⁴** '*pheugete apo*' is more expressive than '*pheugete*' with the accusative; '*apo*' has almost a locative sense: '*flee* pagan temples where you might fall into idolatry.' '*Phēmi*' = 'I declare', is a slightly emphatic term, but is not so solemn here as in 7²⁹.—'*Phronimoi*' (**10¹⁵**) may have a slightly ironical sense since the Apostle is speaking essentially to those who are 'puffed-up'; but it is not certain.—Why do we find in **10¹⁶** the accusative '*ton arton*' for the nominative '*ho artos*' = 'bread'? It can only be an instance of what grammarians call 'inverse attraction' (a noun influenced by the case of the relative pronoun), although such constructions are rare in New Testament Greek.[35]

The passage **10¹⁶⁻²²** contrasts the Christian Eucharist with pagan banquets. Let us first remember that the mystery of the Holy Supper is one of those which has most resisted theological explanation. Even the Pauline texts can illuminate it only partially. For the texts presuppose in the primitive Church experiences of a supernatural kind, to which the Apostle alludes without describing them. All that the commentator can do is to attempt a faithful interpretation of the texts whilst shunning the temptation to add elements of thought borrowed from later theologies—Thomist, Lutheran, Zwinglian or others.

The first difficulty is set by the apparently pleonastic expression '*to potērion tēs eulogias, ho eulogoumen*' = 'the cup of blessing which we bless'. Is there some tautology? There would be, if '*eulogia*' meant a blessing (or thanksgiving) pronounced by us. But '*eulogia*' can very well refer to a blessing (or thanksgiving) pronounced by the

---

[35] See Matthew 21⁴², and BLASS-DEBRUNNER, *Grammatik des N.T.-lichen Griechisch* (1921), §295; R. KÜHNER, *Grammatik der griechischen Sprache*, II.ɪɪ (1904).413ff.

Lord according to **11²⁴**. This meaning seems the more probable. The sense would then be: 'the cup blessed by the Lord, which we bless in our turn,' or : 'the cup through which the Lord gave thanks and for which we give thanks in our turn.' It is difficult to choose between these two senses, since '*eulogein*' and '*eucharistein*' are often synonymous and 'to bless the cup' seems to mean 'to bless God for the cup', that is 'to thank God'. The blessing pronounced over the cup is moreover an important element in the Jewish Passover rite, in which the third cup is called 'the cup of blessing'.³⁶ But it must be noticed that the blessing of the cup also played a part on the Sabbath day,³⁷ and possibly in all meals.³⁸ Our text does not therefore allow us to settle finally, one way or the other, whether St Paul considered the Lord's last meal as a Passover meal.

Allusion to a blessing is absent from the mention of the bread. According to Justin, the bread was also the object of thanksgiving;³⁹ but the expression '*arton klan*' = 'break bread' (without '*eulogein*') is explained by the fact that Judaism even at this time attached some importance to the breaking of bread,⁴⁰ and Christians even more so (*v.* Mk 6⁴¹ and par., Lk 24³⁰, Acts 2⁴⁶).

But the main problem is set by the word '*koinōnia*' = 'fellowship'.⁴¹ Is it only fellowship between believers created by sharing the body and blood? Certainly this idea is paramount for Paul, because Christians, as **10¹⁷** shows, form the body of Christ. But this union can come about only because each person is in communion with Christ. Was this communion simply a table fellowship? The idea is equally valuable, for it is probable that for the early Christians the Eucharistic meals celebrated by the disciples with the risen Lord were up to a point the model of the Eucharistic cult in the Churches, where Christ is supposed to be present, although invisibly so.⁴²

However, the express mention of the body and blood makes us believe that the Apostle is thinking in addition of a metaphysical union of the believer with Christ, as is moreover presupposed in Chapter **5**. What then is the role of the blood of Christ? To understand the Apostle's ideas on this point it must be remembered that the part played by the Spirit of the risen Lord in the Church—which is the body of Christ—is equivalent to that of the regenerating blood.

---

³⁶ כוס הברכה, *v.* STRACK-BILLERBECK, IV, *Excursus* IV, pp. 41–76.

³⁷ Mishnah BERACHOT 6⁵⁻⁶, GOLDSCHMIDT, I.185.

³⁸ Ber. Rabba 8 on Genesis 1²⁸, WÜNSCHE, *Bibliotheca Rabbinica*, 2nd and 3rd fasc., pp. 35 and 510; Kohelet Rabb. 8¹², WÜNSCHE, ibid., 1st. fasc., p. 116.

³⁹ '*Hē eucharistheisa trophē*', *MPG* VI, col. 428 C.

⁴⁰ MERX, *Die Evangelien nach ihrer ältesten Textgestalt*, II.II.417; cf. DREWS RE, V.563. On all these questions see F. GAVIN, *The Jewish antecedents of the Christian Sacraments* (London, 1928).

⁴¹ See JOURDAN, '*Koinōnia* in 1 Corinthians 10.16', in *JBL* (1948), pp. 111ff. Paul may have compressed three ideas into this term: (*a*) the communion of Christians in Christ (sharing together in Christ); (*b*) a reminder of the death of Christ; and (*c*) the messianic hope.

⁴² O. CULLMANN, '*La signification de la Sainte Cène dans le christianisme primitif*'. *RHPR* (1936), pp. 1–22.

If we possessed this verse only, such an interpretation might even suffice. But **11**[24] shows that communion through the blood has some connection with the death of the Lord, and that it is through this communion that believers can appropriate the benefit of His Cross.

In the case of '*sōma*' = 'body', no reference is made to death; so the appropriation of the powers of the resurrection are primarily meant. That is why the cup is mentioned before the bread (which is Godet's explanation).

10[17] stresses the fellowship of believers among themselves and the formation of the Church = the body of Christ, the result of fellowship with Christ. But how are we to think of the construction of this sentence? Are we to take (the first possible construction) '*hoti*' with the previous verse and translate, 'fellowship with the body of Christ, because there is one loaf'? This idea would not be clear; the identity of the loaf would better explain the fellowship of believers among themselves, a point dealt with later. That is why many follow another interpretation and see in '*hen sōma . . . esmen*' the result of '*heis artos*': 'because there is one loaf, we form . . .', the omission of '*estin*' after '*artos*' being nothing extraordinary (cf. for e.g. **15**[39]). But a third construction seems to us even better. We shall take '*heis artos*' as an attribute of the subject '*hoi polloi*', in the same way as '*hen sōma*': 'because we are one loaf and one body.' In Chapter **5** the Corinthians are indeed compared to unleavened bread and the dual equation 'bread = body of Christ = Church' makes this terminology quite possible though at first sight it may seem strange to our mind.[43] The sense of '*hoti*' is then the following: 'For, after communion, we form One loaf, One body: consequently the rite implies a sharing in the body of Christ' (**10**[16]).[44] As for the preposition '*ek*' (**10**[17]), it must be explained as a Hebraism (= מִן).

10[18]. Before moving on to examine pagan sacrificial meals, the author glances at Jewish sacrifices, the term 'Israel according to the flesh' meaning simply and without any pejorative nuance, historical Israel as opposed to spiritual Israel, that is the Christian Church. He makes it clear that participants in Jewish sacrifices (considered as 'eaten sacrifices' naturally) entered into communion with the Deity. In the first place he thinks of the priests and Levites, but in the second place of the people as well. But what is the exact meaning of the expression '*koinōnoi tou thusiastēriou*' 'participants of the altar'? And why '*thusiastēriou*' = 'of the altar' and not '*Theou*' = 'of God'?

---

[43] It will be noticed that if the first clause '*hoti heis artos*' were meant to provide the reason for the second ('*hen sōma . . . esmen*'), we should rather expect the conjunction '*epei*' or '*epeidē*', normally used when the relative clause with a causal sense precedes the main clause.

[44] J.W. considers the possibility of looking on '*hen sōma*' as a gloss, but without making a definite pronouncement on this. The hypothesis seems unnecessary.

Philo also uses the expression '*koinōnoi tou bōmou*'.[45] J.W. concludes
from this that the expression 'participants of the altar' (*Genossen des
Altars*) was a current expression in Hellenistic Judaism. But this
inference seems quite gratuitous. What seems certain is that Paul, in
conformity with Jewish susceptibilities, avoids speaking of '*koinōnoi
Theou*'. He prefers a circumlocution (in other cases '*to onoma*' or
'*hē megalōsunē*' were used for God). At the same time '*thusiastērion*'
foreshadows the communion table.

10[19-21]. The Apostle is rebutting an objection which could be expressed
thus: 'But then are you admitting that the meat is really sacrificed to
the idols and consequently that the idols exist?' Such a supposition
would obviously be contrary not only to Chapter 8, but to all
Pauline teaching. '*Alla*' at the beginning of 10[20] has the force of
'No, but'. The Greek gods do not exist. The question is then to
know who receives the pagan sacrifices. Is it God? No. But there is
another category of beings who substitute themselves for the gods
of Olympus (who do not exist). They are the '*daimones*',[46] and this
term is not used in a good sense as in Plutarch or Celsus, who saw in
them perfectly commendable though inferior deities. In the New
Testament they are always spirits of an inferior and disquieting
nature, and they are the ones who share in the banquets. More than
that, believers run the risk of entering into intimate communion
with them. It is unnecessary to think here about totemic meals, in
which the victim is expressly identified with the deity; in any case a
dangerous relationship is set up with the forces of evil.[47]

Consequently there is incompatibility between the table of the
Lord and the table of demons. The background of the Apostle's
thought is therefore not only of a moral order, but once more of a
metaphysical kind. It is not only treachery to take part in pagan
religious banquets, but there is also the risk of defiling the body of

---

[45] *De specialibus legibus*, I.§221, COHN AND WENDLAND, ed. min., V.45.

[46] Jewish opinion of the time and the common opinion of the Fathers were
slightly more naïve: the pagan gods are demons. Deuteronomy 32[17]: '*ethusan
daimoniois kai ouk theō, theois, hois ouk ēdeisan*' ('they sacrificed to demons and not
to God, to gods whom they did not know'). They were demons who were taken
as real gods, cf. Psalms 105(106)[37] and 95(96)[5]: '*pantes hoi theoi tōn ethnōn daimonia*'
('all the gods of the pagans are demons').—Origen, *contr. Celsum*, III.29 (KOETS-
CHAU, I.226), also explains that people who had little knowledge of demonology
take demons as gods: '*hoi men epi gēs daimones para tois mē paideutheisin nomizo-
menoi einai theoi*'; cf. his *Exhortatio ad martyrium*, Ch. 45. The philosopher
PORPHYRY (*de abstinentia*, II.42, TEUBNER, pp. 171–2) also holds that demons
wish to be gods ('*boulontai gar einai theoi*') and that sacrifices offered to them
endow them with real strength (TEUBNER, ibid., p. 169) '*hōsper hupoduntes ta tōn
allōn theōn prosōpa tēs hēmeteras aboulias apolauousin*'.—ATTO DE VERCEIL (*MPL*
CXXXIV, col. 374 C): '*Quamquam nihil sit idolum, diabolus tamen est aliquid,
qui simplices et pravos homines deficiens fecit se in illis adorari.*'

[47] CLEMENT OF ALEXANDRIA, *Paidagogos*, II 1.§8.3 (STAEHLIN, I.159), is convinced
that demons fall like flies upon the meat of sacrifices, in the manner of the
departed souls in Homer, whom he quotes at this point. The horror of Christians
in presence of these defiled meats can then be understood.

(23) *Everything is permissible, but not everything is expedient; every-*
thing is permissible, but not everything is helpful. (24) Let no one seek
his own advantage, but that of others. (25) Eat of anything sold in the
market, without asking questions prompted by scruples of conscience.
(26) For 'the earth is the Lord's and all that fills it'. (27) If a pagan
invites you out and you decide to accept, eat of all that is offered to
you without asking questions prompted by scruples of conscience. (28)
But if someone were to say to you: 'This is meat which has been sacri-
ficed', then do not eat it, out of respect for the man who told you, and

Christ to which the Christian belongs and of being cut off from it
like a gangrenous limb. So we have here an exact parallel with the
warnings of Chapter 5 according to which debauchery risks bringing
expulsion from the body of Christ; even more strongly would it
apply to idolaters.

It remains now to justify our translation of 10^{19}. We have presumed as correct the text given by Nestlé. Now the exact drift of the
second part of the verse is challenged. Nestlé, following the majority
of witnesses, gives '*ē hoti eidōlon ti estin*'. But P 46, $\aleph$, A, C, and
Epiphanius (ed. Holl, II.165), omit this question. J.W. is inclined to
erase it, apparently because '*thuousin*' (10^{20}) would follow on from
'*eidōlothuton ti estin*'. But this reason does not seem absolutely conclusive. Furthermore, there is a question of the accent on the word
'*estin*' in 10^{19a} and in 10^{19b}. Must we read '*ti éstin*'? In that case we
should have to translate, 'that meat sacrificed to idols really does
exist' or 'that idols really exist'. These questions would agree quite
well with 8^{1-6}. But it seems to us that '*ti*' would be superfluous in that
case. We prefer then, like Nestlé, '*ti estin*'. Then '*estin*' is the copula
and '*ti*' the attribute (see our translation).

'*Parazēloumen*' in 10^{22} (cf. Deut 32^{21}) = 'provoke the Lord by
disobedience and notably by idolatry'. The remark is addressed to the
'strong', as is shown by the sarcastic end of this question: 'Are you
so strong that you will be stronger than God?' Instead of the indicative in '*-oumen*', the subjunctive in '*-ōmen*' would be preferable. But
it may be admitted that a badly formed subjunctive is in question as
in Galatians 4^{17} ('*hina zēloute*'), or in 4^6 ('*hina phusiousthe*'), or again
in John 11^{47} ('*ti poioumen*').

In 10^{23a} '*panta . . . sumpherei*'[48] is a word-for-word repetition of a
phrase in 6^{12}. Here, as there, '*panta exestin*' = 'everything is permissible', could be a party cry of the 'strong'. But '*ou sumpherei*' =
'is not expedient' does not have quite the same force in the two
places. Whereas 6^{12} speaks of the danger which threatens the gnostic
himself, here the effect of his conduct on those around him is being
spoken about.[49]

[48] The Textus Receptus has '*moi exestin*' in both places. But this reading is not
well attested and can easily be explained by the influence of 6^{12}.

[49] It is not, however, impossible that 10^{23a} as far as '*sumpherei*' is a gloss, since
the phrase duplicates 10^{23b} where the point of view of '*oikodomia*' is put first. But
6^{12} also contains two phrases which follow one another in this way.

*on grounds of conscience; (29) yet by 'conscience' I mean not my own,
but that of the other person. For by what right should my freedom be
judged by another conscience? (30) If I eat of food with thankfulness,
why should I be slandered about that for which I give thanks? (31)
Therefore, whether you eat or drink or whatever you do, do it all to the
glory of God.*

*(32) Do not be a stumbling-block, either to Jews or Greeks or to the
Christian Church. (33) It is thus that I give satisfaction to everyone in
all circumstances, not seeking my own advantage, but that of the greater
number, in order that they may be saved. (11¹) Become imitators of me,
as I am an imitator of Christ.*

Immediately, as J.W. points out, we feel ourselves back in the
same atmosphere as in Chapter **8**. The Apostle's main preoccupation
is no longer caused by the danger of the '*eidōlothuta*' in themselves,
but by the consideration due to the 'weak'. This anxiety stems very
naturally from the altruistic principle of Christian ethics classically
stated in **10²⁴**. In practical terms the Apostle envisages two cases:
Firstly, the purchase of meat in the market ('*makellon*' is the Hel-
lenized form of the Latin noun '*macellum*'). Secondly, the invitation
of a Christian to a pagan's house. The third case, namely partaking
in temple meals, envisaged earlier (**8¹⁰**) as possible in principle, is
not referred to again. Taking these in turn—

(1) It must be recalled that secular slaughtering of animals was not
widespread in Greece. For the most part an animal killed for eating
was also an animal killed in a temple, which had abattoirs as out-
buildings. Scrupulous Christians might then feel impelled to go
without meat altogether or else find out in each individual case the
source of the meat[50]—a very burdensome and almost ridiculous thing
to do. The Apostle authorizes his flock to buy meat without any
qualms and quotes, on this point, the first verse of Psalm 23 (24). It
is the ultimate source of the food which matters, and from this point
of view it is a gift of God—unless the word '*kurios*' in Paul's interpretation means Christ here as it often does elsewhere (*v.* especially
8⁶).

(2) Private invitation from pagans. '*Kalein*' is a technical term for
'invite'. There was a current phrase '*eis deipnon kalein*' = 'to invite
to a meal'. Naturally, there is no need to give the rest of the phrase
('*ei thelete poreuesthai*'). The possibility of refusing is expressly mentioned, a reply which the weak will do well to give. But if the invitation is accepted, the guest must be sure of himself and not ask useless
or absurd questions. Even so, the Apostle goes on, a weak Christian
might find himself sitting at the same table. If such a one should

---

[50] Jews escaped from this dilemma by organizing their own slaughtering according to the prescribed ritual. The Christians probably did likewise, if the decision
recorded in Acts 15²⁹ really did forbid pagan slaughter. But it is doubtful whether
this decision ever had the importance ascribed to it by the author of Acts. In any
event the Epistles of Paul make no reference to it whatsoever.

make a special point of calling your attention to the idolatrous source of the meat,[51] abstain from it because of the conscience of this weak person.

But before ending, the Apostle seeks to define limits for the respect due to the weak. Already **10**[29a] recalled that the liberty of conscience of the man who yields through consideration remains free and independent. **10**[29b] expressly underlines this fact by forbidding the weak to judge the strong,[52] or even more strongly to insult them (**10**[30], '*blasphēmein*', as in Romans 3[8] = 'to calumniate, speak ill of'). For the Christian principle, which is stated once more, is that all food, for which we give thanks to God, is permissible.[53]

10[31] summarizes the advice in one sentence which throws a valuable light on all these difficult problems. It echoes Colossians 3[17] and can be seen as a practical application of the principle given in Romans 14[17]. The discourse could have ended here. But the Apostle on re-reading the letter, or on having it reread to him, must have had the impression, not of having gone too far, but of possibly being misunderstood. So he adds a further exhortation, wrapped up, it is true, in a more general injunction: 'Do not be by your conduct a stumbling-block for Jews, Greeks or the Church of God.' This may be directed as much at the 'strong', who might scandalize other Christians as well as Jews (particularly fastidious over the question of meat), as at the weak who, through over-scrupulousness, might needlessly shock pagans whom it was hoped to win; '*aproskopos*' is indeed a man by whose conduct no one is caused to stumble ('*proskoptō*' = 'strike against, stumble'), and who gives no cause for any adverse criticism.

The Apostle himself (**10**[33]) has striven to have the good of others always in view, by following the example of Christ. This remark might lead us to think that he may have known Christ when He was alive. But the conclusion is not inevitable. Nevertheless, it is remarkable how much importance he attaches to the earthly life of Jesus and consequently how erroneous it would be to interpret the well-

[51] It will be noticed that the 'weak' Christian is considered to be polite enough to speak of '*hierothuton*' and not of '*eidōlothuton*'.

[52] The transition from **10**[29a] to **10**[29b] is quite easy, and it is difficult to see the reason for the quantities of ink used on the supposed difficulties of linking **10**[29b] to what goes before. In '*hina ti*', '*hina*' is used neither as adverb nor conjunction, but as a preposition. '*Hina ti*' here means literally 'to what purpose, what is the use?' But the purposive force of the phrase is not obvious, as is shown for example in Plato's *Apology of Socrates* (Ch. 14) in which Socrates addresses Meletus in these words: '*Hina ti legeis touto*' ('Why, by what right, do you say that I am an atheist?'). The Authorized Version has a very good rendering of **10**[29b]: 'Why is my liberty judged?'

[53] We must not push the discussion to the extreme of asking how did the Christian behave in offering thanks to God in a pagan house. The point concerns the general attitude of the Christian with regard to the gifts of the earth, an attitude classically expressed in the Eucharist.—'*Chariti metechein*' is sometimes interpreted, e.g. by Calvin, as 'to share in grace'. This translation is possible. But the context is such that we choose the rendering of the majority of scholars.

known text 2 Corinthians 5^{16} as expressing lack of interest in the *'imitatio Christi'*.

To return to the question of relationships between these three groups of texts—(*a*) 8^{1-13}, (*b*) 10^{1-22}, (*c*) 10^{23-33}—we have the impression that the transition from (*a*) to (*c*) would be easy. In the one as in the other it is Christian liberty tempered by charity which is the recurring theme, and we do not understand why these two passages, which form a whole, are separated. Passage (*b*) is of a strict type. It is no use to say, like Godet, that all this shows a fine strategy on the Apostle's part, who asks little at first, (*a*), then more, (*b*), only to yield again in the end over secondary points, (*c*). We cannot get rid of the impression that the passage 10^{1-22} (and undoubtedly Chapter **9** too) was not dictated for inclusion in its present setting. It seems then that (*a*) and (*c*) originally belonged to a different letter from (*b*), as we have explained in our Introduction.

CHAPTER XI

(2) Now I commend you for remembering me at every opportunity and for keeping the traditions as I passed them on to you. (3) But I want you to know that the head of every man is Christ; the head of a woman is the man; and the head of Christ is God. (4) Any man who prays or prophesies with his head covered brings shame on his 'head'. (5) But a woman who prays or prophesies bare-headed brings shame on her 'head'. For this attitude lowers her to the level of a woman who shaves her head. (6) Indeed, if the woman is unveiled, let her also cut her hair; but if it is shameful for a woman to crop her hair or to shave her head, let her use a veil.

(7) A man, however, should not cover his head, since he is the image and copy of God. But the woman is the copy of man. (8) For in the first place it was not man who was taken from woman, but woman from man; (9) secondly it was not man who was created because of woman, but woman because of man. (10) That is why the woman should wear a strong protection on her head, because of the angels. (11) However, in the Lord, man exists as little without woman, as woman without man. (12) For just as woman was taken out of man, man comes into the world through the intermediary of the woman; but all comes from God.

(13) Judge for yourselves: Is it seemly for a woman to pray to God bare-headed? (14) Does not nature itself teach us that if a man lets his hair grow, it is a disgrace? (15) But that if the woman does so, it is a source of pride for her? For hair was given to her as a kind of veil. (16) If however, anyone thinks it good to pursue the discussion, well, we do not have that habit, any more than the Churches of God.

11$^{1-16}$. As he often does, the Apostle begins by praising his flock before putting his finger on their faults. '*Mou*' is obviously the object of '*memnēsthe*'. The translation 'you remember all that comes from me' is not now accepted. This verse could be considered as the beginning of a new letter. J.W. thinks it to be the beginning of the letter prior to the first canonical epistle. But we may also understand this verse as the beginning of a resumption of the dictation which may for some reason or other have been interrupted for some time. '*Paradosis*' is the *oral tradition*, either on a point of doctrine, ethics or cult. Where did Paul learn it? It is usually and uncritically said to have been in Jerusalem. Nothing could be less certain. We know from the Epistle to the Galatians that he was only infrequently in touch with Jerusalem, and that his connections were not of long standing or very definite. It was at Damascus, that is in the Judaic Christianity of the Syro-Arabian dispersion, that the Apostle was

initiated into Christianity, and he stayed in that area longer than elsewhere (Gal 1 and 2).

In any case, there is one point on which the Christians of Corinth, or rather the women among them, refused to conform to the tradition. They were becoming emancipated and because of that were creating serious problems for the Apostle. (J.W. even supposes that they formed the nucleus of the group of 'libertines', though this may be going too far.) It was especially over the matter of the women who wished to speak bareheaded in the meetings that the Apostle had to take sides in the fight against feminist tendencies. He calls to his aid three lines of argument: (a) Theological arguments to show that woman, in the order of creation, is farther than man from God. (b) Moral arguments appealing to the rules of propriety and feelings of decency. (c) An argument drawn from angelology. The three groups overlap and it is difficult to pick out the trains of thought, the more so because the Apostle uses rather emotive language.

A further difficulty is created by the ambiguity of the word 'kephalē', which can mean 'head' in the anatomical sense, or in a figurative sense, just in the way that 'head' can in English, thereby opening the way to certain puns.

11³ plunges us headlong into a very complicated theological question. If Christ were called the 'kephalē tēs ekklēsias' = 'head of the Church', as in the Epistle to the Ephesians, all would be clear, since the Church is the body of Christ. But in what sense can Christ be called the head of man, namely (a) not of the Christian, but of every man, (b) not of man in the sense of 'anthrōpos', but of man in the sense of 'anēr' only?

On (a): It must be borne in mind that the creation of mankind takes place through Christ, who being the Heavenly Man, is the supernatural pattern of empirical man (8⁶).

On (b): Our only source is the account in Genesis 2 (not Gen 1!), to which the Apostle makes express reference in 11⁸. Woman was created by God (or by Christ) only indirectly; for she came from man—a statement which is obviously unfavourable to the feminist cause. Only the male was directly created by the Deity. Then it can be understood why woman is in some degree farther removed than man from the Creator. Yet if man ('anēr') is 'kephalē gunaikos' = 'head of the woman', it is not in quite the same sense as when Christ is called 'kephalē andros' = 'head of the man (male)'. For man did not exactly create woman. 'Kephalē' is taken here therefore, in a wider sense: man is superior to woman; as 'anēr' has the article, the primary emphasis is not on an abstract relationship between man and woman, but on the submission of the woman to her husband. When God is called the head of Christ, there is no allusion to a creative act; for Christ was begotten before the world appeared ('huios theou; prōtotokos', Col 1¹⁵) and He was not created, as were

the universe and mankind. But the term clearly indicates the Son's subordination to the Father.

In any case, the Apostle feels that he has proved two theses: (1) the inferiority of woman; (2) the necessity of her subordination to man. Both are in line with Judaism, but we shall have to enquire how the Apostle reconciles his contention with statements like Galatians 3²⁸.

From the doctrines put forward in 11³, 11⁴ draws a practical conclusion. It is somewhat surprising—for what is the connection of the question of the 'covered head' (which for a woman means essentially a veil) with the thesis of woman's inferiority? First it must be noted that for the man, as well as for the woman, only their dress in religious meetings is under discussion; it was in such meetings that prophets generally appeared. Consequently prayer should also allude to public prayer. But why does the point not involve all Christians who take part in the meetings? Because it is in prayer or inspired preaching that the Christian man or woman penetrates more deeply into the supernatural world and comes in some degree face to face with Deity. Any inappropriateness in dress then becomes more glaring and dangerous. Yet, it does not seem to have been the Apostle's wish to apply these restrictions only to the charismatically endowed. For the boundary between the two groups is very fluid— anyone might be called to speak. Moreover 11⁶ and 11¹⁴ suggest many matters of a general nature.

First, what is the meaning of the expression 'kata kephalēs echōn'? 'Echōn' has no complement. Willy-nilly 'something' must be supplied. 'Kata' with the genitive generally means 'coming down from'. But some examples have the sense of 'on'; it might be derived from the meaning 'descending upon', which seems equally ancient.[1]

The expression 'tēn kephalēn autou' = 'his head' at the end of 11⁴ really seems to suggest a pun: the man who is covered dishonours his head, and Christ too. The verse is rather obscure. We guess that the man, being nearer than the woman to God, has the right to appear bareheaded in God's presence (contrary to Jewish conceptions, which only allow men into the synagogue with their heads covered), and that non-observance of this privilege implies a kind of dishonour inflicted by the man upon himself. For he treats his head as something devoid of honour which should be covered.[2] But at 11⁷ we find real

---

[1] For the meaning 'descending upon', see HOMER, *Iliad*, V.696 (cf. XX.213): 'Darkness came upon their eyes ("*kata ophthalmōn*").' For the sense 'on': ARISTOPHANES, *Clouds*, 177 (TEUBNER, I.177, *Belles Lettres*, 171) '*kata tēs trapezēs katapasas leptēn tephran*' ('after sprinkling a fine layer of ashes on the table').— PLUTARCH, *Apophthegmata regum*, 200E, '*kata tēs kephalēs echōn to himation*' (TEUBNER, II.79) (= 'having his cloak over his head').—Esther 6¹², '*lupoumenos kata kephalēs*' (= 'observing mourning by having something on his head', ashes doubtless).

[2] The sense of '*kataischunō*' is not only 'to take away someone's honour', but also 'to shame someone, to make him blush' (H. ESTIENNE: '*pudefacio*'). This applies to the situation when a person is treated as though he deserved no honour.

clarification of our text. A man has nothing to hide because his face displays the image of God. Yet he is not only called the '*eikōn*' = 'image' but also the '*doxa*' of God. If the word '*doxa*' = 'glory' could mean 'reflection', the term would be synonymous with '*apaugasma*', which is found in the Epistle to the Hebrews (1³). But this sense of '*doxa*' is unknown. Moreover, it is certain that the Apostle must have been thinking about Genesis 1²⁶: '*kat' eikona kai kath' homoiōsin*' = 'in his image and likeness'. We are impelled to enquire then whether '*doxa*' is not synonymous with '*homoiōsis*' and at the same time definitely synonymous with '*eikōn*'. That is why we shall accept the hypothesis that '*doxa*' is a copyist's error for '*dogma*', which in Aramaic means a 'copy'. This suggestion was put forward by M. Ginsburger.[3] It is indeed known that the word '*dogma*' passed into Aramaic and took the sense of the Greek '*deigma*' = 'image'. This fact is attested by the texts quoted by J. Lévy,[4] as well as by S. Krauss.[5] But a particularly interesting point is that the Targum Pseudo-Jonathan on Genesis 1²⁶,²⁷,[6] expressly gives these Aramaic nouns בְּצַלְמָא כְּדִיוּקְנָא to explain the Hebrew words בְּצַלְמֵנוּ כִּדְמוּתֵנוּ which are respectively equivalent to '*eikōn*' and '*homoiōsis*'. It may be understood then that Paul, whose mother tongue was Aramaic, may have used the word '*dogma*' in the Aramaic sense; but it is quite conceivable also that a copyist, not understanding the term, replaced '*dogma*' by '*doxa*', as suggested by 11¹⁵.

If the word '*doxa*' is retained, it must be supposed that man as he was created, does honour to God—a point which forbids him to cover his head. How then is this statement to be reconciled with Romans 3²³, where all men 'lack glory' ('*husterountai tēs doxēs tou Theou*')?

From 11⁷ onwards, the author seems to have in mind a situation in which the man would *veil* himself ('*apokaluptesthai*'); but here the verb is chosen only by analogy with 11⁵ and 11⁶, where woman is under discussion.

11⁵. Why does a woman shame or dishonour her head by refusing to veil herself? If '*kephalē*' is taken in the natural sense, it is difficult to make this verse agree with 11¹⁵. For if (as in 11¹⁵) long hair is a 'glory' for a woman, given to her as a kind of garment, it can certainly be understood that she should not cut her hair ('*keiresthai*'), nor shave her head ('*xurasthai*'); but we do not altogether appreciate the necessity of veiling this 'glory'. Consequently a figurative sense

[3] *RHPR* (1932), pp. 245ff.
[4] *Neuhäbräisches und Chaldäisches Wörterbuch*, I.376.
[5] *Griechische und lateinische Lehnwörter in Talmud, Midrasch und Targum*, I.68, 165,175, and particularly II.187 (דִּיוּקְנָא = deformation of the Greek word '*dogma*' = 'pattern, copy, resemblance').
[6] Ed. M. GINSBURGER (Berlin, 1903), p. 3.

must be given to '*kephalē*' in this context. The woman who presents herself bareheaded dishonours her husband, by wishing to be his equal. In some degree she is challenging his superiority, by seeking to take a privilege reserved for him alone.

But what is the meaning of **11^5b** ? Why should the woman who displays her hair be placed on the same level as the one who cuts it or shaves her head, that is to say the one who does almost the opposite ?[7] Let us enquire first why the woman with cropped hair or shaven head was held in contempt. We know from Plutarch[8] and from other texts that a Greek woman would cut her hair as a sign of mourning; but this custom shows at most the abnormal character of such a coiffure. We should think rather of the 'mannish' woman of whom Lucian speaks in his *Dialogues of the Courtesans*. Women with shaven heads were held in even greater contempt.[9]

Further, among the Jews, it was also considered as a punishment to compel a woman to remove her veil, at least according to the usual interpretation of Numbers 5^18.[10] It is certain that among the Jews, as among the Greeks moreover, it was, for one reason or another considered as lacking in decency for a woman or girl of good family to appear bareheaded in public. Even so, the Apostle must have felt that his proof was not sufficiently convincing: that is why a fresh argument is brought forward in **11^10**, which seems to reveal what is in the back of his mind.

But first let us deal with **11^6-9**. They introduce nothing new with

---

[7] The expression '*hen gar kai to auto tē*', etc., is elliptical. The situation in which she is placed is the same for her as if she cut her hair, etc.

[8] *Quaestiones-Romanae*, 14 (TEUBNER, II.281).

[9] See LUCIAN, *Dialogues of the Courtesans*, V.13 (TEUBNER [1887], III.244), '*kathaper hoi sphodra tōn athlētōn andrōdeis apokekarmenē*'. ALLO reads '*hai*' here instead of '*hoi*'. This conjecture would give to Lucian's text a more precise and forceful meaning. But we are not sure that the word '*athlētēs*' could be used in the feminine. LUCIAN, *Drapetai*, §27 (TEUBNER, III.297), even speaks of manly women who shaved their heads '*gunaika en chrō kekarmenēn eis to lakōnikon, arrhenōtikēn kai komidē andrikēn*'. Among the Germani, according to TACITUS, an adulteress's hair was cut (*Germania*, Ch.19, TEUBNER, ed. maj., p. 48). It is also known that the heads of women accused of treason were shaved after the liberation of France in 1944.

But we must not in connection with **11^5** use as evidence as does J.W. (copying from WETTSTEIN) the text of APULEIUS' *Metamorphoses*, VII.§6 (TEUBNER, p. 158): '*tonso capillo in masculinam faciem reformato habitu.*' For the context makes it clear that the author is speaking of an extremely virtuous woman ('*quaedam rarae fidei atque singularis pudicitiae femina*'), who decides to follow her husband into exile, and to scorn the pleasures of the town ('*spretis atque contemptis urbis luxuriae deliciis*'). If she dresses like a man and cuts her hair, it is because of the dangers of the journey.—We quote this error to illustrate the false impressions that may creep in when quotations are copied without being checked.

[10] According to this text, the priest should unveil the woman suspected of adultery before subjecting her to certain tests. The Midrash Bammidbar, parasha IX (ed. WÜNSCHE [1885], p. 183), thinks that it is to dishonour her: 'Since she shows no respect for the honour of God, no respect can be shown for her honour.' In the Mishnah (Baba Quamma 8^6, GOLDSCHMIDT, VII.308), to unveil a woman's head was a serious offence (fine: 400 pieces of silver).

reference to **11⁵**; they only develop the main idea of that verse; in **11⁷** the expression '*doxa Theou*' presents, as we have already seen, almost insurmountable difficulties. The same situation obtains with the expression '*doxa andros*' in **11⁷ᵇ**. Here again the contrary would be more expected: since the man is the head of the woman, she could boast of having him as her master. Now since '*doxa*' in **11⁷ᵇ** must have the same sense as in **11⁷ᵃ**, we must again either accept M. Ginsburger's conjecture and read '*dogma*' = 'copy' or admit that '*doxa*' has the sense of 'reflection', which is unfortunately not attested.

But the author's thought remains somewhat obscure. The central idea must be that the woman, being taken from man, is inferior to him. It is even truer that she was created because of man, which means that the purpose of her existence is not in herself. Further according to the Genesis narrative, to which the Apostle alludes, the woman is expressly the man's helper ('*boēthos*', Gen 2¹⁸,²⁰), which underlines her inferior position. All of this reasoning must have deeply displeased the Corinthian feminists.

11¹⁰ surprises us for two reasons. First we do not see why prudence with regard to the angels should result from woman's ontological and social inferiority. An ellipsis must therefore be again conjectured: 'From all this, it follows that the woman is a weak being, therefore . . .' We wonder what the angels have to do with the situation.[11] The traditional explanation identifies the angels with the priests. It does not go as far back as Chrysostom, who gives no opinion on this problem. But we find it in St Ephrem: '*angelos*' = '*sacerdotes*'[12] in Ambrosiaster: '*Angelos episcopos dicit, sicut in Apocalypsi Johannis*';[13] also in Pelagius,[14] in Hervé de Bourg-Dieu[15] and in many others.—Theodoret of Cyr[16] is much nearer the truth, in thinking of guardian angels and the respect due to them.

But the Apostle must have been thinking particularly about the danger into which women might come because of certain other angels—and *vice versa*. Paul may very well have remembered the story of the angels seduced by the beauty of women, which is summarized at the beginning of Genesis 6 and more fully developed in

[11] 'A surprising development', BACHMANN, p. 363.—It is pointless to discuss or even to list the many quite superfluous conjectures which have been made about this point, e.g. '*dia tas agelas*' ('because of the crowd'). The list can be found in the commentary by A. P. STANLEY, *The Epistles of St Paul to the Corinthians* (London, 1876), p. 186.

[12] *Commentarii in epistulas D. Pauli* (Venice, 1892), p. 70.

[13] *MPL* XVII, col. 240 C.

[14] *MPL* XXX, col. 750 A.

[15] *MPL* CLXXXI, col. 926 D–927 A.

[16] *MPG* LXXXII, col. 312 D–313 A.—St THOMAS AQUINAS, op. cit., above (Ch. 10, note 9) (p. 722), admits the possibility of these two interpretations: (*a*) '*angeli caelestes*' as in Psalm 137¹ (138¹), (*b*) '*sacerdotes*', without giving a definite opinion, and without any explanation about the danger threatened by the angels.

the Enoch literature.[17] It is true that it was primarily the women's beauty which attracted the angels. But their weakness, their relatively greater distance from God, could encourage them. Now, it was in the cult, notably when inspiration was being spoken of, that contact was made with the supernatural world and the angels. 'Before the angels (*'elohim*) I will sing thy praise', says the Psalmist in Psalm 137¹ (138¹)—with no intention of referring to a canticle sung after death. According to Origen,[18] angels surround Christian assemblies. It was at least seemly therefore to wear a veil, if only to avoid leading the angels into temptation. This also explains why the Apostle does not say that any covering of the head is sufficient, but specifies a veil which was to conceal the hair and part of the face (at least the forehead).

But since it is not certain that the Corinthians were well acquainted with Jewish beliefs, it is permissible to suppose with Dibelius,[19] and those who have followed him, that there is here an allusion to Hellenistic ideas, according to which a woman in an ecstatic condition (as in sleep) was through her weakness particularly exposed to the attacks of certain spirits which might cause cases of possession. Then the dominating idea would be that the woman ought to be protected against the angels. But in what way was the veil a protection? And is that really the sense of the word '*exousia*'? No one denies that the word means 'power' or 'authority'. There has been a desire to deduce from that that the veil was a sign of power or authority, a sign that the woman belongs to her husband and that she was in some way untouchable.[20] But ought the unmarried woman who also prophesied sometimes (*v.* Acts 21⁸⁻⁹) not to be protected too? And where is it said that the veil was a sign of marital power or authority?

How then are we to explain the curious expression 'to have a power (authority) on her head'?[21] A variant in Irenaeus gives '*kalumma*' = 'a veil';[22] It occurs again in Jerome,[23] who reads, '*velamen*'. Origen[24] has combined both readings: '*velamen et potestatem.*' The reading '*velamen*' is perhaps an attempt to circumvent

---

[17] See Eth. Enoch, Chs 6–7, 67–8, 106¹³⁻¹⁴ (KAUTZSCH, *Pseudepigraphen* [1900], pp. 238ff, 274ff, 309). Slav. Enoch, Ch. 7¹⁸ (BONWETSCH T.U.44.2, pp. 6–7 and 16–17). Testament of Reuben 5 (KAUTZSCH, op. cit., p. 462). Jubilees 5¹ (ibid., p. 48). Apoc. of Baruch 56⁸⁻¹³ (ibid., p. 434).—Remember too the story of Tobit 6¹⁰⁻¹⁸ and 8¹⁻⁸, in which the demon Asmodaeus has killed several men, probably through jealousy.

[18] *De oratione*, Ch. 31 (KOETSCHAU, II.398).

[19] *Die Geisterwelt im Glauben des Paulus* (Göttingen, 1909).

[20] But this meaning is very doubtful. '*Basileia*' in the sense of 'royal crown' (= 'a sign of royal power') has been quoted as a parallel; but there the power of its wearer is meant and not the power of another person. BENGEL refers to Genesis 20¹⁶, where the LXX translates כְּסוּת ('veil'?) by '*timē*'. Could not the noun '*exousia*' have the same sense? But the exact meaning of the Hebrew word at this place is uncertain. And it is very probable that the LXX took it as a synonym of 'price' or 'ransom', which is the normal sense of '*timē*'.

[21] Some moderns have made conjectures. Should the Latin word '*exuviae*' more or less Grecianized be read? But did this noun really have that sense?

[22] *MPG* VII, col. 524 B.   [23] *MPL* XXV, col. 439 A.   [24] *MPG* XIII, col. 119 B.

the difficulty of the original text. Nevertheless the identification of 'exousia' with 'kalumma' is defensible. For Buxtorf[25] shows that שְׁלְטוֹנִיָא = שְׁבִיס = 'vitta, reticulum capitis, ornamentum muliebre'. Now שְׁלְטוֹנִיָא might easily be = 'exousia'. If this identification is not accepted, it must be supposed that 'exousia' here means 'a means of exercising power'. As this sense is common for the word 'dunamis' in Hellenistic literature and is perhaps also presupposed in Deuteronomy 8[17] and Revelation 18[3], it is not inadmissible to make the same supposition for the word 'exousia'.[26]

But was the veil considered as a means of giving proof of power, and that more particularly against invisible enemies? According to Dibelius,[27] that is precisely what was universally admitted by the beliefs of the time.[28] It would be wrong to form the idea that the Apostle shared these ideas. Our knowledge of the invisible creation is so poor in comparison with that of the ancients and the peoples of the East, that we should do well not to display too rashly our rationalist convictions, which may be only prejudices.

In conclusion, let us also recall that against our interpretation, the fact could be adduced that 'anggeloi' might refer to good angels only, who by definition are untouched by desire. But we have already had the opportunity of discovering that the rough and ready distinction between good and bad angels does not take into account the complexity of the Pauline angelology. Nothing permits us to believe, indeed, that the angel descending from heaven to announce another Gospel (Gal 1[8]) is a bad angel. On the contrary, it is because he is good in principle, although not infallible, that his teaching runs the risk of leading men into error. Similarly it is not said that the powers called 'archai' and 'stoicheia' are powers of darkness; they are angels in the process of falling because they oppose the Gospel. And is there any need to recall that the angels of Genesis 6 were also good angels, before they allowed themselves to be misled?[29] According to Fitzmeyer, Greek women could be present at religious assemblies bareheaded. In this case the women apparently did not make any innovation and it is quite understandable that they may have wished to retain the custom. But we must not advance too far along a road which has few signposts.—But why are angels involved here? Fitzmeyer supposes, on the strength of several Qumran texts, that any defect of physique or dress is offensive to the angels. But then the main problem still remains: Why do the angels regard the lack of a veil as reprehensible?

In 11[11] and 11[12] the Apostle answers an objection which must have come to the minds of all his readers: Is not the equality of man and

[25] Lexicon (1639, col. 2416 and 2312).

[26] Cf. GERHARD KITTEL, Die Macht auf dem Haupte (Arbeiten zur Vorgeschichte des Christentums, I.3 [Leipzig, 1920]).

[27] Loc. cit., pp. 233ff.

[28] Cf. FEHRLE, Kultische Keuschheit im Altertum (Giessen, 1910), p. 39.

[29] With reference to 11[10] see also J. U. FITZMEYER, 'Features of Qumran Angelology and the Angels of 1 Corinthians 11.10' in NTS, 4 (1957).

woman nevertheless taught by Christianity? If the Corinthians had been able to know the Epistle to the Galatians, they would have been able to quote 3[28] from it. In any event, the drift of Chapter 7 of our Epistle, which so carefully lays down the equality of duties and rights for both sexes, appeared to support the feminists. Yes, says the Apostle, that is true—'*en kuriō*', that is to say, on the Christian plane: there, neither can exist without the other; they give mutual support to one another. This truth fixes the limits of man's domination. So the words '*en kuriō*' which J.W. would delete are absolutely necessary. They explain how the truth of **11[11]** can coexist with that of **11[8]** and **11[9]**, to which it seems opposed.[30]

Yet we regret the fact that the Apostle did not give a more detailed exposition of the limits of the two orders—the natural order which makes an inferior being of the woman, and the Christian order which makes her man's equal. It is even more troublesome that **11[12]** again brings forward, so as to prove the truth pronounced in **11[11]**, an argument taken straight from human nature: if woman came from man at the beginning of creation, the opposite is true now. Indeed, '*dia gunaikos*' can mean only: man comes into the world 'through the intermediary of woman'.

The phrase '*ta panta ek tou Theou*' = 'all comes from God' is written in the same spirit as 3[23] and 10[31]. These words can mean: everything, that is the universe (in German '*das All*'), comes from God; or else: everything belongs to God. In any case, only by referring everything to God can we fall into the line of the specifically Christian code of ethics.

11[13]. As in 10[15], the author appeals to the good sense, not so much of the women, which would have required '*autais*', but of the whole Church, which, after some thought, will recognize that by standing unveiled before God, a woman acts in opposition to the laws of propriety. If, as we think, it is accepted that Greek women normally were veiled when in the street, the full reach of the argument can be grasped: do not come before God dressed in a way considered elsewhere as indecent.[31]

---

[30] '*Caput autem mulieris vir—secundum ordinem naturalem: ceterum in Christo Jesu neque masculus neque femina.*' PELAGIUS, *Expositio in* 1 *Corinthians* 11 (*MPL* XXX, col. 749 C = *Texts and Studies*, ed. ROBINSON, IX. 2 [Cambridge, 1926]. 187).—'*Plēn*' almost always has an adversative sense in the New Testament: see our '*Royaume de Dieu*', p. 113 and note 1.

[31] The specialists, it is true, do not seem to be altogether agreed about the usual headdress of a Greek woman in public. See COMTESSE DE VILLERMONT, *Histoire de la coiffure féminine* (Brussels, 1891), pp. 41 and 56; DAREMBERG AND SAGLIO, *Dictionnaire des antiquités gréco-romaines*, I.II.1355 and V.670; MÉNARD and SAUVAGEOT, *La vie privée des anciens* (Flammarion, n.d.), III.289ff; SMITH, *Dictionary of Greek and Roman Antiquities* (2 vols, London, 1890). It seems to us that iconography shows a distinction: the long veil covering the face and part of the bust was only worn in exceptional circumstances (mourning, marriage, dangerous journeys). But the short veil concealing the hair, the ears and the forehead seems to have been obligatory in good families.

The Apostle also tries to prove the unseemliness of the attitude under review, by a new argument presented in 11^{14} and 11^{15}. This brings forward a serious difficulty, over which J.W. skates rather rapidly and which we have already pointed out. If a woman's hair can be used as a head-covering and even as a garment provided by nature, why the veil? Is it not rather man, deprived of long hair, who should cover his head? As it is not possible either to give any meaning to '*koman*' but 'wear long hair', we can see only one possible explanation; nature by endowing woman with abundant hair has shown the desire that she should be covered. Civilization should to some extent complete the work of nature by following the direction indicated by nature. We agree therefore with the view of Allo, but without accepting the general thesis of the conformity of nature and grace. Conversely a man who lets his hair grow would pass (and actually did pass) as effeminate.

11^{16} ends this discussion on a slightly resigned note. The Apostle realizes the difficulty of convincing the Corinthian women who are of a contentious turn of mind ('*philoneikeis*').

He states his wish to conform to the usually more peaceful customs of the Christian Churches; this means that he will make no further replies to retorts and attacks which will be undoubtedly provoked by the page he has just written.

In the Christian Churches, until our own day, the Apostle's instructions have been generally observed, women covering their heads, men going bareheaded—apart from Catholic and Orthodox priests. But the motives for this are in part very different from those of the Apostle. A man who fails to remove his hat on entering a place of worship would not be considered as despicable but as insolent because he lacked respect.[32] Further, among women the motive of inferiority to men, as well as that of the fear of the angels, has had little significance. There remains the motive of propriety: so long as a bareheaded woman was considered as improperly dressed, she was not admitted into a church. But here we are in the realm of the relative, as was pointed out by Calvin whose remark[33] about 14^{35} may be aptly applied to this passage: '. . . it is the part of the prudent reader to consider, that the things of which he here treats are intermediate and indifferent, in which there is nothing unlawful, but what is at variance with propriety and edification.'

Today, in the majority of European countries, almost no one is shocked by women who go bareheaded or with hair cut short.

[32] Exceptions are, however, shown in Calvinist churches in France, especially in the south. See PAUL DE FÉLICE, *Les protestants d'autrefois* (Paris, Fischbacher, 1897), pp. 61ff. The same thing occurred in the Low Countries. Further, the skullcap is generally admitted, and BENGEL thinks that when its wearing is justified by baldness or illness, the Apostle would not forbid it were he to return in our time.
[33] *Comm.*, E.Tr., p. 469.

(17) *While making these recommendations, I cannot praise you about the fact that your meetings are harmful to you, instead of being profitable.* (18) *Indeed in the first place, reports reach me which say that when you meet as a congregation, divisions can be found among you, and in part I believe it.* (19) *For there will of necessity be factions among you, in order that those who can stand the test may show up in your midst.* (20) *But in view of the way in which you meet as a congregation, you cannot possible eat what should really be the Lord's Supper.* (21) *For each of you hastens to eat his own meal, and one suffers hunger while another is drunk.* (22) *Have you no houses in which to eat and drink? Or do you consider the Church of God of so little account that you do shame to the poor? What am I to say to you? Shall I praise you? No, on this point I can give no praise.*

(23) *For, on my own part, I have received a tradition which goes back to the Lord and which I have already transmitted to you. It is this: The Lord Jesus on the night in which he was betrayed, took bread, (24) and having given thanks, he broke it and said: 'This is my body which is for you. Do this in remembrance of me.'* (25) *Similarly the cup after supper saying: 'This cup is the new covenant in my blood. Do this in remembrance of me each time that you drink it.'*

(26) *Therefore, each time you eat this bread and drink from this cup, you proclaim the Lord's death, until he comes.* (27) *Consequently, anyone who eats the bread or drinks from the cup of the Lord unworthily will make himself guilty in relation to the body and blood of the Lord.* (28) *So let a man examine himself, and after so doing, let him eat and drink of the cup.* (29) *For anyone who eats and drinks without discerning the body, eats and drinks his own judgment.* (30) *That is why there are among you so many sick and ailing, and a considerable number have died.* (31) *But if we examined ourselves, we should not be judged.* (32) *Further, if we are judged by the Lord, it is for our correction, so that we may not be condemned with the world.*

(33) *Therefore, my brothers, when you come together to eat, wait for one another.* (34) *If any one be hungry, let him eat at home, so as to avoid behaving at the meeting in a way that would bring condemnation.—As for the other matters, I will deal with those when I come.*

11¹⁷⁻³⁴. This section introduces a serious question of a different kind. It concerns abuses which had crept into the celebration of the Lord's Supper. The author's remarks on the subject provide information about his conception of the Eucharist, and in this lies the passage's chief value to us. We must not however read into it a complete, dogmatic statement about this sacrament (see also on this point our observations on **10¹⁶ff** above).

11¹⁷ has four different readings, according to whether one or other of the verbs is used indicatively or participially.

(1) *'Touto de paranggellō . . . ouk epainōn'* in A, C, vulg., pesh.

(2) '*Touto de paranggellōn ouk epainō*' in E, F, Chrysostom (*MPG* LXI, col. 225).

(3) '*Touto de paranggellō ouk epainō*' in D.

(4) '*Touto de paranggellōn ouk epainōn*' in B. This line is missing in P 46.

Readings (3) and (4) may be discarded as copyists' errors. (2) is preferable to (1) for the following reason: '*Touto*' can hardly be attached to what follows, because we must look too far forward to find the contents of the '*paranggelia*'. The pronoun ought then to speak of a recommendation just made by the author (and to be followed up later). It seems more natural then to put '*paranggellein*' in the participial form. The main idea is blame concerning the abuses mentioned between 11¹⁷ and 14⁴⁰. It is expressed by '*ouk epainō*' = 'I cannot praise'.³⁴

'*Sunerchesthai eis to kreisson*' or '*eis to hēsson*' is a rather condensed expression, but its meaning is quite clear: 'Your meetings do not bear the moral fruit which should be expected.' '*Kreisson*' signifies moral good as in 7⁹; Philippians 1²³ (cf. '*hēttēma*' as a synonym for moral defect in 6⁷).

'*Prōton men*' = 'in the first place indeed' in 11¹⁸ is not followed by '*deuteron de*' = 'in the second place', nor by an equivalent expression. We agree with Bachmann's view that '*prōton*' introduces the list of abuses which continues through Chapters 12 to 14.

'*En ekklēsia*' obviously has no local sense, since there existed at that time no place bearing the name of 'church'. '*En ekklēsia*' is the assembly which comes into being by the mere act of meeting together ('*sunerchesthai*'). '*Sunerchesthai epi to auto*' could on the other hand have a local sense (= 'come together in the same place'), though we are not sure of it; for '*epi to auto*' could be a synonym for '*en ekklēsia*' = 'to form a single body,'³⁵ and it was only in this case that the Corinthians were subsequently able to understand that the Apostle wishes to speak of Eucharistic assemblies.—Has the word '*schismata*' the same sense as in the first chapter or must we think in terms of divisions into groups which threatened the unity of Eucharistic meals? Both hypotheses could be supported; but in any case *schisms* from the cultic angle are envisaged here. They do indeed threaten the unity of the Church at the very moment of the celebration of the Lord's Supper.

The fact that the Apostle also speaks, in 11¹⁹, of '*haireseis*' = 'factions', might also suggest doctrinal disputes; but as we shall see

³⁴ What is the force of '*hoti*' in v. 17b? One is tempted to translate by 'because'; but in that case the verb '*epainō*' should be followed by the accusative '*humas*'. '*Hoti*' therefore means 'that'.

³⁵ In 7³ '*epi to auto*' does not exactly suggest a locative sense, nor does 1 Clem 34⁷ where there is a question of spiritual unity: 'Bringing you together on the plane of conscience with a feeling of unity' ('*en homonoia epi to auto sunachthentes tē suneidēsei*'). In Barn 4¹⁰ there may be a local sense; but on the other hand it is doubtful in the frequently quoted texts from Plato, *Republic* 329A, and Xenophon *Ath. Rep.*, II.2.

later, the reference in question here is not aimed specifically at the Church in Corinth. Once more, the Apostle condemns divisions, but his judgement is at the same time calmer ('such things must happen') and more pitiless than in Chapter **1**: 'for those who come through the test victorious will stand revealed' (*'dokimoi'*, cf. 2 Cor 10¹⁸, 13⁷, Rom 14¹⁸, Jas 1³), the others will be rejected. Even if we did not assign our chapter to a different letter from Chapter **1**, it would be necessary to suppose that more recent rumours on this subject had reached the Apostle ('*akouō*'). If he does not write at greater length and generality on these divisions, it is because he considers the question to have been adequately treated in the first chapter.

Even if the reports are not all true ('*meros ti pisteuō*'), the situation is serious. A curious point is that the prophecy in **11**¹⁹, '*dei gar kai haireseis en humin einai*' = 'for there will of necessity be factions among you' is quoted by the *Syriac Didascalia* (6⁵), as a saying of our Lord,³⁶ as well as by Justin in his *Dialogue with Trypho*³⁷ and by Didymus.³⁸ We might very well have here an '*agraphon*', that is an authentic saying of our Lord's unrecorded in the Gospels.³⁹

The expression '*kuriakon deipnon*' is clear, after all that has been said in Chapters **8** and **10**. It is the meal to which the Lord summons us. Analogy with the expression '*kuriakē hēmera*' (*Did.* 14) might lead us to believe that the meal was observed on Sundays only. But it is very possible that in Corinth, as in Judaea according to Acts 2⁴⁶, the meal was observed more frequently.

11²⁰. What is the meaning of '*ouk estin*'? The idea of purpose ('it is not to celebrate') is inadmissible; for the Corinthians do intend to observe the Lord's Supper. The expression might mean: 'That is no way to observe the Lord's Supper.' In this case the word '*estin*' could only be the copula. But then a subject could be expected expressed, for instance, by '*touto*', which is omitted. We prefer therefore to render '*ouk estin*', etc., by 'it is not possible that you are eating the Lord's Supper in the conditions desired by the Lord'.

11²¹ and **11²²** show very clearly two of the reasons for which Eucharistic meals, which were still real meals at the time, had to be gradually reduced to ceremonies from which worldly elements had to be more and more excluded. Firstly social inequality was shamefully displayed, and that at a time when brotherly unity should have been stronger than ever. Instead of waiting until all were present and the food brought by each member was fairly shared out, the

---

³⁶ = Chapter 23, p. 118, in the translation by ACHELIS AND FLEMMING, TU, 25.1 = N.F., 10.2 (1904).

³⁷ Chapter 35 (*MPG* VI, col. 549 C).

³⁸ *De Trinitate*, III.22 (*MPG* XXXVII, col. 920 A).

³⁹ Should we, with ATTO DE VERCEIL (*MPL* CXXXIV, col. 378 C) refer to Matthew 18⁷, or to 2 Peter 2¹? But neither of these texts provides real evidence.

more affluent hurried to eat their share without waiting for the
arrival of the poor, who might have been detained longer by their
work. That is the meaning of the phrase '*prolambanein to idion
deipnon*'.

The second abuse alluded to in **11²¹** is that the rich ate and drank
too much; this was scandalous and ran the risk of stripping the
assemblies of their solemn character. **11²²** clearly states the principle
which has caused the Eucharist's evolution in the direction we know
today: if hunger and thirst are to be appeased, it is better to stay at
home. Consequently, the observance of the Lord's Supper could be
reduced to its simplest terms. The motive indicated in **11²²ᵇ** underlines the morally unpleasant side of the customs condemned in **11²¹**:
it is an offence to the poor ('*kataischunō*' = 'you do them shame', as
in **11⁴** and **11⁵** above); it is moreover contempt of the Church ('*kata-
phroneō*'). It is true that the evolution of the rite was to bring some
attenuation of the idea of a fraternal meal, which should have been
an excellent opportunity for the poor to eat their fill. But we know
that the Churches, while giving the Lord's Supper the sober solemn
character called for by the Apostle, continued to celebrate love-
feasts before or after the Eucharist.[40]

In **11²²** the majority of witnesses, including ℵ, A, C, and D, read
'*epainesō*' (future), whilst P 46 and B, F and G have '*epainō*' (present);
the meaning does not differ essentially. The few words '*epainō*' (or
'*epainesō*') '*humas*' could be a statement = 'I will praise you'; but
the context, as well as the many rhetorical questions which precede,
makes us favour the generally admitted question mark. Yet there is
more involved here than a purely rhetorical question. For the
Apostle answers it, at least in part, by censuring the Corinthians for
their manner of observing the rite.

'*Gar*' at the beginning of **11²³** is not, strictly speaking, the justification of blame; its justification has already been given. This particle
presupposes an unexpressed thought: 'If you had been faithful to the
traditions which were passed on to you (**11¹**), you could not have
behaved in this way. For—I repeat it—this is the tradition, etc. . . .'
There has been much discussion about the exact meaning of '*apo tou
kuriou*' = 'which goes back to the Lord'. Our view, together with
that of the majority of critics, is that the author purposely turned
down the preposition '*para*', which might have been expected. '*Para*'
would mean rather 'from the Lord's mouth' and would suggest a
direct revelation.[41] '*Apo*' = 'on the Lord's behalf' indicates the
source of an item of information, which must have passed along the

---

[40] For the history of the Lord's Supper readers are referred to the following
works: MAURICE GOGUEL, *L'eucharistie des origines à Justin Martyr* (Paris, 1910);
HANS LIETZMANN, *Mass and Lord's Supper* (Tr. Reeve, Leyden, 1953); OSCAR
CULLMANN, '*Le culte dans l'Eglise primitive*', *CTAP*, No. 8 (*Early Christian Worship*, London, 1953) and the literature cited therein.

[41] For this use of '*para*' see Galatians 1¹², Philippians 4¹⁸, 2 Thessalonians 3⁶,
2 Timothy 1¹³, 2², 3¹⁴, and many other New Testament passages.

channel of tradition before reaching the Apostle. In fact he must have received it at the time of his conversion, that is at Damascus.[42]

Our Epistle is the oldest Christian document about the Lord's Supper. So it is perfectly fair to give this passage a pre-eminent and almost exclusive place in Protestant liturgies. It is even more important to make a close examination of its meaning. Obviously it is out of the question to give here a survey of the controversies which the text has provoked, or to study its exact connection with the Synoptic texts.

The chronological indication ('the night in which . . .' etc.) says nothing about the day or date of the Lord's last meal. The expression '*arton klan*' = 'to break bread' could be related to the Passover rite (although '*artos*' is not accompanied by '*azumos*' = 'unleavened'), but also to other solemn meals. We learn that the cup was not the only thing to be blessed, as might be believed according to 10^{16}; for it is certain that the rite was observed according to the outline given here. What is curious is that the formula (11^{25}) of 'consecration' of the cup '*touto to potērion*', etc., does not correspond exactly to that of the bread. After '*touto esti to sōma mou*' = 'this is my body' we might expect '*touto esti to haima mou*' = 'this is my blood'. But we find a much more complicated phrase: '*touto to potērion hē kainē diathēkē estin en tō emō haimati*' = 'this cup is the new covenant in my blood'. This lack of exact parallelism seems to argue in favour of the antiquity of the formula recorded here by Paul.[43] It is identical with the one given in most of the manuscripts of Luke 22^{20}, and this is not surprising since the third Evangelist must have reproduced the tradition known in Antioch, that is in the milieu with which the Apostle lived in close contact. But it can be understood that requirements of an aesthetic and ritualist nature caused this text to evolve in a way which progressively blurred the differences in the formulae concerning the bread and wine respectively. With Justin Martyr,[44] this ideal of harmony is reached: in his work the phrase '*touto esti to haima mou*' has replaced the Pauline wording, and becomes an exact parallel of '*touto esti to sōma mou*'.

The formulae recorded by Mark (14^{24}) and Matthew (26^{28}) fall between the two extremes. The first two Evangelists say in effect: '*touto esti to haima mou tēs diathēkēs*.'[45] This text is reminiscent of

---

[42] As J.W. points out, there is no contradiction with the Apostle's general statement that he received the Gospel directly from Christ. Indeed, on the Damascus road, Christ revealed Himself to Paul as crucified and glorified. For the historical details, it is natural that Paul had recourse to traditions received from his elder brethren in Christianity.—For all matters concerning the connection between '*euanggelion*' and '*paradosis*' in Paul's writings, see MOLLAND, *Das paulinische Evangelium* (Oslo, 1934) (pub. Acad. Sect. phil, 1934:3).

[43] With the possible exception of '*huper humōn*' added to '*to sōma*'.

[44] *Apology*, 66^3 (*MPG* VI, col. 429 A).

[45] As many exegetes have pointed out, there is a genitive too many in this formula. In our view '*tēs diathēkēs*' is original. '*To haima tēs diathēkēs*' was a post-Pauline but pre-Markan expression, and constituted the first attempt to balance the two parts of the words of institution; the noun '*haima*' was therefore already in the nominative like '*sōma*'; moreover the expression fitted the pattern

the Pauline formula, but is to some extent moving towards the definitive text of Justin.

Moreover the text given by Paul in 10¹⁶ is to be taken into account only for the interpretation which Paul gave of the words of institution and not for the reconstitution of those words. We have already seen that the idea of a close communion with Christ dominates Paul's concept. We should also like to know in exactly what sense the Apostle understood the relationship between the bread and the body. The many questions asked by Catholics and Protestants on the subject are well known. Unfortunately the Apostle gives no definite indication. A clear impression is even given that what interests him primarily in the doctrine of the body is its presence in the Church, which is founded on the communion with Christ actualized in the Eucharist. That is why we find no explanation of the manner in which the body is present in the bread. All that can be said is that genuine communion with the dead and risen Christ is made possible by the bread.[46]

In Chapter 10 we had the impression that the cup alludes rather to the death, the bread to the resurrection. This truth must not be forgotten. Yet it remains to be noted that the three words '*to huper humōn*' added to '*sōma*', even if they are not entirely original, are characteristic of the concept accepted by Paul. Indeed '*huper humōn*' can hardly mean anything other than 'given for you, for your salvation'. To express the simpler idea that the bread was distributed to those present, the *dativus commodi* '*humin*' would have been adequate. Consequently it is not unreasonable to think that the Apostle already saw in the breaking of the bread an allusion to the death of Christ.[47]

Before discussing the exact meaning of '*anamnēsis*' = 'remembrance', which is involved in the subjects of both the bread and the wine, let us ask what is the meaning of the expression '*hē kainē diathēkē hē en tō emō haimati*'. And first of all, what is the meaning of '*diathēkē*'? Covenant? Or Testament? '*Hē kainē diathēkē*' is obviously a contrast to the old '*diathēkē*'. What is it? It is impossible not to think of the text in Exodus 24⁸ which has been quoted already. After sacrificing some '*moscharia*' = 'young bulls', Moses poured part of their blood into a receptacle and sprinkled part on the altar. Then

---

given in Exodus 24⁸: '*idou to haima tēs diathēkēs.*' The genitive '*mou*' was introduced to conform with '*sōma mou*' in Mark and Matthew, and eventually ousted, in Justin's form, the rival genitive.—For the entire passage see the important study by F. LEENHARDT, *Le sacrament de la sainte Cène* (Neuchâtel and Paris, 1948).

[46] To those interested in comparative studies we would mention a work which has in all probability not attracted their attention. Mme ALEXANDRA DAVID-NÉEL (*Parmi les mystiques et les magiciens du Thibet* [Paris, Plon, 1919], p. 134) points out that in Tibet a candidate for a certain initiation must pronounce these words: 'I give my flesh to those who hunger, my blood to those who thirst. . . .' But it is to demons that this sacrifice is made in the course of an exercise in imagination in which the candidate visualizes himself torn by demons.

[47] Perhaps Jesus Himself gave this meaning to the breaking of bread at the last meal; for He could expect to be stoned by the Jews, the usual punishment for religious crimes.

he read the 'book of the covenant', and made the people promise to
observe its commandments. Finally, he sprinkled blood on the
people and declared: 'This is the blood of the *covenant* (בְּרִית =

'*diathēkē*') which the Lord has established with you concerning these
words.' But if the word '*diathēkē*' has the force of 'covenant', who
exactly are the contracting parties in the new covenant? Usually the
difficulty is turned by giving to '*diathēkē*' the sense of 'testament',
which would be a very acceptable idea since Jesus to some extent
passed on His last wishes by the institution of the Lord's Supper.
Unfortunately this sense, justifiable as it is in the texts of Mark and
Matthew, is inadmissible in our context by the use of the adjective
'*kainē*' and by the parallelism with Exodus 24 which is implied. For
neither the Sinai covenant nor the 'book of the covenant' were ever
presented as a testament of Moses. Reference to Galatians 3[15],
where '*diathēkē*' really means 'testament' is of no help whatsoever;
for that text is concerned with promises made to Abraham, which
had no connection with a sacrifice.[48]

We must therefore take the decisive step of affirming that here
again a covenant between God and His people is meant; but this
time 'people' is taken in the spiritual sense as the Christian Church.
For its centre this new covenant has, not the Law, but Christ Himself, who replaces the victim of the old covenant.[49]

Where must '*en tō emō haimati*' be attached? To '*potērion*'? Or
to '*diathēkē*'? Or to '*estin*'? The first solution (the cup containing the
blood) is difficult to support for reasons of style, '*potērion*' being
widely separated from its so-called complement; further, the sense
of '*en*' would be quite unusual in that event. The third solution is
supported by J.W. and Allo. The sense would then be: 'If the cup is
a cup of the covenant, it is because of my blood.' This is a defensible
meaning. But it seems more natural to us to take the second construction as Godet does. Indeed, we do not see why '*en tō haimati*'
should not provide a very good complement to the idea of בְּרִית, as

is foreshadowed in Exodus 24. The covenant was made and continues to be made in blood.[50]

Which is meant? The material blood of the Crucified? Or the
supernatural blood of the Risen One, which is destined to circulate
in that body which is the Church? Here again the task is not to
explain the meaning of those words in the Lord's mouth, but in that
of the Apostle. In the light of all we have just said, the dominant

[48] We are well aware that Hebrews 9[16] very cleverly combines both senses of
the word '*diathēkē*'. But it seems contrary to good method to use this Epistle
without due care in commenting on Pauline or Synoptic texts.

[49] On this point there is naturally absolute conformity between the Epistle to
the Hebrews and Paul. But Romans 3[25] and 5[9] must also be borne carefully in
mind. Although these texts affirm more than the words of institution, we think
that they support our translation of '*diathēkē*' as well as our reading of 11[25].

[50] On the synonymity of '*en*' and '*dia*' (with the genitive) there is nothing more
to be added after our discussion on 4[21].

allusion is to death. By the wine of the Lord's Supper, the Christian is mysteriously linked to the benefit which emanates from the Cross, that is the cancellation of sin, and deliverance from the powers of evil, although the participle '*ekchunnomenon huper humōn*' = 'shed for you' (Luke) or *ekkechunnomenon huper pollōn*' = 'shed for many' (Mark) or '*ekkechunnomenon eis aphesin hamartiōn*' = 'shed for the remission of sins' (Matthew) is absent here.—However, the second sense is not untenable on that account and would not be so even if the Apostle understood the participle to be '*ekkechunomennon*'; for is not the spirit of Christ which must circulate in his new body also a gift made to Christians among whom it is spread abroad?

Finally, what is the meaning of the commandment to do this 'in remembrance of me' ('*eis tēn emēn anamnēsin*')? As is known, it is absent from Mark and Matthew, but present in Luke for the bread only and in Paul for both elements. For the cup Paul also adds '*hosakis ean pinēte*' = 'each time that you drink'. Without this fresh hint it would not be clear to what '*touto*' = 'this', the object of '*poieite*' = 'do', refers, since no act of our Lord's is mentioned. For the bread on the other hand '*eucharistēsas eklasen*' = 'having given thanks he broke (it)' makes the meaning of '*touto poiein*' quite clear. There is, however, a slight difference in nuance between 11^{24} and 11^{25}, if they are taken literally. The definitive action which must be repeated in remembrance of the Lord is the blessing and breaking of the bread on the one hand, and the drinking of the wine ('*hosakis pinēte*') on the other. But the importance of this lack of parallelism must not be exaggerated.

Once more we have before us a tradition independent of the one recorded by Mark's Gospel. It is difficult to say which is the more ancient. If Luke has reproduced it in part, is he drawing on the same tradition as Paul? Or did Luke originally have the Marcan tradition, and were the words '*touto poieite*' added later by Pauline Churches using the Third Gospel? A very difficult question to settle.

What is the meaning of '*anamnēsis*'? The term does not refer to a persistent memory, but to a 'reminder' (Allo). This accords quite well with the fact that from one point of view, the Lord's Supper was a representation and a repetition of the last meal of our Lord who was held to be present through the Spirit, after His appearances at the time of a meal in the manner of Luke 24^{41} had ceased. The Passover festival instituted as a reminder of the Exodus from Egypt[51] may be cited as an analogy. It is understandable why the celebration of the Eucharist is considered by Paul as a 'proclamation of Christ's

---

[51] '*Estai soi sēmeion kai mnēmosunon*' (Ex 13^9).—Lietzmann also thinks of the commemorative meals for the dead in the Graeco-Roman world: these meals created a kind of communion of the survivors between themselves and with the deceased. As it is unlikely that Jesus was acquainted with this custom or that Paul attached much importance to the analogy, we cannot argue from these banquets instituted by testament to translate '*diathēkē*' by 'testament'; even less when, as has already been shown, it is impossible to see in that case what the adjective '*kainē*' can mean.

death' (*'katanggelete'* is in the indicative), 'until he come', that is until the Parousia. This point was calculated to induce the Corinthians to observe the utmost seriousness during the ceremony.

The force of the particle *'gar'* is less clear; it links **11²⁶** to **11²⁵** which ends the quotations taken from tradition. Once more an ellipsis must be postulated: 'If this happens, then beware. For each time that . . .'

An attempt could be made to interpret the whole rite (in its Pauline meaning) in the light of the injunction to 'do this in remembrance of Christ'. The Eucharist would then be a memorial ceremony. But we have already seen that it seems to imply a reminder in the sense of an evocation, and the expression 'table of the Lord' has strengthened us in this view. Further, it is impossible to integrate the expression *'touto esti to sōma mou'* and the analogous, though not identical, expressions concerning the wine, into the framework of this over-narrow interpretation, nor the ideas relating to *'koinōnia'* with the Church, regarded as the body of Christ.

If then we are asked to state whether the meaning of the Pauline rite is realistic, symbolic, significative, mystical or ethical, we shall answer that all these interpretations are valid, on condition that they are not separated from one another. For to St Paul, the Lord's Supper has all these meanings at the same time. It is realistic, because it puts the believer truly (and not in thought only) in contact with Jesus Christ, dead and risen. It is symbolic because it is a representation of His last earthly meal; it is significative because the powers of renewal which the Christian receives are the guarantee of the final resurrection and of entry into the Kingdom of God; mystical because it creates and feeds the body of Christ, the Church; and ethical because it produces between Christians a brotherly communion which must be confirmed and strengthened in it.

But it also seems to us that even if someone should feel impelled to select just one of these interpretations, as is often done, he cannot avoid asking what is the nature of the event which has to be actualized, symbolized or signified by the Eucharist. In the first place it is improbable that this event is purely 'spiritual', using the word in the modern sense, that is of a purely immaterial nature, concerned only with the Christian's consciousness. Descartes' distinction between *'res cogitans'* and *'res extensa'* was—fortunately we might say, if it were permissible to state some personal convictions which cannot be justified here—unknown in the Apostle's time. It is always the whole human reality which preoccupies him. But when he speaks of the inner man, he means a new, complete, though hidden, man.

Further, if the powers emanating from Christ were to be solely directed to the conscious awareness, we could not see why a sacrament of the word would not be perfectly sufficient. Why choose a ceremony which employs actions as down to earth as eating and drinking? If on the other hand the grace is intended to penetrate into the depths of our being, of those regions which feed our subconscious (as modern psychologists say), the meaning of the rite becomes clear.

And we have already established in discussing Chapter 5 that belonging to the body of Christ is for the Apostle indeed a metaphysical reality (or ontological, if it is preferred, to avoid the barbarous word 'existential').[52]

This interpretation is confirmed by the next passage, namely 11^{27-30}, and notably 11^{30}, which links the many sicknesses and deaths in Corinth with the unworthy way of eating the body and drinking the blood of Christ. For what is involved here is not a punishment, justified but rather arbitrary, by God. It is the metaphysical result of misusing the Lord's Supper. 11^{29} says in effect that he who does not distinguish the body of Christ from a simple piece of bread, that is he who eats only to feed his body (as the Corinthians do), eats and drinks his own condemnation: *'esthiōn kai pinōn krima heautō'* (*'krima'* = 'the sentence which is pronounced', here a sentence of condemnation). This expression, of a 'terrible realism' (Allo), is very characteristic: there is a real causal connection between the sin and the punishment.

What exactly constitutes the sacrilege? In 11^{27b} it is said that he who eats and drinks unworthily is *'enochos tou sōmatos kai tou haimatos tou kuriou'* = 'guilty of the body and blood of the Lord'.[53] *'Enochos'* with the genitive appears again in Matthew 26^{66} (*'enochos thanatou'*), where the adjective means 'worthy of being punished', the genitive giving the punishment ('death'). In the Epistle to the Hebrews 2^{15} (*'enochoi douleias'*) on the other hand, the same adjective means 'subject to' (and this is undoubtedly its original meaning), the genitive indicating the master. Neither of these examples is of any help in the exegesis of our text. But the Epistle of James 2^{10} explains to us that he who transgresses the Law in a single point (*'en heni'*), while observing it in every other point, is guilty of violating (or: accused of violating) all the commandments, *'enochos pantōn'*. It is in this sense that our verse must be interpreted. The unworthy Christian will commit a sin against the body and blood of Christ. Of the nature of this sin we learn nothing precise. It must consist both of lack of respect and a certain abuse of grace. An immanent justice will bring punishment, though it is not said that it will take always the exact form foreseen in 11^{30}. Therefore the Christian will do well to examine himself (*'dokimazetō'*) beforehand,[54] that is to

---

[52] Let no one accuse us of imputing to the Apostle a magical conception of the sacrament. Here indeed the opposite is the case. For magic consists in influencing the supernatural through nature; here it is grace which must penetrate into the natural world.

[53] The Textus Receptus together with D, F and G inserts a second *'anaxiōs'* (after *'pinōn'*). But this adverb is a mere repetition here of the participle *'mē diakrinōn'*. A, B and C do not have it in their original text, nor does P 46. It is true that in ℵ and C a later hand has interpolated it; but that does not increase our confidence in the reading.

[54] *'Exetazetō tēn dianoian'*, as is very well explained by THEODORE OF MOPSUESTIA (*MPG* LXVI, col. 889 A). It does not mean that this Father read *'exetazetō'* in our text, as Migne's edition suggests. It seems rather that a happy paraphrase of *'dokimazetō'* is in question.

ask himself whether he is in the requisite religious frame of mind. Above all, he must not come '*mē diakrinōn to sōma*' = 'without discerning the body'. Further, as Theodoret of Cyr points out, he must ask himself whether he has betrayed Christ by fornication (Ch. **5**), or by sharing in demonic meals (Ch. **10**).[55]

11[32] softens the terrible impression produced by **11**[29] and **11**[30]. Even the judgement to which it refers does not mean rejection by the Lord (nor other similar judgements). On the contrary, if we are 'trained',[56] it is to allow us to escape the destruction of the world and of all those who are subject to it. More than that, we may even avoid the judgement ('*ouk engkrinometha*'), if we are willing to examine ourselves ('*diakrinomen*').[57]

11[33–4] recapitulate the exhortations implicitly contained in **11**[21] and **11**[22]. Other details which the Apostle has not been able to touch in this letter will be put in order by word of mouth (**11**[34b]).

It has often been asked to what extent precise information about the way in which the Eucharist was observed may be drawn from this pericope. Did the blessing of the bread precede that of the cup? Did the cup go round more than once? At what precise moment were the words of institution recalled? We do not think that our Epistle takes us further forward in our knowledge of these details. On the other hand, it does provide us with a glimpse of the experiences which Christians had in it as well as of the ideas which were linked with it. With reference to the whole passage, Leenhardt asks (in *Le sacrement de la sainte Cène* [Neuchâtel and Paris, 1948], pp. 108ff) whether the sacrament was for Paul a symbol or a sign, and he decides for the latter. Quite possibly he is right. But we would insist upon the prior need of clarification about the supernatural events for which the sacrament is either the actualization, the symbol, or the sign. For us this is the crucial point. Our suggestion is that it is a matter of grace descending to the very depths of our subconscious mind.[58]

---

[55] *MPG* LXXXII, col. 318 AB.—It goes without saying that there is no question here of an examination of the dogmatic conviction about the manner in which Christ is present in the 'elements'. How much heartache would catechumens have been spared, if this ridiculous interpretation had not been expatiated upon.

[56] A euphemism for 'chastise for our good'; see for example 3 Kings (1 Kings) 12[11, 14], as well as many texts in Jewish Wisdom literature, as Proverbs 3[11–12], cf. Luke 23[16, 22]; 2 Corinthians 6[9], 2 Timothy 2[25], Hebrews 12[6–10], Revelation 3[19].

[57] On the exact sense of '*krinō*' and its compounds, see the very complete article by BÜCHSEL in KITTEL, *TWNT*, III.920-55. Let us merely repeat here that '*krinō*' = 'judge'; '*katatkrinō*' = 'condemn'; '*diakrinō*' = 'examine'; '*anakrinō*' = 'conduct an enquiry'; '*sungkrinō*' = 'to compose'. '*Diakrinō*' in a bad sense ('to be unable to make up one's mind, to doubt') is found in Mark 11[23] and James 1[6].

[58] Cf. *RHPR* (1953), p. 290. We regret that we were unable to use, for the first part of this chapter, a study which came to us too late: FRANZ J. LEENHARDT, '*La place de la femme dans l'Eglise d'après le N.T.*' (*ETR* [1948], No. 1). The reader will notice a fundamental agreement between us on the majority of points, notably also on what concerns 14[34].

CHAPTER XII

(1) *I do not wish you to be in ignorance, brothers, on the subject of spiritual gifts.* (2) *You know how, when you were pagans, you were drawn astray to dumb idols.* (3) *That is why I tell you that no one speaking under the influence of the Spirit of God says 'Jesus is anathema', and that no one can say 'Jesus is the Lord', if he is not animated by the Holy Spirit.*

In order to understand the exhortations in Chapters 12 and 14, we must bear in mind an ability latent in the human organism, of becoming a means of expression for beings (good or bad) of the invisible world. Sometimes the 'medium' loses consciousness during these 'supranormal' states, sometimes on the other hand his consciousness is seemingly intensified. This ability has of itself no religious significance. But at times of religious enthusiasm or in circles where such ecstatic phenomena are cultivated, these potentialities may be awakened and are then supposed to help in the transmission of messages from the Holy Spirit. This has occurred quite frequently in the history of Christianity. Apart from early Christianity, we may mention the Montanists and the inspired enthusiasts of all periods, and for the history of Protestantism the Camisard prophets, the beginnings of Irvingism, and the Welsh revival, as well as the different forms of Pentecostalism.[1]

The Apostle will warn the Corinthians against valuing these phenomena too highly. Yet he has no doubt that the Holy Spirit may in principle speak through such charismatics. But he urges his readers to distinguish between the spirits.

From another point of view, the reader must be on his guard against modern prejudices which simply set these phenomena aside as 'unhealthy'. Even when the inspired person shows signs of disturbance, this may be a *result* of a previous internal shock.

12¹ Discussion of the gender of the adjective (or noun) '*pneumatikōn*' will probably never cease. With Calvin, we favour the neuter ('spiritual things' or 'spiritual gifts') (like '*pneumatika*', 2¹³) rather

---

[1] From the important literature on ecstatic phenomena of a religious order, the following may be mentioned: WEINEL, *Die Wirkungen des Geistes und der Geister, im nachapostolischen Zeitalter bis auf Irenaeus* (Tübingen, 1899); S. MASIMAN, *Das Zungenreden* (1911); ANTOINE COURT, *Histoire des troubles des Cévennes* (1760); JEAN-DANIEL BENOIT, *Les prophètes huguenots* (Montauban, 1910); CH. BOST, '*Les prophètes des Cévennes*' (*RHPR* [1925], pp. 401-30); HENRI BOIS, *Le réveil au Pays de Galles* (Toulouse, *Société des publications morales et religieuses*, n.d.); EMILE LOMBARD, *De la glossolalie chez les premiers chrétiens et des phénomènes similaires* (Lausanne, 1910, Doctor of Theology thesis at Neuchâtel).

than the masculine ('spiritual Christians'); for when the Apostle uses this word in the masculine ('*ho pneumatikos*', 2^{15}, and also doubtless '*tois pneumatikois*', 2^{13}), it has a different sense, namely to refer to those Christians who are, or who think themselves to be, more advanced than the rest. But here charismatic gifts are in principle granted to all in one form or another. Later, moreover, the question turns on a distinction of gifts rather than of Christians.— In the phrase '*ou thelō . . . agnoien*', the verb '*agnoien*' has no object; it is therefore used intransitively = 'to be in ignorance'.

In 12^2 the juxtaposition of '*hoti hote*' lacks elegance. But what is more serious is that '*hoti*' is an unnecessary repetition of '*hōs*' (after '*ta aphōna*'). The particle '*an*' is also very troublesome; for there is no question of a conditional construction. Several solutions are theoretically possible:

(1) '*Hōs*' is considered as referring back to '*hoti*', from which the development of the sentence had moved too far (an explanation put forward by J.W.).

(2) '*Hōs*' is translated by 'as' and '*hōs an ēgesthe*' is looked on as a relative clause, which is then rendered by 'according to the impulse which took hold of you'. But then the clause introduced by '*hoti*' and continued (putting things in the best light) by '*apagomenoi*' has no finite verb. It would then be necessary, as Allo does, to introduce a supposed second '*ēte*' (after '*apagomenoi*'), which is rather clumsy.

(3*a*) '*Hōs*' and '*an*' are reunited, as though originating from '*hōsan*', an adverb = 'so to speak', and translated: 'you were, so to speak, led away' (Bachmann). '*Hōsan*' may also be attached to the participle '*apagomenoi*'. In this way '*an*' would also be disposed of. But is the adverb '*hōsan*' used before a verb in this way? It is very doubtful. Further there is a more elegant way of disposing of '*an*':

(3*b*) '*An*' and '*ēgesthe*' may be reunited. Indeed '*anagesthai*' seems to be a technical term for a snatching away into the invisible world by supernatural powers, see Luke 4^5: '*kai anagōgōn auton edeixen autō*', etc. (cf. Mt 4^1).[2] This seems a good solution so far as the difficulty created by '*an*' is concerned. However, the problem posed by '*hōs*' still remains unsolved. So we must have recourse to solution (1) or seek new ones.

(4) One may delete '*hoti*' as the Textus Receptus and some other witnesses do.[3] Authority for this reading is not good, but we incline to the view that the editor of the Textus Receptus made an intelligent

---

[2] Similarly '*analambanō*' is used in Ezekiel 11^1: '*kai anelaben me pneuma kai ēgagen*', etc.; cf. the Emperor JULIAN, *Orationes*, V.172 (TEUBNER, p. 223).

[3] JOHN CHRYSOSTOM (*Homily* 29, *MPG* LXI, col. 241) first quotes the text as given in Nestlé. But in the commentary (ibid.) he gives: '*oidate hote Hellēnes ēte, pōs apēgesthe*', etc. '*Hoti*' therefore appeared unnecessary in his opinion. As for the particle '*an*', he ignores it because it raised a problem. Further, he emends '*hōs*' to '*pōs*'. '*Hōs*' is indeed less correct here, but can be justified (*v.* PREUSCHEN-BAUER, *Dictionary*).

cut. For '*hoti*' could be little else than an interpolation made by a copyist who was looking for a conjunction which could depend on '*oidate*', and did not realize that '*hōs*' (a long way away) fulfilled this function.

(5) On the other hand '*hote*' might be deleted.[4] In this case one may without qualm and without interpolating '*ēte*', make '*hōs an ēgesthe*' into a relative clause, as solution (2) suggests: 'You know that you were pagans drawn to dumb idols according as you felt the impulse.'

(6) '*Hote*' might be emended to '*pote*', with Wescott and Hort, and the translation would be similar to (5) with the addition of 'formerly'.[5]

To sum up, solutions (4) on the one hand and (5) and (6) on the other seem the best. If we prefer (4), it is because '*hote*' seems necessary to us, in view of the fact that the state of paganism recalled by the Apostle is not a sufficiently central idea to need expression in a main clause.

As for the particle '*an*', we shall attach it to '*ēgesthe*' as in solution (3*b*). We shall read therefore: '*oidate, hote ethnē ēte, pros ta eidōla ta aphōna hōs anēgesthe apagomenoi.*' The juxtaposition of '*anēgesthe*' and '*apagomenoi*' seems less shocking than the reading '*ēgesthe apagomenoi*', where the sense of '*ēgesthe*' would be very colourless.— But if '*anagesthai*' signifies mystical abduction, what is then the meaning of '*apagesthai*'? Here it must be noticed that '*apo*' often has a bad sense = 'away from the right track'. Moreover '*apagesthai*' is used to speak of victims dragged to the altar, which is a very apt idea here; for pagan ecstatics are the victims of demons. Thus a play on words is intended: you thought you were being transported to heaven ('*anēgesthe*'), but really you were the victims of the forces of evil ('*apagomenoi*') which were leading you astray.[6]

It is very natural that the Apostle should recall here the ecstatic phenomena of a pagan past; it is to remind the Corinthians that they are not in themselves a manifestation of the Holy Spirit. From it there emerges already his own wise position, which is not a negative one, however, with regard to these phenomena.

But how can 'dumb'—that is, lifeless—idols have such a pernicious influence? Here we must remember that according to the Apostle (see Ch. **10**) demons substitute themselves for the so-called pagan gods, in order to subdue the faithful. So all inspiration does not come from God.

12³ gives a partial criterion for distinguishing among the spirits. A

---

[4] With G, Peshitto, Coptic, ATHENAGORUS, *MPL* XVII, col. 244 C.
[5] P 46 is damaged and is of no help.
[6] For this, cf. 'ATHENAGORUS, *Legatio pro christianis*', *MPG* VI, col. 950 D: '*hoi daimones . . . peri ta eidōla autous helkontes.*'

(4) Now there is a variety of gifts but a single Spirit; (5) and there is a variety of ministries, but a single Lord; (6) and a variety of activities, but it is the same God who produces them all in all. (7) But to each there is given for the common good some manifestation of the Spirit. (8) To one is given, through the Spirit, a word of wisdom, to another a word of knowledge, according to the same Spirit; (9) to a third, faith according to the same Spirit, to still another, powers of healing in the one Spirit; (10) to another the power to work miracles, to another prophecy, to another the distinguishing of spirits, to another the gift of speaking various tongues, and to yet another the interpretation of tongues. (11) But all these effects are products of one single Spirit, and he distributes the gifts to each separately, as he wills.

charismatic who cried 'Jesus anathema'[7] can be possessed only by an evil spirit, whatever the personal value of the 'medium' may be in other connections. The sense of *'anathema'* is fixed by the LXX, which uses it to translate the word חֵרֶם = 'curse'. We feel that the

Apostle would not mention this case unless it really had occurred.— Further the exclamation *'kurios Iēsous'*, which is like the essential confession of the Christian faith,[8] is a guarantee that the Holy Spirit has spoken. The third case, namely that good angels may have inspired the utterances of charismatics, is not expressly brought forward, presumably because in that case the message could be considered as indirectly inspired by the Holy Spirit. Obviously the suggested criterion is not sufficient. For either of the formulae may be absent from a spiritual utterance. In that case it will be necessary to appeal to other charismatics who have the gift of distinguishing between spirits (see below, 12[10]).

In 12[4] *'diaireseis'* signifies both the variety of gifts as such, and their distribution among many individuals. The Apostle wants to stress the fact that no Christian can boast of possessing all the charismatic gifts. Even if the chapter contained this sentence alone, it would give invaluable advice to Churches, which too often demand from a single person an almost impossible combination of gifts. The word *'charisma'* is rather rare in secular Greek, where it means a 'gift'. It is

[7] P 46, together with D, G and the Textus Receptus read *'anathema Iēsoun'*. In that case the accusative depends on *'legei'*, and it would be necessary to translate 'no one calls Jesus anathema'. We hold that the other reading is preferable, for it reproduces verbally the exclamation of the inspired person. JOHN CHRYSOSTOM (*MPG* LXI, col. 242) reads the accusative. At the end of the same verse, D, F, G, the Textus Receptus and CHRYSOSTOM have the double accusative *'kurion Iēsoun'*, but P 46 gives the nominative.—GODET refers to the Ophites who, according to Origen, cursed Jesus, according to *Contra Celsum*, VI.28 (KOETSCHAU, II.98).

[8] See W. BOUSSET, *Kyrios Christos* (1913, 2nd edn, 1921); O. CULLMANN, *The Earliest Christian Confessions*, E. Tr. Reid (London, 1949) and *RHPR* (1931), pp. 77-110; J. HÉRING, *Le Royaume de Dieu et sa venue selon Jésus et l'apôtre Paul*, *EHPR*, No. 30 (1938), particularly Chs 8-10.

in just this sense that the Apostle Paul uses it, for he is speaking of a gift from God. The variety of gifts, on which he so insists, seems to indicate moreover that the Christian does not receive the Holy Spirit *in abstracto*, but always in the form of a specific aptitude which he should put at the Church's disposal. Sometimes charisms are understood in such a wide sense that every Christian, even the most unassuming, is considered as having one (12^{22}) which will be useful to the community. But in the first part of the chapter (12^{4-11}) the writer uses the word with a more limited connotation: he is thinking of the manifestations which bring a section of the community's members (*'ta dokounta melē'*, 12^{22}) into particular prominence. In 12^9 it seems that *'charisma'* may have an even more restricted sense, because the author seems to contrast *'charismata'* = 'gifts' with *'energēmata'*. But this distinction must not be over-stressed, since cures (*'iamata'*) obviously do not constitute the only charisms; the word 'cures' is used, because no more precise term occurred to the author's mind, whilst *'dunameis'* here designates other *miracles*, undoubtedly the driving out of demons, for which *'energēmata'*[9] is particularly appropriate.[10] As for *'diakoniai'*, from which developed the institution of deacons (1 Tim 3^{8ff}), either administrative or charitable work is meant, perhaps both, as in Acts 6^{1-4}.

It is much more difficult to give precisely the respective meanings to *'logos sophias'* and *'logos gnōseōs'*. *'Logos'* must denote the genus; *'sophia'* and *'gnōsis'* permit identification of the precise species. Taking Chapters 1 and 2 into account, the sense of theoretical knowledge may be given to *'sophia'*, whilst *'gnōsis'* may denote, as in Hellenism, a sort of 'mystical intuition' of higher truths, exactly the kind on which the gnostics in Corinth had prided themselves.

But the Peshitto translates *'sophia'* by *'hokmātā'* and *'gnōsis'* by *'yada'tā'* (which may denote some particular knowledge). Allo sees in *'sophia'* the knowledge of God's intimate plans, whilst *'gnōsis'* could have as its object 'the disposition of partial truths adapted to the understanding'. If we have recourse to the language of the LXX, which is perhaps a relatively sure path, we can admit that *'sophia'* denotes moral teaching, whilst *'gnōsis'* indicates theological knowledge, the legitimacy of which is affirmed by 2^{10-11}. *'Logos'* should be something like sacred eloquence or the power to proclaim truths, which here are truths revealed by the Spirit.

Between the two groups which have just been analysed, namely

---

[9] J. W., *Kraftentladungen*, p. 301.

[10] *'Dunameis'* in the New Testament designates all miracles, including cures. No attempt should be made therefore to oppose *'dunameis'* to *'iamata'*. Cures are one type of miracle, and are in a distinct class. Is there any need to say that *'dunamis'* never has the philosophical sense which we usually give to the term 'miracle'? What is meant is simply an intervention of supernatural powers, anticipating the conditions of the new world-age. But early Christianity did not enquire how far this intervention did or did not make use of the ordinary laws of human nature. See ANTON FRIDRICHSEN, *Le problème du miracle dans le christianisme primitif*, *EHPR*, No. 12.

the two '*logoi*', on the one hand (**12⁸**), and the '*iamata*' (**12⁹ᵇ**) and '*dunameis*' (**12¹⁰**) on the other, is placed '*pistis*' (**12⁹ᵃ**) as a particular gift. Evidently this cannot refer to 'saving faith', as in the Epistle to the Romans; this latter is considered to appertain to all Christians. We must therefore take the word in the intensive sense which Mark 9²³ and Matthew 17²⁰ can help us to glimpse: it does not refer to the faith which anyone may or may not have, but to faith which may be possessed in a more or less intense degree. When it is animated by great fervour, it may be considered as a particular charism. How is it deemed to manifest itself? We may suppose, especially by miraculous cures.—It goes without saying that this list is not systematic. The terms may overlap one another. There is, however, a clear contrast between '*heterō*' (**12⁹ᵃ**) and '*allō*' (**12⁹ᵇ**); it shows that the author must have been thinking also about other concrete manifestations of '*pistis*', perhaps of the effects of the prayers of those who were animated by a particularly ardent faith, and who might have objectives other than cures or exorcisms.

In **12¹⁰** prophecy must not be confused with glossolaly. According to **14³** the aim of prophecy is to edify, exhort and encourage. It coincides therefore to a large extent with what we call a sermon today. The Apostle does not identify 'prophecy' with 'foretelling the future', as we have it in Acts 11²⁸. But if this is so, and if moreover women are expressly allowed to prophesy (Ch. **11**), we cannot see why Churches should claim support from the opinion of the apostles in order to forbid women from preaching sermons; as for the well-known verse **14³⁴**, this does not have the meaning commonly given to it (see below).

There remain to be examined the three last gifts in this list, namely: '*diakrisis pneumatōn*' = 'the distinguishing of spirits'; '*genē glōssōn*' = 'various kinds of tongues'; '*hermēneia glōssōn*' = 'the interpretation of tongues'. We have already seen that distinguishing between good and evil spirits, which might speak through the mouth of an inspired person, is not easy. It can be understood then that the ability to make distinctions in specific cases was looked on as a charism. Moreover, evil spirits were the more dangerous because they might try according to 1 Timothy 4¹ to deceive Christians wilfully.[11]

Glossolaly and its interpretation ('*hermēneia*') are problems which have claimed the particular attention of exegetes and psychologists. What is the exact meaning of the expression '*genē glōssōn*' (also **12²⁸**)? In every case a multiplicity of *languages* is indicated. To grasp the meaning, we must compare it with other expressions: '*glōssais*' (or '*glōssē*') '*lalein*' = 'to speak in tongues' (**12³⁰**, **14²,⁴,⁵,⁶,¹³,²⁷,³⁹**,

---

[11] According to 1 John 4¹ ('*dokimazete ta pneumata, ei ek tou Theou estin, hoti polloi pseudoprophētai exelēluthasin eis ton kosmon*'), it is especially a question of the spirits of the prophets, as in the Didache 11⁷⁻¹². The Apostle Paul seems to have thought of an examination of inspiration in general. Further, in the First Epistle of John as in the Didache the word 'prophecy' is taken in a fairly wide sense.

Acts 10⁴⁶); *'glōssan echein'* = 'to have (a gift of) tongues (to exercise)' (14²⁶); *'proseuchesthai glōssē'* = 'to pray in a tongue' (14¹⁴); *'logon didonai dia tēs glōssēs'* = 'give a speech "by the tongue"' (14⁹); *'lalein tais glōssais tōn anthrōpōn kai tōn anggelōn'* = 'to speak in human or angelic tongues' (13²); *'lalein heterais glōssais'* = 'to speak in other tongues' (Acts 2⁴); *'glōssais lalein kainais'* = 'to speak in new tongues' (Mk 16¹⁷). There can be no question of interpreting *'glōssa'* as the organ of speech (*'die Zunge'*). Speech itself or language is meant. The clearest expression is the one in Acts 2⁴, 'to speak in other tongues'—that is, to speak in languages foreign to those normally spoken in the assembly, but foreign also to the language or languages which the subject could speak in his normal psychological condition. Thus, according to the account of Pentecost, men from Galilee began to speak Latin, Arabic, Coptic, Cretan and a number of other languages (from which Greek is probably omitted solely because its use seemed less extraordinary).

In certain cases, however, the speech seemed to differ from all known human languages. It was then thought that the language of the angels was in question (see 13¹; Testament of Job 48–50:¹² *'hē anggelikē dialektos'* and similar expressions).¹³

But how is the abbreviated expression *'lalein glōssais'* (or *'glōssē'*) to be explained? It is relevant to note here that in the Hellenistic world, *'glōssa'* had already become a technical term to designate an archaic language, often used in a cult, and sometimes speech that was incomprehensible like that of the Pythia of Delphi.¹⁴

We point out this fact not to imply that the *'glossai'* at Corinth may have been nothing but speeches in an archaic language, but simply to explain that the expression *'glōssais lalein'* = 'to speak in tongues', enigmatic at first sight, was well known to the Greeks and could therefore be used by Paul as a synonym for the more complete expression, *'heterais glōssais lalein'* = 'to speak in other languages'.

---

¹² Given by ROBINSON, in *Texts and Studies*, V.i.135ff.

¹³ Here again the history of Pentecostalism provides some interesting parallels. Take, for example, a translation into the language of the angels of the first strophe of Count Zinzendorf's hymn, *Jesu geh voran*: '*Ea tschu ra ta u ra tori da tschu rikanka oli tanka bori ju ra fanka kullikatschi da ur: tu ra ta*' (borrowed from *RGG*, IV.1153).

¹⁴ GALIEN (ed. Bâle, V.705, ed. Kuehn, XIX [1821].62-3) defines *'glōssai'* in the following way: 'We speak of expressions as "*glōssai*" which were current in olden times but which are no longer used.' PLUTARCH, *De Iside*, LXI.375 F (TEUBNER, *Moralia*, II, fasc. III.60) defends poets against the accusation of using barbarisms and calls their speech 'tongues' ('*hoi glōttais ta toiauta paragoreuontes*').—According to QUINTILIAN, *Institutions*, I.35 (TEUBNER, I.11), little-used expressions belonging to esoteric language ('*lingua secretior*') are called *'glōssai'* by the Greeks.—Let us point out too that, according to PLUTARCH, *De pythiae oraculis*, 24, 406 E.F (TEUBNER, *Moralia*, III.52), the Pythia in ancient times used '*epē kai glōssas kai periphraseis kai asapheian*', that is verses, 'tongues', periphrases, in a word, obscure language. In connection with QUINTILIAN, J. W. has not distinguished between the two following quotations: (*a*) I.i.8, *'glōssemata'* (less interesting) and (*b*) I.i.35, *'glōssai'*.

(12) *For just as the body is one, while having many limbs, and as the limbs of the body, though many, form only one body—so it is with Christ.* (13) *For we have all been baptized in the same Spirit, so as to form us also into one body, whether we be Jews or Greeks, slaves or free men. And we were all made to drink of one Spirit.* (14) *So also the body is not composed of one member, but of many.* (15) *If the foot were to say: 'Because I am not a hand I am not part of the body', it would not, for that reason, cease being part of the body.* (16) *If the ear were to say: 'Because I am not an eye, I am not part of the body', it would not, for that reason, cease being part of the body.* (17) *If all the body were eye, where would the hearing be? If all were hearing, where would the sense of smell be?*

The Apostle is to return later to glossolaly; but in his list (which is not at all exhaustive and which must be completed by the list in 12²⁸⁻³⁰), we see that speaking in tongues and its interpretation occupies the last place. We can sense the Apostle's relatively reserved judgement of the value of this gift. But what preoccupies him above all in the passage 12¹⁻¹¹ as well as later, is the danger of these manifestations, or more exactly the danger of a certain notoriety to which they gave rise and which ran the risk of aggravating the menace of discord in the Churches. Against this risk the Apostle reacts strongly by underlining the unity of the spirit which animates all true charismatics.

In the whole of this passage, the language rises to a poetic level. 12⁴⁻⁶ contain three sayings constructed in the same way, as can be easily seen. It is the same Spirit, the same Lord, the same God, who give the inspiration. This strophe is constructed on a trinitarian pattern which is not without theological significance, while it says nothing about the exact relationship of the Holy Spirit with the Father and the Son respectively. The gender of '*pasin*' in 12⁶ is uncertain. As charisms rather than charismatics are meant in the preceding verses, we agree with the Synodale Version and the Authorized Version and favour the neuter (as against the Peshitto and Luther).

In 12¹¹ a new idea comes to light after the list of gifts: the Holy Spirit distributes them according to His pleasure, that is—through pure grace. Consequently—this is the conclusion that presents itself —there is no reason to see personal merit in any particularly outstanding charism. We now guess also why gifts gave rise to disputes and rivalries which threatened the unity of the Church.

This unity in diversity, the Apostle thinks, is as necessary to the Church as is the unity of the organs in an 'organism'. Indeed, in 12¹²⁻²⁶ the author retells the fable of the body and the limbs, which seems to have been well known in antiquity and which Menenius Agrippa[15] told to the plebeians in Rome when they had become dis-

[15] According to Livy, II.32 (Teubner, I.93ff).

contented with their inferior social status and seceded by withdraw-
ing to the Sacer Mons.[16]

What is more curious is that the Stoics were very quick to adapt
this fable to political life, regarded in its supranational and cosmic
aspect, which was so dear to later Stoicism.[17] Yet the analogy with
the Stoic doctine should not blind us to the radical difference between
their teaching and that of the Apostle: here it is not nature which
makes us members of one organism, but grace. Nor has the point of
view of creation anything to do with that organism which is the body
of Christ. It is the Spirit communicated through baptism which binds
the individual to this body. If then national or social differences
cannot play any part in it (12[13], 'eite Ioudaioi', etc.), this is not for the
same reason as in the world-wide republic of the Stoics.

Some have considered 'epotisthēmen' = 'we were made to drink'
(12[13b]) as an allusion to the Lord's Supper. But this connection is
rather strained. 'Epotisthēmen', which is dependent on 'ebaptisthēmen'
= 'we have been baptized' (12[13a]), relates to the actual act of baptism, whilst 'ebaptisthēmen' insists on the result, namely attachment
to the body of Christ. But this unity in diversity is an ordinary fact,
which should neither puff up those who have received more outstanding gifts, nor discourage the others who do humble but equally
necessary services to the Church. It seems that the Apostle is giving
a new twist to the famous fable: he is not so much afraid of a possible
revolt of the inferior members, but of the pride of the 'superior', who
perhaps squabbled among themselves about the excellence of their
respective gifts.

The necessity of diversity is developed in 12[14-20], which are so
clear that detailed comment is superfluous. Note, however, that the
exact force of 'para touto' at the end of 12[15] is debated. According to
whether these words are linked to 'ouk estin', or to the negation of
this negative statement by the first 'ou', it would be necessary to
translate either 'because of that', or 'in spite of that'. We think that
the first sense of 'para', though rarer, is more natural here, in view
of the place of 'para touto' in the construction.[18]

The next section (12[21-5]) develops a second fundamental idea, namely
interdependence of the members on one another. But here again,

[16] The fable seems to have had a very ancient origin. LIETZMANN states that it is
to be found in Egypt as early as the twelfth century.—Only a faint echo of it is
heard in Aesop, who is usually quoted in this connection (v. ed. Belles Lettres,
No. 159, p. 70: 'koilia kai podes'). Also there is a similar fable, given in the form
of a dream, in the Midrash Tehillim to Psalm 39[2] (pub. BUBER [Vilna, 1891], p.
255). Lack of space prevents reproduction here of this 'dispute of the organs'.

[17] 'Politēs ei kosmou kai meros autou', EPICTETUS exclaims (Dissertations, II.x.3;
TEUBNER [1894], p. 131): 'You are a citizen of the world and one of its organs.'

[18] The exact force of 'para' is therefore the same here as that of the Latin 'prae'
preceding the statement of the cause of a negative fact ('prae multitudine sagit-
tarum solem non videbitis').—PREUSCHEN-BAUER, Dictionary, after giving good
examples for 'para' = 'because of', translates our text rather strangely by 'therefore nevertheless'.

(18) *But in fact, God has arranged the members by assigning to each one its place in the body according to his will.* (19) *If they all formed only one member, where would the body be?* (20) *But in fact, there are many members, but only one body.* (21) *And the eye cannot say to the hand: 'I have no need of you', nor can the head say to the feet: 'I have no need of you'.* (22) *But much more are those members which seem to be the weakest especially necessary.* (23) *And the members of the body which we judge less honourable, we dress with the greater care. Our least presentable members, enjoy more attention,* (24) *whilst the presentable members have no need of this care. But God has arranged the body so as to give more honour to the members which lacked it,* (25) *in order to avoid division in the body and on the contrary to establish the interdependence of the members in the care of one another.*

the danger of a secession by the inferior members is less than the risk of seeing their services rejected by others who are too proud of their superiority: the eye cannot do without the hand, nor the head without the feet (12²¹). 12²² is introduced by *'pollō mallon'* = 'much more.' A gradation must therefore be involved. Consequently the supposedly weak organs (12²²) are something other than the extremities named in 12²¹. Only the digestive organs can be intended, here presented as especially despised, whilst in the fable of Menenius, it is the stomach which represents the aristocracy (as the term was used in antiquity), or the middle-class (in the modern sense). These organs of vegetative life have no protection and consequently have rights from certain points of view; they are dressed with care (the only possible sense of *'timēn paratithenai'*).

12²³ᵇ refers more particularly to the organs of excretion and reproduction. We are quick to clothe these also. However, the exact meaning of *'euschēmosunēn echein'* is not clear. Preuschen-Bauer (see under *'euschēmosunē'*) explains: 'These members receive (from the very attention that we give them) greater respectability'; but no proof-references are given for this sense of *'echō'*. We prefer to interpret it as 'they enjoy more attention' and thereby become respectable, in the same way as the others, because they are not exposed. Moreover, the organs, respectable of themselves (like the hands, the legs, the head) can forgo this attention, except for the restriction of 11⁵, which has other reasons.

It is more difficult to grasp the idea of 12²⁴ᵇ, in which God Himself is held to bestow particular regard to the ill-favoured organs. One wonders when and how. There are only two solutions of this difficulty—a difficulty largely unnoticed by the exegetes. It will be recalled that according to 12²² it is only because of human opinion (mistaken) that certain organs are more worthy than others. That is not God's idea. According to the fable of Agrippa, the inferior organs are the very ones for which the others, in the order of nature, are obliged to work and to pay tribute (*'timē'*) in some degree. If this explanation is rejected, it must be admitted that the aorist *'dous'* does

(26) *Thus, if one of the members suffer, all the members suffer with it; and when one of the members is honoured, all the members rejoice with it.* (27) *Now you are the body of Christ, and his members, each in his own way.* (28) *And God has established in the Church: first, some as apostles, secondly prophets, thirdly teachers, then those who have the gift of miracles, then those who have gifts of healing, of charitable works, of administration, as well as the gift of speaking in various tongues.*

(29) *Are you all apostles? all prophets? all teachers? do all perform miracles?* (30) *Do all have the gift of healing the sick? do all speak 'in tongues'? are all interpreters?* (31) *No, but aspire earnestly to the higher gifts.*

not have here a past but a present sense: God, by inspiring in men certain feelings of decency, obliges them to do justice to those organs. In any event, the main idea of the parable is clear: in the natural body, all the organs must work together for the common good.

The two words '*huper allēlōn*' (**12²⁵**) may seem troublesome in conjunction with '*to auto*'; if each one thinks of the others, all do not think precisely the same thing. '*Merimnōsin to auto*' must therefore be taken, rather as the expression '*to auto legein*' in 1¹⁰, in the general sense of 'being agreed', and that in the common interest.

12²⁶ brings us back from the ideal of **12²⁵ᵇ** to the level of facts: interdependence among the members is unfailing in sickness or in health. Whether '*eiti*' or '*eite*' is read here, the sense is the same.[19]

12²⁷ takes us back to spiritual reality, the essence of which has been explained through the figure of the natural organism. The diversity of gifts in the body of Christ is as natural as the diversity of functions in the natural body; if all wanted to have the same gift, the Church could not live.[20] Let each one exercise his gifts in all humility, thinking about the edification of the Church. It is on this point that the Apostle gives a second list of gifts, which does not altogether agree with the one we have studied. (We see once again therefore that such lists are given only as samples.) He begins by naming three groups of charismatics, but continues with a list of the charisms themselves,

[19] A word on the logical structure of the parable. It is the specific application of the fable, either to the political organism or to the Church, which makes these considerations into a parable. The narrative itself was not taken in antiquity as a parable, but as the true description of the organism, each organ of which was represented as animate and enjoying a certain autonomy. It is good to remember this fact also in connection with what is said of 'members' in Romans 7²³.

[20] The reading '*ek melous*', presupposed by the Vulgate in **12²⁷** and attested by D, as well as by some of the Fathers, especially the Latin Fathers, is obviously a mistake in copying or dictation for '*ek merous*'. '*Melē ek merous*' gives moreover a thoroughly acceptable meaning: 'You are members, and each one should play the part accorded to him.'

probably because masculine nouns were lacking or were little used to designate the bearers of *'dunameis'* and of the *'genē glōssōn'*. At the head appear the Apostles, designated in general terms by Christ Himself to be His witnesses and to found and administer Churches (cf. Ch. **3** especially). In the Pauline Churches, there is no question of bishops, administrative functions being exercised by those who could be called *'kubernētai'* = 'directors' (**12**[28]).

The prophets (see **11**[4ff] above) come second, then the teachers. In comparison with the sermon of the prophets, the teachers' task must have been more theoretical and consisted to a great extent of exposition of the Scriptures, that is of the Old Testament books in Greek. The other charisms have already been listed above (**12**[8–10]), except for the *'kubernēseis'* = 'administrations', here distinguished from the *'antilēmpseis'* = 'works of charity'.

12[31a] gives preliminary notice of a distinction not between the more or less legitimate charisms (we have seen that they are all of the same value), but between gifts which are more or less useful for edification. This is the meaning of *'ta meizona'*, as is shown in Chapter **14**. It should therefore not be surprising to see the phrase continued by *'mallon de hina prophēteuēte'*, which we find in **14**[1]. It is surprising to see that Chapter **13** praises not one particular charism already mentioned, but a Christian virtue which has not previously been envisaged as a charism, and which is moreover supposed to be granted to all.[21]

---

[21] For the translation of Chapter **12** we have followed quite faithfully the Synodale Version, which here seems particularly good.

CHAPTER XIII

We have just seen that this chapter obviously interrupts the discussion on spiritual gifts. The two sentences added at the beginning and the end by an editor are in fact typical examples of editorial linkages. The first states: *'kai eti kath' huperbolēn hodon humin deiknumi'* = 'and in addition I will show you a royal road' (12³¹ᵇ). As *'eti'* already expresses the idea of an addition, perhaps even of a comparative ('more than that'), we must attach *'kath' huperbolēn'* to *'hodon'* ('a super-eminent way'; Luther: *'Einen köstlichen Weg'*; Vulg.: *'excellentiorem viam'*). The point is that agapé is to be placed above the charismatic gifts so much vaunted by some Corinthians. That is certainly the idea of Chapter 13, but it is quite unrelated to Chapters 12 and 14, which deal only with the reciprocal value of the 'gifts'.[1]

At the beginning of Chapter 14 we shall find another transitional link inserted by the editor, which will serve to bring the discussion back to the subject. It could be argued therefore as certain that Chapter 13 did not originally occupy its present place in the Epistle. There is, however, no valid reason to doubt its Pauline origin. Did it form part of another epistle, or was it an isolated sheet which some editor (possibly Sosthenes himself?) may have inserted here? That is something which we shall probably never know.[2]

But we must be profoundly grateful to the unknown interpolator for saving this treasure of early Christian literature, about which a Spanish Jew, a physician, once said that he wished it were written in letters of gold and 'that every Jew were to carry it with him wherever he went'.[3] And we may add: the Christian too, for even stronger reasons.

---

[1] It is true that Dˣ and even P 46 read *'ei ti'* instead of *'eti'*, and this reading has again been recently defended by A. DEBRUNNER (*Coniectanea Neotestamentica*, IV, in honour of A. FRIDRICHSEN [Lund and Copenhagen, 1947], p. 37). But the phrase introduced by *'eiti'* has no verb . Then *'zēloute'* (the verb used in 12³¹ᵃ) must be understood, a comma must be inserted after *'huperbolēn'*, and the translation should read: 'And if you seek something extraordinary, I will show you a way.' But we cannot rid ourselves of the impression that the use of *'hodos'* without article or complement would not be good Greek. That is why we have not retained this reading. We also recognize that it is to some extent a matter of personal preference.

[2] J.W. holds that it followed Chapter 8 where spiritually inflated people who lacked love were condemned. But in that case, it could also be attached to Chapter 10.

[3] Quoted by A. P. STANLEY, *The Epistles of St Paul to the Corinthians* (4th edn, 1876) p. 242, who refers to John Wesley (*Sermons*, III.46).

(12³¹ᵇ) *And in addition I will show you a royal road:* (1) *Though I speak 'with tongues'—human or angelic—if I lack love, I am merely a sounding gong or a tinkling cymbal.* (2) *Though I have a gift of prophecy and understand all mysteries and all knowledge; though I have faith absolute enough to remove mountains—if I lack love, I am nothing.* (3) *Though I distribute all my goods to feed the poor, though I give my body—if it is for my own glory and I lack love, it is of no avail to me.*

It is a hymn glorifying agapé.[4] In style and the structure of the stanzas, it is reminiscent of Hebrew poetry in the LXX translation. The rhythm of Greek poetry is naturally absent; but the choice of imagery, the careful balance of phrases, the warmth of the author's emotive reactions in presence of the truths he enunciates, give it an impressive beauty.[5] It must not be forgotten, however, that the Apostle's first aim is not the expression of personal feelings, but the description of spiritual realities. In this sense, it is didactic rather than lyric poetry. Thus the passage contains or presupposes an analysis of agapé which we shall call phenomenological and not psychological. For it is the essence of Christian love which is studied here, independently of its more or less perfect fulfilment in the life of the Christian in general, or of such-and-such a type of Christian in particular.[6]

The first stanza of our hymn comprises verses 1–3, each one being constructed on the same pattern, which is too obvious to need analysis. The phrase 'to speak with the tongues of men or of angels' is a fuller and more correct expression to designate the phenomenon normally called 'to speak with tongues' or 'glossolaly'. This gift, practised by a person lacking Christian love, would make of him a gong or a cymbal—that is a noisy religious instrument. The first of

[4] The word 'agapē' is rare in secular Greek literature, though not unknown. The LXX often speaks of God's *agapē*. Christianity took and used the word to designate a love differing from both 'erōs' ('desiring love') and from 'philia' ('natural sympathy'). See *TWNT*, and the monograph by the Swedish theologian A. NYGREN, *Agape and Eros*, Pt I (Tr. HERBERT, London, 1932); Vol. 1, Pt II (Tr. WATSON, London, 1939). Also: R.P.C. SPICQ, *L'agapé de* 1 *Cor. XIII. Un exemple de contribution de la sémantique à l'exégèse néotestamentaire*, (Paris, 1955); and his *Agapé dans le N.T.* (3 vols; series *Etudes bibliques* [Paris, 1959]).

[5] The eulogy of Wisdom in Wisdom, 7²²⁻³⁰ belongs to the same literary genre. It cannot be quoted in its entirety through lack of space. But we will recall two typical verses: (7²⁹): 'She is more beautiful than the sun, and excels every constellation of the stars. Compared with the light she is found to be superior, (7³⁰) for it is succeeded by the night, but against wisdom evil does not prevail.'

[6] It is rather surprising that Nygren's book referred to above did not make more use of Chapter **13**. He may have thought wrongly, that it was a purely psychological analysis. About Nygren see the critical study by J. D. BENOIT, published in *RHPR* (1946), No. 1, pp. 89ff; and also the book by MAURICE NÉDONCELLE, *Vers une philosophie de l'amour*, (Paris, Aubier, n.d.).—It is known that Nygren had predecessors such as SCHOLZ, *Eros und Caritas* (Halle, 1929), and particularly MAX SCHELER, *Wesen und Formen der Sympathie* (Bonn, 1923; French edition under the title *Nature et formes de la sympathie* [Paris, Payot, 1928]).

these two instruments ('*chalkos*') was hung in temples, or on trees
as in the sacred grove at Dodona. According to the sophist Zenobius
the expression '*dōdonaion chalkeion*' even seems to have been an
ironical technical term to designate empty rhetoricians. 'It is said of
people who speak much and never reach the end.'[7] Here the metaphor
also indicates the lack of vitality in these soulless speeches.[8]

'*Kumbalon*' corresponds to cymbals which are used in pairs in
modern orchestras and are held in the hands. '*Alalazon*' is an onoma-
tapaeic verb expressing a sound possibly less reverberant than
'*ēchōn*' = 'resounding', but equally lacking in proper musical significance. As these instruments, as well as others of a similar kind,
played a part in some mystery religions, notably in the cult of the
goddess Cybele, it is possible that this comparison refers to pagan
customs in a way that would displease intensely the glossalalists at
whom Paul is aiming.[9]

13² (the second line of the first stanza) shows a gradation. Even
prophecy and knowledge, which are much more useful gifts than
glossolaly, and understanding of 'mysteries', even faith 'to remove
mountains', are not enough to turn a man into a Christian; he must
have love. What are the mysteries referred to? Comparison with 2[7]
and 15[51], as well as with Romans 11[25], makes J.W. believe that the
reference is especially to revelations of an eschatalogical order.
'*Mustēria*' and '*gnōsis*' might very well then refer to almost the same
thing. As for the '*pistis*' = 'to remove mountains', it is impossible
not to think of the word recorded in Mark 11[23] (and Mt 21[21]). As
this phrase occurs neither in the Old Testament nor in Jewish
apocryphal or Talmudic literature, it may be presumed that Paul
was acquainted with this saying of Christ's, through oral tradition.[10]

In the third line of the first stanza (13[3]) the verb '*psōmizō*' = 'to
distribute' presents no difficulty. Here the accusative is used, as
sometimes in the Greek of the LXX, for the thing given to the poor,
the whole fortune in a word, and not the person who enjoys the gift,

----

[7] '*Eirētai de epi tōn polla lalountōn kai mē dialeipontōn.*' ZENOBIUS, Proverbs
6[5] (*Corpus* paroemiographorum, pub. Leutsch and Schneidewin I [Göttingen,
1839], p. 162).

[8] '*Anaisthēton ti kai apsuchon*', as CHRYSOSTOM says (*Homily* 32.3 = *MPG* LXI,
col. 268).

[9] Cf. ATHENAEUS of NAUCRATIS (beginning of the 3rd cent. A D.), the texts of
Deipnosophistai (*The Learned Banquet*), 336 A and 361 E (TEUBNER, II.291 and
III.403), as well as the description by the historian HERODIAN (3rd cent.) of the
entry into Rome of the Emperor Heliogabalus, *Ab excessu divi Marci* V, 5.9
(TEUBNER, [1922], p. 146).

[10] According to STRACK-BILLERBECK, I.759, the term 'uprooters of mountains'
was used for rabbis who were particularly subtle in discussions. Here, however,
Faith is in question.—We would also bring to the notice of those fond of legends
that the Christians of Asia pointed out to the famous traveller MARCO POLO a
mountain which shortly before had been miraculously moved by the prayers of
a great saint. See Chapter 2 of his book *Le divisament du monde* (crit. ed. by L. F.
Benedetto [Florence, 1928], p. 22).

as Romans 12²⁰ (*'psōmize auton'*). Similar sacrifices are recorded in
the Acts of the Apostles, concerning Barnabas for example (4³⁶). At
first sight, it is curious that anyone should conceive the possibility of
performing such an act of charity without love; but it is not impossible
for it to be done through spiritual pride or in expectation of a
heavenly reward.

Once started on this road, could one not go even farther? Might
there not have been Christians who had sold themselves into slavery
in order to give the price of their person to the poor?[11] Preuschen[12]
thinks that the phrase *'ean paradō to sōma mou hina kauthēsomai'* =
'if I give my body in order that I may be burned' contains a reference
to this possibility. But let us first examine the traditional explanation
of this phrase. According to this explanation we must accept the
reading *'kauthēsomai'* as do the Textus Receptus, the Latin Fathers
and the Vulgate, and translate 'in order that I may be burned'.
Then we should have either an allusion to some fakirs from India
(called gymnosophists by the Greeks), who took the course of self-
immolation, or to Christian martyrdom. In support of the first
hypothesis the example of a certain Calanos is cited; he is stated to
have burned himself in the presence of Alexander the Great;[13]
similarly a certain Zamorkos is reported to have done the same
thing,[14] or again Lucian's celebrated 'Peregrinus Proteus' (who may
be a merely fictitious character). But such a custom, though it may
not be surprising among Hindus, is unthinkable in the realm of
Christianity, which would have held the act as suicide and consequently as a mortal sin.[15]

But reference to martyrdom by fire is no less improbable. True,
we know about the martyrdom of the three young men in the fur-
nace, recorded in the Book of Daniel, Chapter 3; the Second Book
of Maccabees (Ch. 7) tells of similar martyrdoms, expressly cited by
Origen in his *Exhortation to Martyrdom*. Yet this punishment was
unknown in the Graeco-Roman world. It would seem rather strange,
then, for Paul to select just this case as his example. This is why
Preuschen, while retaining the reading *'kauthēsomai'*, saw in it a
reference to the hot iron with which the bodies of slaves were
branded. Then it might indeed refer to Christians who had sold

[11] The Epistle of CLEMENT OF ROME to the Corinthians 55² speaks of many
Christians as having sold themselves and as having fed the poor with the money
obtained from the sale (*'Polloi paredōkan heautous eis douleian kai labontes tas
timas autōn heterous epsōmisan'*).
[12] *ZNTW*, XVI.127ff.
[13] See CICERO, *Tusculanes*, 22.2, TEUBNER, XLIV.308.
[14] DIO CASSIUS, *Hist. rom.* 54.9, TEUBNER, III.229.
[15] It is true that a text from CLEMENT OF ALEXANDRIA is often quoted in this
connection. He says in the fourth book of his *Stromateis*, Ch. 4, §17.1 (STAEHLIN,
II.256): 'Some who belong to us in name only, are eager to deliver themselves,
(understood: to martyrdom), *'kathaper hoi tōn Indōn gumnosophistai mataiō
puri'*. But it is very doubtful whether the dative *'mataiō puri'* really refers to the
Christians. CLEMENT probably wished to compare the exaggerated zeal of some
Christians to that of the Hindu ascetics who burned themselves.

> (4) *Love is full of long-suffering and kindliness; love knows no jealousy or presumptuousness; it is not puffed-up with pride.* (5) *It does nothing ill-mannered, is not self-seeking; it does not blaze out in anger, it keeps no reckoning of evil.* (6) *It does not rejoice over unrighteousness, but finds pleasure in truth.* (7) *In all circumstances, it is full of forgiveness, full of faith, full of hope, full of patience.*

themselves, and this would constitute a perfect gradation in comparison with those who give all their goods to the poor, but not their liberty.[16]

But all these explanations suppose '*kauthēsomai*', a very doubtful reading, as Robertson and Plummer strongly stress in their commentary. For the oldest manuscripts, namely P 46, ℵ, A, and B read '*kauchēsomai*'.[17] It seems impossible to set aside without very good reason, a reading which is so well attested. Further, and this fact has not received sufficient notice, in the first place, a word in the third person singular might be expected: 'I should give my body in order that *it* might be burned (or: branded).' If on the other hand we read '*kauchēsomai*', that is 'in order that I might be glorified', the use of the first person singular is reasonable and even necessary. Now, 'to give one's body' may have a double significance: to strive for martyrdom (without being obliged to do so) or 'to sell oneself', both actions being undertaken for glorification. We prefer the second explanation (to sell oneself as a slave) for the reason that we have indicated: this act constitutes the superlative of charity, the comparative of which consists in the disposal of possessions and the positive in almsgiving. We can manage without Preuschen's ingenious exegesis which has just been mentioned; yet we feel that it would have to be adopted, if the reading '*kauthēsomai*'[18] were to be retained.

After showing in the first strophe that the presence of agapé is an indispensable factor in the Christian's character, the author begins the real description of it in the second strophe (13[4-7]). 13[4a]: '*makrothumia*' is the 'patience' which knows how to bear injustice without anger or despair.[19] '*Chrēstotēs*' can be found associated with '*makrothumia*' in several of the texts quoted in footnote[19]. This word means 'kindliness' and gentle charm (Mt 11[30], Lk 5[39]); it is a kind of

---

[16] With reference to the alleged self-immolation, see DOELGER, *Antike und Christentum* (1929), p. 254, who sets this ancient practice (death by fire, but without love) over against the enthusiastically endured martyrdom of Christians. As against PREUSCHEN, in no degree does he assimilate the Christian attitude to the vainglory of Hindus who spectacularly committed themselves to the flames.

[17] JEROME, who criticized the text in the light of the Greek and Latin MSS, also gives preference to '*kauchēsomai*' (*v. MPL* XXVI, col. 425 A).

[18] Note the tact in the author's use of the first person ('if I gave', etc.) as if to avoid any insinuation that others might more easily than himself fall into the faults he lists.

[19] 2 Corinthians 6[6], Galatians 5[22], Colossians 3[12], 1 Thessalonians 5[14], Ephesians 4[2]. '*Makrothumia*' as a divine quality: Romans 2[4], 9[22], 1 Peter 3[20]; cf. Matthew 18[26, 29].

goodness and courtesy coming from the heart and represents the active counterpart of forbearance.

In $13^{4b,5,6}$, the Apostle, like a good phenomenologist, characterizes Christian love by a series of negative attributes: '*ou zēloi*', etc. '*Zēlos*' in early Christianity can mean an active and well-intentioned enthusiasm. But more frequently this noun, as well as its derivatives '*zēloō*' and '*zēlōtēs*' is used in a pejorative sense, and here it seems to mean 'jealousy'.[20] The Apostle challenges the validity of the common idea that jealousy is one of the proofs of love.

The verb '*perpereuomai*', rare in Greek, is a New Testament hapax legomenon. It is derived from the adjective '*perperos*', which describes a boastful and tactless nature.[21] It is therefore almost synonymous with '*phusioumai*' and denotes one of the practical results of the pride of the 'puffed-up'; this pair of vices, unknown to love, is accompanied by a third at the beginning of 13^5 which should logically have been joined to 13^4: '*ouk aschēmonei.*' This verb (cf. the discussion on the marriage of virgins 7^{35-6} and on the undisciplined glossolalists 14^{40}) indicates wrongs contrary to the requirements of propriety and good order, committed by some ill-mannered members. To this trio of vices is added a second group, from which agapé should also be free: '*ou zētei ta heautēs, ou paroxunetai, ou logizetai to kakon.*'[22] These are (1) the spirit of covetousness, i.e. selfishness, (2) anger which is allowed to lead to unfortunate incidents (cf. the German word '*Jähzorn*', 'sudden anger'), a vice from which the Apostle Paul or the Apostle Barnabas or both were not completely free according to Acts 15^{39}, (3) the habit still widespread even among Christians of keeping a reckoning of the faults of others ('*logizomai*' ='to book a debt', cf. Zech 8^{17}). We may pause, with reference to this verse, to notice the misconceptions caused by the erroneous translation of '*ou logizetai to kakon*' as '*ne soupçonne pas le mal*' (do not suspect evil)—for example, in the Synodale Version 1911; Segond 1917; and Bible du Centenaire 1928. We are not accusing the mistake of having created the prestige of a particular ethical aberration, but of having contributed largely to its standing. We are thinking of the common assumption which looks on unvarying trustfulness as a Christian virtue, an error often responsible for unfortunate catas-

[20] The complete list of the very numerous texts in which the word '*zēlos*' and cognates are found is given in KITTEL, *TWNT*, II.882ff.

[21] See R. ESTIENNE, Vol. VI, col. 996f.

[22] B and CLEMENT OF ALEXANDRIA (*Paid.*, III.,I.§3, STAEHLIN, I.237) read '*ta mē heautēs*'. This would mean: 'Christian love does not covet what does not belong to it.' Only the verb '*zēloō*' does not normally have the sense of 'covet'. Moreover, Clement seems to have had doubts himself about this reading; for in his sermon '*Quis dives salvetur*' (§38, 1, STAEHLIN III.184) he reads '*zētei ta heautēs*' (without '*mē*'). P 46 reads '*zētei to* [sic] *mē heautēs*'; but the '*mē*' has been added at a later date above the '*o*' of '*to*'. (This would be a case for saying, as in 4 , '*to mē huper o gegraptai*'.) We are of the opinion then that this MS rather supports the reading without '*mē*', contrary to the opinion of A. DEBRUNNER (in *Coniectanea Neotestamentica XI in honorem A. Fridrichsen sexagenarii* [Lund and Copenhagen, 1947], p. 41).

trophes in personal life and still more in communal life. It is hardly necessary to point out how far removed indiscriminating trust is from the teaching of the Apostle Paul, and from that of the entire New Testament, by which a healthy mistrust is recommended of all false prophets, 'wolves', 'dogs', 'foxes', and, in general, of all the wiles of Satan and his hordes.

There is a certain modern version of Christianity which, desiring to be more intelligent than the Bible, has started to doubt the existence of Satan and to believe in the goodness of all human hearts. It is most unfortunate that the erroneous translation we have criticized should have seemed to countenance this view.

It is still more unfortunate that the customary and almost universally accepted translation of '*panta pisteuei*' (13[7]) by 'believeth all things' seems to confirm this sophisticated Christian attitude. Does not the Apostle Paul reprove the Galatians precisely for their inexcusable credulity? And is not a critical spirit expressly recommended to Christians in such passages as 1 John 4[1]? Or should Eve, who believed all that the serpent promised her, be taken as the pattern of a believer? In fact, as we have explained, the verse means that the Christian holds to his faith on every occasion. '*Panta*' is not the object of '*pisteuei*', but a different use of the Greek accusative. And '*pisteuei*' naturally means Christian faith, like '*pistis*' (13[13]).

13[6] briefly summarizes the emotive attitude of agapé with regard to the good and evil which happen before our eyes. Neither selfishness nor any other vice will deflect the heart animated by Christian love from its normal reactions which consist in rejoicing at every occurrence of good and in being sad about evil.

Let there be no surprise to find '*adikia*' ('injustice, unrighteousness or wrongdoing' in general) contrasted with 'truth' ('*alētheia*') and not with 'righteousness' ('*dikaiosunē*'). We find the same opposition in 2 Thessalonians 2[12]: 'those who did not believe the truth but had pleasure in unrighteousness.' Galatians 5[7] and 1 Peter 1[22] should also be consulted, and it will be seen that what is meant is obedience to a moral principle. Further, parallels in Judaism and even in the Johannine literature show that 'truth' is often a synonym for what we call 'morality', and '*alēthēs*' a synonym for 'gentleman', 'sincere man'.[23] The use of the noun '*alētheia*' by Paul is the more explicable since '*dikaiosunē*' had acquired in his writings a technical sense connected with 'justification', and as a result had to be avoided (cf. Gal 5[5] contrasted with 5[7]).

This strophe ends with an impressive anaphora: '*panta stegei, panta pisteuei, panta elpizei, panta hupomenei*.' If we could read '*stergei*' = 'to esteem' (unfortunately a poorly attested reading) the sense would be clear,[24] on condition that '*panta*' was taken quite

[23] See KITTEL, *TWNT*, I.233-4.
[24] In fact, CYPRIAN reads '*omnia diligit*' (*MPL* IV, col. 632 A and 733 C), and ZENO of Verona likewise (4th century, *MPL* XI, col. 275 B).

(8) *Love never loses its standing. Are prophecies in question? They*
will be abolished. Or tongues? They will cease. Or knowledge? It will
be abolished. (9) For it is only in our imperfect existence that we exer-
cise knowledge and prophecy. (10) When perfection becomes a reality,
all that is imperfect will be abolished. (11) When I was a child, I used
a child's speech, I had the mentality of a child, the judgment of a child.
When I reached manhood, I put away childish things. (12) Well, for
the present we view truth by means of a mirror, enigmatically; then
we shall view it face to face. At present I have only partial knowledge,
but then I shall know, as I have been known.

(13) *But now there remain for us faith, hope, love, these three; and*
love is the greatest of the three.

naturally as a Greek accusative, which alone would justify this use
of the neuter. Moreover '*stergei, pisteuei*', and '*elpizei*' would well
lead on to the trio of the following verse.

But the reading '*stegei*' seems to be too well attested. The original
meaning of the verb is 'to cover'; here it must mean 'to forgive the
faults of others' or at any rate 'not to make an issue of them'. There
can be hesitation in this case about the exact force of the accusative.
Is the meaning 'to cover all' or 'to adopt on every occasion the particular attitude expressed by "*stegein*" '? To clear up the matter, let
us look at what follows: '*pisteuein*' and '*elpizein*' could have a general
sense: 'to believe everything, to hope everything.' But the allusion to
the 'theological virtues' in 13[13] seems difficult to contest. We cannot
therefore translate by 'love believes all things', a statement which
would be quite contrary to the precepts about judgement of spirits
and distrust of false prophets. Therefore it must refer to the power
that agapé derives from Christian Faith and Hope, which are never
absent from it. From that point on the accusative must be translated
as an accusative of 'limitation', expressing for once, it is true, the
absence of all limits: 'at all times.' Similarly '*panta*' would have to be
translated as the object of '*stegei*' and '*hupomenei*'. '*Hupomonē*' is
synonymous with '*makrothumia*'. As for the anaphora, we have tried,
in our translation, to render it in another, rather less heavy, way.

The third strophe (13[8–10]) affirms the superiority of agapé over all the
other spiritual gifts, and this is shown by its eternal and uncon-
querable power. '*Piptein*' here has an absolute sense and means 'to be
abolished', as in Luke 16[17].[25]

So prophecies and glossolaly will be abolished. When and how?
Could Paul have been thinking about the future of the history of the
Church, as Godet supposes? In this case the Apostle's forecast might
very largely have been achieved, since 'inspired' people are becoming
rarer and rarer. But the Apostle reckoned with the early return of the
Lord. It is better then to think of the consummation of all things in

[25] Some witnesses read '*ekpiptei*', which makes no change in the meaning.

the Kingdom of God. Then the imperfect forms of relationship between man and God will end. Then our partial and obscure knowledge of God will give place to a vision 'face to face', as 13^{12} expresses it.

The general sense of 13^{9-10} is clear. The words '*ek merous*'[26] may be regarded as depending on an '*ek pantos*' which is lacking; but in any event this expression must explain the essentially imperfect character of our prophetic inspiration. Further on (13^{10}) the expression is used as a noun and contrasted with '*to teleion*', to denote the imperfect nature of our religion in comparison with what it will be in the Kingdom.

The fourth strophe (13^{11-13}) elaborates the idea of the progress which will take place in the realm of knowledge. In so doing the Apostle opposes the claims of the mystery religions which promised perfect enlightenment here and now to their initiates. But what is the meaning of '*di' esoptrou*' = 'by means of a mirror' (13^{12a})? Even if imperfection is granted to Greek mirrors—which seems quite unproved—this would not be enough to explain the expression '*en ainigmati*' = 'enigmatically'. Moreover, in the ordinary use of a mirror, it is not usual to look at things other than oneself. We think therefore that Achelis[27] has put us on the right track: there is an allusion to the magical use of mirrors, which was fairly widespread in antiquity,[28] and is still in modern times for that matter.[29] Some sorcerers make a speciality of conjuring up in a mirror persons or scenes distant in space or time. As visions of the future are especially in question, this practice provides a metaphor which is quite in keeping with the text, in which the Apostle contrasts our present imperfect knowledge with the vision of God which we shall have later. The fact that our knowledge of God is a result of the knowledge that God has of us, has already been mentioned above in connection with 8^3.[30]

But 13^{13} has been an especial perplexity to exegetes. It is generally agreed to contrast '*menei*' (13^{13}) with '*piptei*' (13^8) and to give '*menei*' a future sense. 'Whilst the charismatic gifts will vanish, the three (love, faith, hope) will continue.' But if '*piptei*' has a future sense, it

---

[26] SCHLATTER (p. 361) points out that the Midrash Rabba on Qoheleth 1^8 uses a similar expression: רָאוֹ מִקְצָה, which WÜNSCHE (Biblioth. Rabbin. I.16) translates by: 'To see through a crack in a door.'

[27] 'Katoptromantie bei Paulus' (in *Theologische Festschrift für G. Nathanael Bonwetsch* [Leipzig, 1918], pp. 56-63).

[28] See BOUCHÉ-LECLERCQ: *Histoire de la divination dans l'Antiquité* I.340. According to ADAM ABT, *Die Apologie des Apulejus und die moderne Zauberei* (*Religionsgesch. Versuche u. Vorarbeiten* 4.2 [Giessen, 1908]), catoptromancy was used at every period in Asia and Europe.—See also ALFRED LEHMANN, *Aberglaube u. Zauberei von den ältesten Zeiten bis auf die Gegenwart* (2nd edn, 1908, Stuttgart), pp. 532ff.

[29] See GOETHE, *Faust*, I, *Hexenküche*, lines 95ff.

[30] N. HUGEDÉ in '*La Métaphore du Miroir*' uses the Torah, in particular Exodus 33^{20} and Numbers 12^{6-8}, to contest the idea of the magical character of the mirror. It is simply the opposition between symbolic knowledge and direct vision which is implied. This makes virtually no difference to the meaning.

is only because of the adverb '*oudepote*' which goes with it. We should then expect an '*aei*' modifying the verb '*menei*'. Yet we shall not delay over this difficulty, since all that is necessary is to change the accent without altering the spelling.

But the force of '*nuni de*' = 'but now' is obscure, if the usual interpretation is accepted. It is useless to speak of the very common adversative sense of this expression; all the same it would be very strange to use it in speaking of the eternal permanence of agapé in the future. Moreover, as Allo very rightly points out, for any casual reader, '*nuni de*' stands in contrast with '*tote*' in **13**[12b] and consequently could only have the temporal sense: '*now.*'

If in spite of all, we try to see an allusion to the future in '*nuni de menei*' (that is, to the fact that the triad will continue even into the Kingdom, when the imperfect state of things will have ended), then we face a much more serious problem: for then, according to Paul's teaching, faith ('*pistis*') will disappear to give way to sight ('*eidos*'); this is presupposed in 2 Corinthians 5[7]: '*dia pisteōs gar peripatoumen, ou dia eidous*' = 'we walk by faith, not by sight'. Similarly for hope, cf. Romans 8[24–5], which holds that it will give place to sight: '*tē gar elpidi esōthēmen; elpis de blepomenē ouk estin elpis. Ho gar blepei tis, ti elpizei?*' etc. = 'for we are saved in hope; now hope which is seen is not hope. For why should a man still hope for what he sees?' etc.

Perhaps the problem about faith may best be resolved by noticing that '*pistis*' does not always have the same force in the Apostle's writings. It could be argued, as Luther does, that the word can also denote the new life of the Christian reconciled to God. 'To have faith' would not then be contrasted with 'to have sight', but with 'to lack faith' (as in the discussion about meat sacrificed to idols).[31]

What is to be thought of a 'hope' continuing when all is consummated? Without saying so in so many words, Godet envisages the idea that the fruits of hope and faith will abide. But apart from the fact that the reader is unprepared by the preceding verses to think of such a connotation, it would be very strange that 'love', which can have no analogous sense, should even so be associated with 'hope' and 'faith'.

J. W. and Lietzmann argue that Paul used a formula here which he did not himself coin, but which may have been provided for him by the Corinthians. Hence it would not exactly fit in with his thought, although he may have reshaped it, by omitting the word '*gnōsis*', which may have been present also.[32]

[31] We leave out the extra difficulty caused by the fact that '*pistis*', according to **13** , is listed among the charismatic gifts. This use is exceptional, and in **13**[7] ('*panta pisteuei*') the author seemed to have returned to the normal use.

[32] LIETZMANN points out that the Neo-Platonist philosopher PORPHYRY (*ad. Marcellam* 24 [pub. Nauck, 2nd edn], p. 289) uses the tetrad '*pistis, alētheia, erōs, elpis*'.—Also, the *Oracula chaldaïca* (pub. Kroll, p. 74, line 23 in *Breslauer Philologische Abhandlungen*, R. FORSTER, Vol. VII, fasc. 1, Breslau, 1894) had a formula which resembles Paul's quite closely: '*pistis, alētheia, erōs.*' But these are late texts.

It may also be supposed that the Corinthians, as Clement of Alexandria[33] later, may have known the triad '*gnōsis, pistis, agapē*'. But all this is quite hypothetical. And if the triad was of Corinthian origin, why did Paul use it earlier in 1 Thessalonians 1[3] and 5[8]?

In conclusion then, it seems more natural to break with the usual exegesis of '*nuni de menei*' and to take the eulogy of the triad in a present sense, and as a contrast to the charismatic gifts: 'If we leave aside the charismatic gifts properly so called, there still remain three virtues also created by the Holy Spirit and which are closely linked together.' Why is love the greatest? The main reason, which the Apostle does not need to express since it is implicit, is that faith and hope, understood as we have expounded, will lose their meaning in the consummated world; but this does not apply to agapé.

---

[33] *Stromateis*, III x.§69.3, STAEHLIN, II.227, and VII x.§55.7, STAEHLIN, III.41.

CHAPTER XIV

(1) *Follow after love; aspire also to supernatural manifestations and especially to prophecy.* (2) *For the one who speaks in tongues, does not speak to men, but to God. Indeed no one can understand a word, while in the spirit he is speaking mysteries.* (3) *But the man who prophesies speaks to men: he edifies, he exhorts, he comforts.* (4) *The man who speaks in tongues, edifies himself; he who prophesies, edifies the Church.* (5) *I might wish that you could all speak in tongues, but I prefer you to prophesy. The man who prophesies is greater than the one who speaks in tongues, unless someone can interpret his words, so that the whole assembly may find edification in them.* (6) *Well now, my brothers, I ask you: in what way should I be of profit to you if, on coming to see you, I spoke in tongues, and my words brought neither revelation, nor knowledge, nor prophecy, nor teaching?*

This chapter, following Chapters 11 and 12, indicates further abuses to be avoided in the meetings, notably the harm resulting from placing too high a value on glossolaly, and from the participation of women in discussion.

14¹ provides a link with Chapter 13 which, as has been seen, is a digression. Originally 12³¹, '*zēloute de ta charismata ta meizona*' must have been followed immediately by 14¹ᵇ, '*mallon de hina prophēteuēte*' = 'aspire to the so-called higher spiritual gifts, but still more to prophecy'. The editor (Sosthenes?) inserted '*diōkete tēn agapēn*' = 'follow after love', as a summary of Chapter 13 and repeated 12³¹ (but without '*ta meizona*' and with '*pneumatika*' instead of '*charismata*' before passing on to 14¹ᵇ. Thus, '*mallon*' received the unexpected sense of 'especially', since prophecy is evidently ranked among the '*pneumatika*' = 'supernatural manifestations'. In 14⁵, '*mallon*' has retained its natural sense of 'more than'.

The superiority of prophecy is shown primarily by the fact that the prophet, although inspired, speaks a comprehensible language and, without interpretation, can have a beneficial effect on the meeting (see especially 14³). Naturally, the authenticity of the prophecy must be judged—and that is the task of those who possess the gift called '*diakrisis pneumatōn*' = 'the discernment of spirits (12¹⁰). So prophecy is not infallible, but—other things being equal—it is preferable to glossolaly, which (at best) can be of value only through an 'interpreter' ('*hermēneutēs*'), and this is always irksome. The content of prophecy is not indicated precisely. Its province is messages from the Spirit of God with the purpose of instruction or edification. Glossolaly is not scorned for that reason (14¹⁸), but it is especially useful to the person who possesses the gift. He speaks to God (14²).

This indicates that it is essentially prayer, a supposition which is confirmed by 14¹⁴. It is therefore a gift to be exercised more in private. Yet glossolaly seems to have been so popular that the Apostle cannot do otherwise than grant it a fairly important place in corporate worship (14²⁷). But he demands the same rights for prophecy, hoping that the latter will gradually win increasing appreciation. The impression is conveyed that if he were not dealing with an already existing situation, he would there and then have given a more important place to prophecy. A further argument in favour of prophecy is that the speaker retains control of himself. And so he is self-consciously active, which is not so in glossolaly. The ideal of inspiration according to the Apostle is the development of self-awareness through the Spirit of God, not its atrophy.

14². In this verse '*pneumati*' is ambiguous. It might mean the Holy Spirit, who speaks through the mouth of the inspired person, or alternatively the *spirit* of the person himself, transported in ecstasy. With Godet, we opt for the second alternative, in view of the absence of the article, but we do not say that the former is untenable. The former would indeed be certain if the reading '*pneuma lalei*' = 'the Spirit speaks', given in F, G, a few Latin manuscripts and Pelagius,[1] could be accepted. For if the spirit of the man can be the instrument (dative), the Spirit of God is the author of the utterance. But this reading is perhaps too poorly attested to be retained.

14³. J. W. cites Romans 12 and 13 as an example of '*paraklēsis*' = 'exhortation'; but he might equally well have pointed to many texts in 1 Corinthians. However, the comparison relates only to the contents; for Paul does not claim to have dictated this Epistle in a state of prophetic inspiration, though it may contain the gist of earlier revelations. '*Paramuthia*' is 'consolation'; as a sample of a '*logos paramuthias*', 1 Thessalonians 4¹³⁻¹⁴ might be evidenced, or the letter to the Philadelphians (Rev 3⁷⁻¹³).

14⁵. '*Thelō*' does not express an order, but a concession in the form of a wish unlikely to be fulfilled (cf. 7⁷). '*De*' after '*meizōn*' (14⁵ᵇ) creates a difficulty. The '*gar*' which would be expected is given by the majority of witnesses. But the oldest ones, namely P 46, ℵ, A, and B have '*de*'. However, this conjunction does not always have an adversative sense. In many Gospel texts, expecially in Mark, '*de*' is equivalent to '*kai*'. Moreover, an exactly similar use of '*de*' following '*thelō*' occurs in 14⁵ᵃ, where no one would think of giving it an adversative sense.

What is the subject of '*diermēneuē*'? We do not think it is '*ho lalōn glōssais*'; for normally it is not the same person who *interprets*. But it must be remembered that in Greek the subject '*tis*' = 'some

---

[1] '*Spiritus autem loquitur mysteria*', MPL XXX, col. 759 C.

(7) *It is the same with musical instruments, for example with the flute or the zither. If there is no order in the sounds, how is anyone to recognize the tune played by the flute or the zither?* (8) *Or again: if a trumpet gives only a confused sound, who will prepare for battle?* (9) *Similarly with you, if by your 'tongue' you give no intelligible speech, how will anyone understand what you say? In fact you will be like people who speak to the four winds.*

one', or another easily guessed subject, is often understood, even when it is not expressly given in the preceding sentence.[2]

14[6]. '*Nun de*' here has neither the adversative sense (which would presuppose the prior enunciation of an hypothetical instance), nor the conclusive sense ('*rebus sic stantibus*', see Godet), but means 'well now', i.e. 'let us look at the facts and take a concrete example'.

14[7]. Here, '*homōs*' is 'difficult to understand' (Allo). This particle means 'nevertheless' and presupposes a '*kaiper*' = 'although', as '*tamen*' is balanced against '*etiamsi*' in Latin. J. W. thinks that '*homōs*' should go with '*pōs gnōsthēsetai*' and that the participle '*phōnēn didonta*' might be the equivalent of '*eiper phōnēn didō*'. Then the meaning would be: 'inanimate objects, even if they give a sound, would nevertheless lack meaning if, etc. . . . .' We feel that here we have one of those forced explanations which have produced much harm in exegesis. For to introduce a rhetorical question ('*pōs gnōsthēsetai*' = 'how would anyone recognize?') by '*homōs*' would be extremely odd. Moreover, as Godet has wisely noted, the participle '*phōnēn didonta*' cannot be separated from '*apsucha*', which it determines in the manner of an appositional adjective. These three words mean 'instruments of music'. It is therefore impossible to take '*didonta*' as a predicate replacing a relative clause.[3]

Godet gives the ingenious explanation that instruments, which are *still* only inanimate things, are also subject to this law, etc. . . . But there is no proof that '*homōs*' means 'still' in that sense. Allo is of the opinion that '*homōs*' is in opposition to the implied idea 'in spite of your liking for unintelligible words'; but can the reader be supposed to be sufficiently intelligent to guess this?

To this difficulty there are in our opinion only two solutions: either to amend '*homōs*' to '*homoiōs*' = 'similarly'; or, the solution which we prefer, merely to change the accents, and for '*hómōs*' to

---

[2] Thus '*phēsin*' means 'someone says, it is said' (synonymous with the plural '*phasin*'). Cf. Wisdom 15[12], or 15[52], where the subject of the verb '*salpisei*' is not the trumpet mentioned earlier, but 'someone' or 'the trumpeter', exactly like the example in the *Anabasis* of Xenophon, I.ii.17 ('*epei esalpingxe*' = 'when someone had given the signal on the trumpet').—In other cases, God or the spirit of God is understood as the subject.

[3] The analogy with Galatians 3[15], to which J.W. attaches some importance, proves nothing, because that verse does not contain the difficulty which has just been pointed out in 14[7].

*(10) There are I know not how many sorts of words in the world,
and no kind is meaningless. (11) Yet if I do not know the significance
of the word, I shall be a foreigner to the speaker and the speaker a
foreigner to me.*

read '*homôs*' (the same in meaning as '*homoíōs*'). This is moreover
how the majority of unbiased readers would take it, if they were
given an unpointed text, such as that of P 46 or A.[4]

The meaning of the simile given in 14[7-8] is clear. Of themselves
musical instruments are useful only if they emit clear sounds giving a
precise signal or melody. With even more reason must men be
required to express themselves in an intelligible way. It is permissible
to add: there are instruments which, like gongs and cymbals, make
noise only, and according to 13,[5] those gifted with tongues resemble
them.

14[9b]. '*eis aera lalountes*' means to 'speak into the air' (for all the
understanding I am receiving from my listeners).

14[10]. '*ei tuchoi*' implies a slight attenuation of the statement of
number expressed by '*tosauta*' and at the same time stresses the
writer's unwillingness to declare for a specific number. It may be
translated by 'no doubt', or, better still, 'I know not how many'.—
'*Phōnē*' here means neither 'voice' nor 'language' (in spite of the
Vulgate and Preuschen-Bauer), but 'word', as the French Synodale
Version realized. For 'language', moreover, the Apostle uses
'*glōssa*'. The meaning of '*aphōnon*' was also clearly understood by
the Synodale Version: the sense required by this context is 'inco-
herent' or 'lacking in meaning'. But the neuter '*outhen*' can agree
only with '*genos*' and not with '*phōnē*'. So we must translate 'no kind'
and not 'no word'.—Yet it is not enough that the words should have
meaning, we must also know what that meaning is. This truth is
illustrated in 14[11], which reads like a paraphrase of Ovid's well-
known couplet written in exile:

---

[4] It is true that '*homôs*' is rather archaic; but other derivatives of '*homós*' such
as '*homóse*' and '*homoû*' are found in classical Greek as well as in the LXX. The
Grammar of BLASS-DEBRUNNER, §450.2 (5th edn, 1921), p. 257, and the *Dictionary*
of PREUSCHEN-BAUER prefer to read '*hómōs*', but think that through confusion
with '*homôs*' this adverb may here have taken on the sense of 'similarly'; then
why not adopt openly the reading '*homôs*'?

[5] A snatch of unintelligible glossolaly is given in the Massoretic text of the
prophet Isaiah (28[10]) in these sounds: '*tsaw lātsaw tsaw lātsaw qaw lāqāw qaw lāqāw
ze'er shām ze'er shām.*' The prophet follows it by stating expressly that he is
speaking of people who 'stammer'. Furthermore he says of himself (38[14]) that
there were times when he 'murmured like a crane', 'twittered like a swallow', and
'moaned like a dove'. The widely varied attempts at translation in the LXX and
modern versions should be taken as fanciful, unless they prove that one of the
translators had the gift of 'interpreting tongues' in the particular sense of our
Epistle.

(12) *So it is with you: from the moment that you aspire eagerly to states of inspiration, let it be for the edification of the assembly that you seek to be rich in them. (13) That is why he who speaks in tongues should pray that someone should interpret him. (14) If I pray in tongues, my spirit is indeed at prayer, but my understanding is sterile. (15) What conclusion am I to draw? That I should pray with my spirit, but that I should also pray with my understanding. That I should sing psalms with my spirit, but that I should also sing psalms with my understanding. (16) For if you pronounce the benediction with the spirit, how will the mere layman be able to say Amen in response to your blessing, since he does not know what you are saying? (17) I admit that you may be offering thanks very well, but the other person is not being edified.*

> *Barbarus hic ego sum, qui non intellegar ulli.*
> *Et rident stolidi verba latina Getae.*[6]

Indeed, a barbarian, strictly speaking, is one who does not speak Greek, and anyone who fails to make himself understood may be so termed.

14¹². '*zēlōtai pneumatōn*' = 'those who aspire to spirits' is surprising. We expect '*zēlōtai charismatōn pneumatikōn*' = 'those who aspire to spiritual gifts' (some MSS read '*pneumatikōn*', which is an emendation). Obviously '*pneumata*' here means 'good spirits', which '*diakrisis*' is able to distinguish from bad ones; cf. **14²⁹** and 1 John 4¹: 'test the spirits to see whether they come from God.'

According to the Apostle, each prophet has his particular spirit when he speaks, though naturally this does not mean that it is always the same spirit which inspires him. This view of things is in keeping with the pneumatology of the Hellenistic world; yet none the less it does not contradict the fundamental Pauline conception, according to which Christian prophets are taken to be inspired, in the final analysis, by God.

14¹⁴ seems to imply that the utterance of speakers with tongues was usually a prayer. What, however, does '*proseuchesthō*' mean in **14¹³**? If this verb has the same sense as in **14¹⁴**, we must translate: 'Let him say his prayer with the intention of interpreting it.' But usually someone else acted as interpreter. J. W. explains it thus: the speaker with tongues in his state of illumination should ask God to bestow on him the gift of '*hermēneia*' = 'interpretation'. But this explanation is open to the same objection. Moreover, it would be very curious for '*proseuchesthai*' to be used in **14¹³** as a synonym for '*aiteisthai*' = 'to ask', when it does not have that sense in **14¹⁴**. So we prefer, as in **14⁵**, to take an understood '*tis*' as the subject of '*diermēneuē*': 'that someone should interpret.' Then there is no point in giving '*proseu-*

---

[6] *Tristia*, 5.10, lines 37, 38 (ed. Garnier), p. 200.

chesthai' (**14¹³**) another sense than the one it has in **14¹⁴** and **14¹⁵**. The Apostle is seeking to say in short: 'Let him who prays in tongues be fully aware that the words have no value, if no one interprets them; if he keeps this end in sight he will speak only when he is sure of finding an interpreter, and he will thus not tax the patience of the assembly. The latter will moreover not give a hearing to a second messenger "in tongues", before the first has been interpreted.'

In **14¹³⁻¹⁷** we meet an interesting balance between '*pneuma*' and '*nous*'. Since in **14¹⁴** it is '*pneuma mou*' which is in question, and as in **14¹⁴⁻¹⁷** '*pneuma*' and '*nous*' are inter-dependent as two human faculties, '*pneuma*' cannot here mean the 'spirit of God', nor 'a spirit from the supernatural world'. Consequently, '*pneuma*', as very often in Hellenistic literature,[7] denotes that part of a man which can be carried away into ecstasy and become in some degree the instrument of inspiration. Is this '*pneuma mou*' only to be found in Christians, as a product of the Holy Spirit? Probably, though we can find no account of the matter. The conception of glossolaly here is rather more complex than the one hitherto outlined. But it can be understood as completing and clarifying the former without contradicting it. In contrast, '*nous*' can refer only to the conscious part of man and corresponds to a certain extent to what we call the understanding. According to the Apostle, it is better to speak '*tō noi*', knowing what one is saying, rather than in ecstasy. At the same time the activity of self-consciousness allows the inspired person to control the spirits which might seek to speak through him ('*pneumata prophētōn*', **14³²**), unless '*pneumata*' means here again the spirits of the prophets themselves, i.e. that part of a man which is particularly subject to inspiration. The sense of **14³²** would then be: the prophet can direct his spirit, whereas it escapes from those who speak in tongues when they are in a state of inspiration.

But it is doubtless not going too far to attribute to the Apostle not only motives of a practical order, but also an accurate assessment of the part which should be played by conscious awareness in Christianity. For him the ideal of inspiration is that which renews and develops self-awareness instead of diminishing it.[8]

So far as the construction of **14¹⁴** is concerned, it must be noted that the particle '*gar*' (Nestlé) is absent from some important manuscripts, notably P 46, B, F, and G, and should doubtless be ignored. If it is to be retained, its use might be explained, in our view, by the author's habit of thinking in ellipses. The idea in its more developed form would be approximately: 'In general terms, I do not overesteem glossolaly because in that state the human spirit is inactive.'

---

[7] See especially PHILO, *Quis rerum divinarum haeres*, §249ff (COHN AND WENDLAND, ed. minor, III.48ff). This text is far too long to be quoted here. Briefly, the philosopher-rabbi explains that so long as the '*nous*' is active ('*heōs men oun eti perilampei kai peripolei ho nous*, p. 51), inspiration cannot occur. It must, however be conceded that Philo's terminology is, as always, rather variable.

[8] Cf. ROBERT WILL, *Le culte*, I.140ff. *EHPR*, X(1925).

(18) *Thanks be to God, I speak in tongues more than you all.* (19) *But in an assembly I would rather say five words with my understanding in order to instruct others—than ten thousand in a 'tongue'.* (20) *Brothers, do not be children in intelligence, but be babes in evil; be mature in intelligence.* (21) *In the Law it is written: 'I will speak to this people in foreign tongues and with lips of foreigners, but even then they will not listen to me', says the Lord.* (22) *Consequently the 'tongues' serve as signs not to those who are becoming believers, but to those who disbelieve; prophecy, on the other hand, will be a sign not to those who disbelieve, but to those who are becoming believers.* (23) *If then the whole Church meets together in assembly and all speak in tongues, and if novices and pagans come in, will they not say that you are mad? (24) But if all prophesy and a pagan or a novice enters, he is reproved by all, called to account by all.* (25) *The secrets of his heart are discerned, and so he will prostrate himself and worship God, proclaiming 'Truly God is among you'.*

14^{16} returns to arguments of a practical kind, and varies them. This time the concern is not with the reaction of believers to a message in tongues, but with that of the '*idiōtai*', i.e. 'the uninitiated'.[9] As they have a definite place in the assembly ('*ton topon tou idiōtou anaplērōn*'), they are not pagans present by chance, but sympathizers who are yet unbaptized, or quite simply 'ordinary' Christians who do not possess any gifts of inspiration. The Apostle is afraid that they might be repelled by unintelligible ecstatic speech. They will be unable to say 'Amen' (== 'in truth, so be it'), which is the usual response to blessings. This argument is to be taken up again in 14^{23-5} and extended to *apistoi*' == 'unbelievers'.

14^{18-19}. The Apostle again defends himself against certain interpretations of these exhortations. He values speaking in tongues highly enough to practise it himself, but not in Church gatherings. There he would rather speak five words intelligibly. The number 'five' seems to be a synonym for a 'few', like the expression 'half a dozen'.[10] Passages such as Luke $12^{6, 52}$, 14^{19}, and Revelation 9^5 may be called to mind; but we shall be chary of accepting the references to many other texts listed by Kittel.[11]

14^{20}. '*Phrenes*' does not have exactly the same sense as '*nous*'. '*Phrenes*' means rather a quality which has its seat in the '*nous*', and it is naturally attached to the same root as '*phroneō*' (cf. 13^{11}).

[9] This sense for '*idiōtēs*' was current in the vocabulary of philosophy and mysticism. In Aramaic הדיוט means the layman as opposed to the rabbi. Cf. STRACK-BILLERBECK, III.463.

[10] Cf. STRACK-BILLERBECK, III.461, and G. KITTEL, '*Die Fünfzahl als geläufige Zahl und stilistisches Motiv*' (*Arbeiten zur Religionsgeschichte des Urchristentums*, I.III.39ff).

[11] The reader will certainly agree with us over Matthew 14^{17}, 16^9, $25^{2, 16}$ Luke 16^{28}, John 4^{18}, Acts 20^6, 24^1.

'*Phrenes*' is to be found only here in the New Testament; but it is used in the Greek Bible[12] in the sense of 'intelligence'. The Corinthians should, then, develop their intelligence. It follows that the destruction of fleshly wisdom by the Gospel (*v.* Ch. 1) should in no way lead to any dulling of a man. If little children are sometimes cited as patterns for Christians (a probable allusion to the words recorded in Mark 10[14] and par.), it is not with regard to their silliness, but because of their innocence. 'Be like new-born babes in evil' means, then, 'Do not develop that vice'.

14[21-5]. If an 'uncoded' message is delivered, e.g. by a prophet, the '*apistoi*' and '*idiōtai*' will be (*a*) 'reproved' ('*elengchontai*')—that is, convicted of their errors or sins (Godet); (*b*) 'called to account' ('*anakrinontai*'); and (*c*) 'their secret thoughts will be discerned' and put into words by the prophets ('*ta krupta . . . ginetai*'). Judgement presupposes, certainly, that the sinner should first be exposed. Yet the fact that we are here in the presence of a slight '*husteron-proteron*' will not worry us too much in a text of a rhetorical nature.

But a real difficulty is raised by '*hupo pantōn*' = 'by all', as the complement of '*elengchetai*' and '*anakrinetai*'. '*Emprosthen pantōn*' = 'before all' might be expected. It must be conceded that the sinner has the impression that the prophet is speaking in the name of all.

Here, then, there is certainly involved the phenomenon of thought-reading by the prophets in a state of inspiration. Parallels are attested in the history of modern Pentecostalism and in some other revival movements.[13]

But if this is so, why is glossolaly called in **14[22]** a 'sign (*sēmeion*) for unbelievers', and prophecy a 'sign for believers', to follow the usual translation? The exact opposite would be expected.

We think that '*apistos*' in **14[22]** does not have exactly the same sense as in **14[24]**. Indeed, the quotation from the prophet Isaiah (in **14[21]**)[14] speaks of Jews who refused to believe and who were not even impressed by glossolaly. The '*apistoi*' are therefore those who harden

---

[12] Proverbs 7[7] and Daniel 4[34, 36] according to the text of THEODOTION (following RAHLFS numeration).

[13] It goes without saying that thought-reading is not of itself a religious phenomenon. But here again a psychical ability is involved which can be awakened and used by the spirit of God. See HENRI BOIS, *Le Réveil au Pays de Galles*, pp. 417ff, 484, 489.

[14] The quotation does not agree with the LXX text, which gives (Isa 28[11-2]) '*dia phaulismon cheileōn dia glōssēs heteras, hoti lalēsousin tō laō toutō . . . kai ouk ethelēsan akouein*'—'Because they will speak to this people through despised lips, by a strange tongue . . . and they were (sic) not willing to understand.' Could Paul have been quoting from memory? But ORIGEN (*Philokalia* 9, ORIGEN *Opera*, ed. LOMMATZSCH 25 [Berlin 1848], p. 56) claims to have found the Pauline wording in the Greek version of the Old Testament by Aquila (at the time of the Emperor Hadrian). This curious fact seems to indicate that the Apostle used an ancient translation of the prophet, which Aquila also used later. Paul differs still more from the Massoretic Text, which need not be quoted here.

(26) *What then, brothers? When you come together—each one has a psalm to sing, or some teaching to give, or a revelation to bring, or a gift of tongues to exercise, or an interpretation to add—well, let all be done with a view to edifying. (27) If any speak in tongues, let it be done by two or by three at the most, and one after the other, and let only one interpret the message. (28) But if there is no interpreter, let the speaker in tongues remain silent in the assembly; let him speak to himself and to God. (29) As for the prophets, let two or three speak, and let the others judge. (30) But if another, who is seated, receives a revelation, let the first be silent. (31) For you can all prophesy one after another, so that all may be instructed and all encouraged. (32) Moreover the spirits of the prophets are subject to the prophets. (33) And the fact is that God is not for disorder, but for peace. As in all Christian Churches, (34) women should be silent in assemblies; for they are not permitted to speak. They should, on the contrary, keep a subordinate attitude, as the law says indeed. (35) But if they desire information, let them question their husbands at home. For it is unseemly for a woman to speak in a Church assembly.*

their hearts and who remain disbelieving through stumbling. On the other hand the '*pisteuontes*' are those in the process of becoming Christians.[15] However, since the aim of Paul's preaching was not to harden but to convert, it is understandable that later he should develop the theme of the superiority of prophecy.

14[26-33]. This passage gives some details about abuses which were likely to disturb good order. Not only did speakers in tongues speak without being sure that an interpreter was present, but it also happened that several inspired persons might speak at the same time (14[27,31]); that is why they are enjoined to speak one after the other ('*ana meros*'). This can be explained by the fact that sometimes a second person might be seized with inspiration before the first had finished. In such a case the first was to be silent. This recommendation may seem surprising. But by preventing the second from speaking, the hearers ran the risk of not benefiting at all from his message, which could not be postponed. The number of inspired speakers seems to have been very big. So it was necessary to dam these floods of eloquence by limiting the number of speakers in tongues and of prophets respectively to two or three. This is more readily understood since each message in tongues had to be interpreted, and each prophetic message discussed ('*anakrinatōsan*')—which already brought the number of speakers to eight or twelve at least. And suitable allowance of time must also be made for the teachers, the poets (14[26]), for reading from the Bible or of epistles sent by the

---

[15] Concerning the expression 'God is among you' in 14[25], ALLO supposes, not without reason, that some Corinthians considered glossolaly of itself as a sign of the divine presence—an opinion which received little encouragement from the Apostle.

Apostle Paul or by other Churches, as well as for the singing of psalms and for prayers.

It goes without saying that '*hoi alloi*' = 'the others' in **14²⁹** must not encourage everyone or just anyone to take part in the discussion, though as a last resort, the Church as a whole had, in certain cases, to judge the validity of a message. Similarly '*hekastos*' in **14²⁶** (or '*hekastoi humōn*' according to quite a number of authorities) means only 'each one who feels impelled to speak'. There is hardly any need to stress the point that all 'inspired' movements have encountered similar difficulties.

The injunctions of **14²⁴⁻³³ᵃ** are continued in **14³⁷⁻⁴⁰**. But before that the Apostle speaks of the participation of women in discussions.[16]

14³³ᵇ⁻⁵. This passage seems to interrupt the context, and it is understandable that D, and G, followed by Ambrosiaster[17] and several Latin MSS, place the passage **14³³ᵇ⁻⁶** after **14⁴⁰**. This is one of the reasons why J. W. inclines to the view that it is an interpolation. We do not agree with this opinion; for the Apostle has just restated the principle of decorum, which must be observed in Church gatherings (**14³³ᵃ**). So it is quite natural that he should go a step farther and reduce to silence the women who, contrary to Jewish and Greek custom, wished to take part in discussions.

This danger is also in question in **14³³ᵇ⁻⁵**. For **14³⁵** shows that after the messages delivered by the prophets, the company had the habit not only of discussing, but also of asking questions—which was quite natural. Women would be better advised to ask any questions at home; their husbands could have found out or would be able to find out the answers in the assembly (girls would obviously be able to question their fathers). There was no question therefore of imposing silence on women who spoke in a state of inspiration to deliver a message. This contingency is expressly dealt with and passed as permissible in **11⁵**, where women who prophesy or pray are ordered to have their heads covered; and no exegete has ever doubted that the point there concerns women speaking in Church gatherings.

So there is a clear distinction between a preaching woman (using the term in its widest sense), who has the right to bring a message—and a woman who is merely present at worship as an ordinary member of the congregation. The latter should be silent. Hence, the so-called contradiction between **11⁵** and **14³³ff** disappears, and with it J. W.'s second argument in favour of the spuriousness of this passage.

Further, it goes without saying that the reason for this (partial) silence imposed on women must be sought solely in a concern not to violate the rules of propriety that were generally observed at the

---

[16] The article by P. DE LABRIOLLE, '*Mulieres in ecclesia taceant*'. *Un aspect de la lutte antimontaniste* (*Bulletin d'ancienne littérature et d'archéologie chrétiennes* I(1911).3-24, 103-22) was not available to us.

[17] *MPL* XVII, col. 259, note a.

(36) Or was it from you that the word of God went forth, or did it reach you only? (37) If anyone believes himself to be a prophet or to be inspired, let him recognize that my words are a commandment from the Lord. (38) But let him who does not recognize them, not be recognized either. (39) Consequently, my brothers, seek earnestly to prophesy, without hindering speaking in tongues. (40) But let all take place in a decent and orderly way.

time. We are, then, here in the realm of the relative. Calvin was well aware of this.[18] It is permissible to suppose that in our own day, when women enjoy all rights and shock no one by speaking in public, the restriction enjoined by the Apostle no longer has the same force.

However, once more (cf. 11^{16}), the Apostle is conscious of having tenacious opponents in the feminist party of the Church. That is why he recalls quite baldly that he too has the Holy Spirit and that it was through him that the Church first heard the word of God.

In the closing remark (14^{37-40}) he again addresses those who are inspired. This is in no way surprising, since they are concerned in almost every exhortation in this chapter.

The rather sharp tone must have its explanation in disastrous news about disorderly assemblies, which must have reached him. Those who do not recognize his injunctions as valid—that is, those who refuse to conform to them—should not be recognized as truly inspired. The orders given by the Apostle should be considered as orders from the Lord—not as referring to '*logia*' handed-down, but because the Lord has guided him by His spirit. As for 14^{40}, it summarizes once more his directions.

The thought is in close harmony with 14^{36}, where Paul is considered as having brought the '*logos tou Theou*' = 'the Word of God' in his capacity as Apostle; and this strengthens our belief that 14^{33b-6} are in their right place and quite authentic.

---

[18] See the passage of his *Commentary* cited above on 11^{16}.

CHAPTER XV

(1) *I remind you, brothers, of the Gospel which I announced to you, which you accepted and to which you remain faithful. (2) By it also you are saved, if you hold fast the teaching which I gave you—if you do not you have become believers in vain. (3) For I passed on to you above all the tradition which I had received: Christ died for our sins, according to the Scriptures, (4) he was buried, he was raised up on the third day, in accordance with the Scriptures. (5) And he appeared to Cephas, then to the Twelve. (6) Then he appeared to more than five hundred brothers at the same time, of whom the majority are still alive, though some of them have died. (7) Then he appeared to James, then to all the apostles. (8) And lastly, as to an abortion, he appeared also to me. (9) For I am the least of the apostles. I am not even worthy to be called an apostle, because I persecuted the Church of God. (10) But through the grace of God, I am what I am; and the grace which he bestowed on me was not ineffective; on the contrary, I worked harder than all the others—yet not I, but the grace of God which is with me. (11) So whether it be I or they, that was our preaching and that our belief.*

The doctrine of the Resurrection is like the keystone of the structure of the Apostle's religious thought.[1] In it his Christology, soteriology, and anthropology are culminated. We shall distinguish two elements:

(a) The affirmation of the Christian hope in the resurrection. This is ineradicable from souls whose sensibilities have been cultivated by reading the Old Testament. For although the latter has little to say about resurrection, it teaches—contrary to the majority of Eastern and Greek religions—that the creation of the visible world and of the human body was not a regrettable accident linked with a fall of spirits, but a manifestation of divine wisdom, notwithstanding its subsequent Fall. Consequently no eschatology which teaches a mere dissolution of the visible world, contenting itself with the hope of the heavenly immortality of the soul, can do justice to this way of understanding the creation. Therefore it is to 'a new heaven and a new earth', that is to a new creation, that the Christian aspires.

(b) The affirmation that this hope will be fulfilled. On what is this assurance based? The Apostle might have been content to ascribe it to a revelation concerning these mysteries, as he does in the Epistles

---

[1] 'What is disclosed here is Paul's key position', KARL BARTH, *The Resurrection of the Dead* (Tr. Stenning, London, 1933), p. 107.—'The beginning and the end of the Christian message is the proclamation that Christ is risen from the dead', PHILIPPE H. MENOUD, *CTAP* IX (undated), p. 51.

to the Thessalonians. But he is eager to link the assurance with a definite event attested by witnesses, namely the resurrection of Christ, which will bring that of Christians in its wake.

15¹⁻². Our rendering of these two verses is given with great reserve; for the text is certainly not in correct order. Indeed, whatever construction is adopted, it gives only meagre satisfaction. Before all else is the question of knowing to which verb to subordinate the question '*tini logō ēuanggelisamēn humin*'. There are three possible explanations:

(1) Bachmann attaches the clause in question to '*gnōrizō*'. Then we should have a good Greek construction: '*gnōrizō to euanggelion, tini logō*,' etc. = 'I make known to you with what words I announced the Gospel to you'. But then '*katechete*' is left without an object.

(2) As is done by Godet and J.W., '*tini logō*' could be subordinated to '*katechete*' = 'if you hold fast in what way,' etc. This construction is rather awkward: '*ei katechete*' would normally precede '*tini logō*'. Further, as Baljon[2] points out, an accusative would be preferable with *katechō*. However, the construction is not absolutely wrong.

(3) Following John Chrysostom, a full stop may be placed after '*sōzesthe*' and '*tini logō*' made into a direct question, with '*touto*' understood as the object of '*katechete*'. 'With what words did I proclaim it to you? If you hold it fast,' etc. But then we have an anacoluthon to deal with, since the relative clause beginning with '*ei*' is not followed by a main clause.

It is understandable that emendations have been attempted both in ancient times and more recently. Thus D and G read '*opheilete katechein*' in place of '*ei katechete*'. In that case a full stop would also be needed after '*sōzesthe*', and the translation would be: 'You ought to hold fast the words with which I preached the Gospel to you.' It is an attempt to improve the text, which succeeds in overcoming the difficulty, but which seems rather arbitrary. It would be simpler to read '*ho katechete*', as does Alfred Seeberg,[3] and to place it after '*ho parelabete, en hō stēkete, di hou sōzesthe*'. Unfortunately, the last phrase ('*ho katechete*') is separated from the others by '*tini logō*,' etc., and the attachment of this question presents the same difficulties of construction as before.

(4) It could also be supposed that the original text included '*ei katechete kathōs opheilete katechein*'. The text of the majority of authorities would stem from an omission caused by haplography, whereas D and G may have preserved odd scraps of the original text. But this is very hypothetical. We prefer, after full consideration, not to make conjectures, but to adopt Godet's construction (2).

'*Anamimnēsko*' might be expected in **15¹** rather than '*gnōrizō*'. But the verb '*gnōrizō*' can well bear the sense of 'recall', as in Galatians

---

[2] Op. cit. above on 4⁶.
[3] *Der Katechismus der Urchristenheit* (1903), p. 48.

1¹¹.—The gospel proper, that is the message of Jesus–Kyrios, is distinguished here from the words by which Paul proclaimed it. These turn out to be a precise formula, as 15³ᶠᶠ show.

The Gospel was accepted ('*parelabete*'), and the Corinthians remained faithful to it ('*hestēkate*'); but they are really saved by it ('*sōzesthe*') only if they keep in mind the reasons adduced by Paul as a foundation for the faith and without which conversion ('*episteusate*' = 'you began to be believers') would be equivalent to baseless credulity, and to that degree it would be a blind belief, lacking profound conviction, and consequently incapable of really lifting men from the doubt and despair which will attack them sooner or later. So here an examination of the foundations of the Christian conviction of resurrection is involved.

Some exegetes have shied at the accumulation of particles '*ektos ei mē*', as also in 14⁵. It is not clear why; for '*ektos*' means 'outside', and '*ektos ei*', 'apart from the case where' (examples from secular usage are quoted by J.W.).

15³. '*En prōtois*' cannot be masculine. It would be too obvious an exaggeration to rank the Corinthians among the first to be reached by this Pauline '*paradosis*' = 'tradition'. We shall therefore take '*prōtois*' as a neuter = '*in primis*' = 'among the first and most important elements taught.' '*Ho kai parelabon*' = 'which I had received' reminds us, as does 11²³, that the tradition is older than Paul's preaching. The phrase '*para kuriou*' = 'from the Lord' is lacking here. There can be no doubt that the Apostle is restating a Church tradition, which he had doubtless received earlier in Damascus.⁴

Where does it end? At the latest before '*eschaton de pantōn*' (15⁸), where Paul speaks of himself. But probably even before 15⁵; for from this point on, the statement loses its measured rhythm and seems to be added by Paul to give the proof of the preceding affirmations. We believe, then, that 15³⁻⁴ may be identified with the '*euanggelion*' (comparable to the Mishnah) and 15⁵⁻⁸ with the Pauline '*logos*' (as it were, the Gemara).

Examine first the 'Gospel'. It consists of a three-lined strophe, in which the first and third lines include the phrase '*kata tas graphas*' = 'according to the Scriptures'. This is rather perplexing, for it is not easy to find in the Old Testament precise texts proclaiming the atoning death and the resurrection of a Saviour. For the atoning death, one might think of the 'Servant of Yahweh' of Isaiah 53. But we know that the Jews of antiquity never regarded this as an allusion to the Messiah.⁵ Did the Pauline Christians do so? Peter's speeches

---

⁴ On the distinction between two traditions in the statement 15³ᶠᶠ, see PAUL WINTER, *Novum Testamentum* (Leyden, April 1957), pp. 142ff.

⁵ See the all-important but too little known works of DALMAN, '*Jesajas 53*' (Berlin, 1891) and '*Der leidende und sterbende Messias der Synagoge im ersten nachchristlichen Jahrtausend*' (Berlin, 1888). Cf. our article 'Messie juif et Messie

in the Acts of the Apostles, the importance of which for early Christian history cannot be doubted, make no reference to it. The most developed of these sermons (Acts 2¹⁴⁻³⁶) speaks only of an ancient decision of God concerning the ignominious death of Jesus the Nazarene,[6] without referring either to the Ebed-Yahweh, or to any other prediction in the Scriptures. It is true that Acts 3¹³ calls Jesus '*pais Theou*' = 'servant of God' (which is the translation of עֶבֶד יְהֹוָה: in the LXX); but this is not in connection with the death, but only with the ascension, a point which does not arise in Isaiah. In Acts 3¹⁸ Peter refers to a prediction of the passion 'in all the prophets'. This is almost as vague as the Pauline phrase '*kata tas graphas*'. Acts 4¹¹ quotes Psalm 117²² (118²²) and identifies Christ with the well-known stone which the builders rejected; but this is not very precise, however. From Acts 5³⁰ and 10⁴⁰ we might think that the expression '*kremasantes epi xulou*' = 'hanging him on a tree' contains an allusion to Deuteronomy 21²²; but the would involve a very unobtrusive and questionable way of quoting the Scriptures. Further, Deuteronomy speaks only in a general way of those who have committed a sin worthy of death.[7] It is only at the meeting between Philip and the Ethiopian eunuch (Acts 8³²⁻³) that a precise text is brought forward: Isaiah 53⁷⁻⁸, quoted incompletely and notably omitting the phrase 'because of the sins of my people'.

To summarize, it can be affirmed that three phases should be distinguished in the evolution of scriptural proof of the Messiah's death: (*a*) the presentation of Christ's death, so scandalous in Jewish eyes, is limited to the statement that it conforms to the divine plan; (*b*) the conviction that it *must* be in accordance with the Scriptures; (*c*) an attempt, in a groping way, to look for precise texts on the subject in the Old Testament. Our text, **15³**, obviously belongs to the second phase. It is doubtful whether the Apostle ever went beyond that (except for a reference in Galatians 3¹³). Yet he makes extensive use of biblical texts to corroborate other theologoumena, such as salvation by faith, the universality of sin, the tribulation of Christians, predestination, the salvation of the Gentiles.—Similar remarks could be made about supposed scriptural proofs of the resurrection.[8] Another explanation would be that the liturgical formula used by

chrétien', in *RHPR* (1938), No. 5/6, as well as those of SEIDELIN, 'Der Ebed-Jahwe und die Messias-Gestalt im Jesajas-Targum' (*ZNTW* [1936], pp. 194ff), and of PAUL HUMBERT, Le Messie dans le Targum des Prophètes (*RTP* [1910], pp. 420ff and [1911], pp. 1ff).

[6] '*tē hōrismenē boulē kai prognōsei tou Theou*', **15²³**.

[7] Our reasons for ascribing great antiquity to Peter's speeches cannot be developed here. On this subject see our *Royaume de Dieu* (particularly Ch. 9).

[8] The difficulty of finding scriptural proof of the passion and resurrection of the Messiah is one of the strongest arguments in favour of the historicity of these great facts which are at the basis of Christianity. Cf. G. BALDENSPERGER, 'L'historicité de Jésus' (*RHPR* [1935], pp. 193-209).

Paul alludes to some lost apocryphal writings, perhaps of the same sort as were read among the Essenes. An hypothesis of this kind has been advanced in the book by Max Maurenbrecher: *Von Nazareth nach Golgatha*.[9] But it goes without saying that such statements can neither be substantiated nor refuted[10]—in spite of Qumran. Why does the formula insist on the burial of Christ?[11] Doubtless it was to combat gnostic and docetist ideas which contested the reality of Christ's death.[12] Or is there here a veiled allusion to something like the descent into 'hell'? Without passing judgement on the original meaning of the formula, which we shall perhaps never know, we consider it improbable that Paul had this doctrine in mind—a doctrine to which he never refers.[13] The mention in 15[4] of the third day has released floods of ink; for the question has been raised whether the rare allusions or supposed allusions to the third day in the Old Testament justified this precision.[14] But after what we have just explained about the force of *'kata tas graphas'*, we can no longer ask such questions, and even less when it is very doubtful whether the reference to Scripture relates to this chronological detail. If the formula stresses the third day, it is simply to state an historical fact. The second or the fourth might just as well have been spoken of, if the event of the resurrection had taken place on another day.[15] For it was not with ideas, but with facts that the oldest narrative about Christ was written.

The meaning of *'egēgertai'* = 'he was raised up' will become clear in the light of the following verses. From 15[5] onwards the Apostle gives proofs of the historicity of the resurrection, not by the empty tomb, of which he never speaks, but by the appearances. In order to understand their full significance, we must not give a subjective sense to *'ōphthē'* = 'he appeared'. In ancient usage this verb can be

---

[9] Berlin, Schöneberg, 1909.

[10] The height of thoughtlessness is reached by VOLLMER, *A.T.-liche Zitate bei Paulus* (Freibourg and Leipzig, 1895), who thinks that Paul quotes no texts, because they were too well-known (pp. 52ff).

[11] *'Kai hoti etaphē'* is not followed by *'kata tas graphas'*. Perhaps this omission is evidence of the secondary character of this part of the sentence; but there is no room for doubting that it formed an integral part of the formula known to Paul.

[12] On the antiquity of the docetist danger, see G. BALDENSPERGER, 'La gnose', in *Trois études sur le Christianisme primitif*, III. (*RHPR* [1939], pp. 214ff). In the confession of faith of IGNATIUS OF ANTIOCH, an antidocetist concern is shown even more clearly; see *The Epistle to the Trallians*, §9: *'alēthōs egennēthē'*, etc.

[13] Philippians 2[10] (the *'katachthonioi'* will bow before the Kyrios) proves nothing; for this is a future event. Moreover, as LOHMEYER has shown in *Kyrios Jesus* (*Sitzungsberichte der Heidelberger Akademie, philol.-histor. Klasse* [1927-8], No. 4), the psalm in Philippians 2[6-11] was borrowed by Paul from an earlier tradition.

[14] Hosea 6[2]: 'He will heal us after two days; and the third day we shall rise up again' (*'en tē tritē hēmera kai anastēsometha'*). On the other hand, Mark 8[31], 9[31], 10[34] and par. give *'meta treis hēmeras'*.

[15] The Hebrews, like the Greeks and Romans in such cases, counted the starting day as the first. Thus the Sunday was the third day after the Friday.

employed for an objective vision, that is, for an appearance not discernible by the eyes of all.[16]

The first appearance, the one to Peter, is doubtless the one referred to in Luke 24[34]; we do not know why the Synoptic writers do not attach more importance to it.

The second appearance is the one to the Twelve. Here we have two readings: (*a*) D and G read '*meta tauta tois hendeka*' = 'then to the Eleven'; (*b*) almost all the other authorities give '*eita*' (or '*epeita*') '*tois dōdeka*' = 'then to the Twelve'.[17] Since some manuscripts give a combination of the two, J.W. draws the conclusion that this appearance was not mentioned at all in the original manuscript, but that this lacuna was filled in two different ways by readers of a generation after A.D. 70, who knew of the appearance to the Twelve through the Gospels. But this duality can be easily explained in the following way: reading (*b*) is ancient, but a rather pedantic copyist replaced twelve by eleven for reasons of historical accuracy; similarly '*eita*' was replaced by '*meta tauta*', for reasons of style, in order to avoid the repetition '*eita-epeita*' (or '*epeita-epeita*') in 15[5] and 15[6]. As the Gospels record several appearances of this type, it is difficult to identify the one referred to in this verse.

The appearance to the five hundred is not mentioned either in the Gospels or in Acts, unless it is equated to the descent of the Holy Spirit recorded in Acts 2[18]; but such a suggestion seems very speculative. It may refer to an appearance in Galilee where Jesus must have had many disciples. Nevertheless, it is obvious why the Apostle insists on the fact that the majority of these five hundred are still alive.

The fourth vision is the appearance to James, perhaps also in Galilee; here we can guess why the Synoptics and the Acts do not speak of it, for these writings seek to bring to the fore the authority of the Twelve and especially of Peter and to play down that of James, who was the real head of the Church in Jerusalem.[19] The

---

[16] In connection with 15[5-8], J.W. remarks that the Apostle is unaware of the tradition of Acts (1[8]), according to which the risen Christ lived forty days continually with the disciples. But it is not certain that the expression '*optanomenos di' hēmerōn tessarakonta*' has this sense. It might merely recall that there were sporadic appearances spread over a period of forty days. However, we will grant to the illustrious scholar that the remark as given in Acts 1[3] suggests a greater number of appearances than that given by Paul. It goes without saying that the definite references of the Apostle give us an older tradition than Acts 1[3]. Cf. on this subject and on all connected questions, C. R. BOWEN, *The Resurrection in the N.T.* (London, 1911), and M. GOGUEL, *La foi en la résurrection de Jésus dans le christianisme primitif* (*Bibliothèque de l'Ecole des Hautes études, sciences religieuses*, Vol. XLVII [Leroux, 1933]). O. CULLMANN, *La foi à la résurrection et l'espérance de la résurrection dans le N.T.* (*ETR* [1943], pp. 3ff), *Immortality of the Soul or Resurrection of the Dead?* (London, 1958).

[17] P 46 is defective.

[18] E. v. DOBSCHÜTZ, *Ostern und Pfingsten* (Leipzig, 1903), pp. 33ff.

[19] See M. GOGUEL, 'Tu es Petrus', *Bulletin de la Faculté Libre de théologie protestante de Paris* (July 1938); also his *The Birth of Christianity* (Tr. Snape [London, 1953], Ch. 2).

(12) But if Christ is preached as raised from the dead, how is it that some of you declare: 'There is no resurrection of the dead'? (13) If there be no resurrection of the dead, then Christ has not been raised either. (14) Now if Christ has not been raised, then our preaching is baseless, and so is your faith. (15) And we find we are false witnesses of God, for we witnessed before God that he had raised up Christ—whom however, he did not raise, since 'the dead are not raised'. (16) For if the dead are not raised, neither is Christ risen. (17) Now, if Christ be not risen, your faith is illusory, you are yet in your sins, (18) and moreover the dead Christians are lost. (19) But if it is only within the bounds of this life that we had placed our hope in Christ, we should be the most wretched of all men.

Fourth Gospel similarly favours the disciple 'whom Jesus loved'. This appearance is also mentioned in the Gospel according to the Hebrews.[20]

The fifth appearance, the one to all the apostles, is in no way a mere repetition of the second; for Paul, who does not know of appearances in great numbers, insists on mentioning two successive appearances. Further, '*pasin apostolois*' includes a wider group than the Twelve, and in particular the Lord's brothers, perhaps Barnabas also, and others, to whom Paul did not refuse the title of apostles.

15⁸⁻¹¹. The vision on the Damascus road is assimilated to the earlier ones, though it took place later than the Lord's ascension recorded in Luke's Gospel and in the Acts. But it is the last ('*eschaton . . . kamoi*'). '*Ektrōma*' is not a 'late birth', as the context might suggest, but the very opposite. And so the point of comparison does not lie in the timing of the Apostle's conversion, but in the idea of inferiority and unworthiness. In fact '*ektrōma*' was an offensive word. The article '*tō*' before '*ektrōmati*' might even suggest that others had already applied this coarse and insulting word to him; but a Semitism might also be involved, since Hebrew likes to use an article in comparisons ('to roll up the heavens like *the* book' says Isaiah 34⁴ in the Massoretic text). In any event the Apostle accepts or adopts the term, because he had persecuted Christians (Gal 1¹³, Acts 9¹⁻²). It is even more certain that he owes his apostolic position, his perseverance in the work ('*perissoteron . . . ekopiasa*'),[21] the success of his preaching ('*ou kenē . . . egenēthē*') solely to the grace of God. But in 15¹¹ the author returns to the main topic, the content of the Christian '*kērugma*' (cf. 15³⁻⁴), which is the same in the mouths of all the apostles.

15¹²⁻¹⁹. Some Corinthians, without denying the resurrection of

---

[20] See M. R. JAMES: *The Apocryphal N.T.* (Oxford, 1926), p. 3.
[21] SCHLATTER (p. 403) thinks that Paul is alluding to those of his fellow-workers who had left him on the journey, such as Mark (Acts 13¹³), Barnabas (Acts 15³⁹) and possibly others.

Christ, declared that of Christians to be impossible, for reasons of a general nature. The Apostle replies by a *reductio ad absurdum*, which he first develops in 15^{12-15}, and resumes in 15^{16-17}. This argument takes place in two stages: (1) If resurrection, in a general sense, is impossible, that of Christ is not real either (15^{13} and 15^{16}). This conclusion supposes that Christ was raised as a human being—a view in conformity with the whole of Paul's Christology. The incarnate Christ had divested Himself of His divine glory to be merely the servant of God. His resurrection is therefore a miracle of God. This miracle could not have taken place, if resurrection were absolutely impossible.

(2) But without the Lord's resurrection the Christian faith is empty, i.e. without foundation (15^{14} and 15^{17}). Then Christians would still be in their sins. Now, this conclusion—here is the underlying idea—would be absurd; for we know from the supernatural experience of the Church that the Holy Spirit is a reality and that we are removed from the grip of evil powers.

It goes without saying that with unbelievers this *reductio ad absurdum* would lose all its force. For the conclusion envisaged—the futility of faith—they would accept. Luther saw this very clearly: 'But this seems a very weak dialectic or proof before pagans, who deny not only the article which it seeks to prove, but also all that the Apostle adduces for the proof, and this is called '*probare per negatum et petere principium*'.' [22] But he adds,[23] 'I have stated that it is a preaching-theme for Christians, who believe the article of Christ's resurrection and know its power.'

15^{18-19} complete the argument, showing that the negative conclusion is very saddening. It would have to be drawn, however, if Christ were not risen. Then those Christians who had died already, would have fallen into nothingness, and it is extremely significant that the verb '*apōlonto*' = 'they are lost' is the same one used of unbelievers, to indicate their disappearance into the death that engulfs them.[24] Another conclusion is that Christians would be more wretched than other men. Why? Because the Christian would renounce earthly joy to be a martyr to an illusion.

The translation of 15^{19} is much more difficult than most scholars admit. The perfect '*ēlpikotes esmen*' is certainly quite easy to explain: it is equivalent to a future perfect in an hypothetical construction: 'if it were confirmed that the dead had hoped.' But to which part of the sentence must '*monon*' = 'only' be attached? To '*en tē zōē tautē*' = 'in this life'? But the idea of a hope to cheer us during the future life

---

[22] Erlangen edition, LI.120.
[23] Ibid. p. 121.
[24] '*Apōlonto*' can naturally be taken also as a synonym of '*apōlonto an*'. This would then be a hypothetical construction ('they would be lost'). In that case '*esti*' is naturally also equivalent to '*estin an*'. But this makes no essential change in the reasoning.

(20) *But in truth, Christ is risen from the dead in the forefront of the departed.* (21) *For since it was through a man that death supervened, the resurrection of the dead likewise took place through a man.* (22) *For as all die because of their link with Adam, so shall all be restored to life through their link with Christ.* (23) *But each in his own rank. The vanguard is Christ, then will come those who are Christians at the time of the Parousia;* (24) *then—it will be the end, when he returns the kingdom to God the Father, after utterly destroying every*

as well makes little sense, because that life is envisaged as bringing the fulfilment of all hopes. This consideration impels J.W. to attach '*monon*' to '*ēlpikotes*' and to translate: 'if during this life we have only hoped, etc. . . .', that is, 'if it were confirmed that our hope has no fulfilment'. We, however, cannot get rid of the impression that this way of expressing things is not at all Pauline. The Apostle might rather have said something like: '*hē elpis hēmōn mataia estai*' = 'our hope will be vain'. Moreover it seems to us that the pronoun '*tautē*' calls for the adverb '*monon*': 'in this life only.' In order to avoid the snag seen by J.W., we shall give to '*en tautē*' a rather wider sense: 'within the framework of this life' or 'for this life only.' One can indeed hope in Christ and in God also for this life, in which the Christian continually needs supernatural help. But it is normal that hope should also have an object in the future.[25]

Note also that the two '*en*' in 15[19] do not have the same force.

In 15[20], Paul returns to reality, 'but in truth' ('*nuni de*' has an adversative sense as almost always) 'Christ is risen'. We know it through witnesses and by the reality of His power. However, before drawing the conclusions, the author alludes (15[21-7]) to the contrasting roles of the two Adams, a theme developed at greater length in Romans 5. Adam, by his Fall was the first dead man and drew humanity along in the wake of his death; Christ in His capacity as the second Adam, is the first of the risen; the word '*aparchē*' = 'first-fruits' being almost

---

[25] KARL BARTH rightly quotes Luther (Erlangen edn, LI.132-5), who brings in the same verdict as the Apostle. The quotation is too long to be reproduced here.—We might also see in 15[19] proof that Paul would have rejected with horror Pascal's famous wager, because he wants certainties. But this would omit the fact that the wager was proposed to unbelievers only, whereas the Apostle is speaking to believers. So there is no common factor in the two lines of reasoning.

Elsewhere, W. BOUSSET (*Die Schriften des N.T.*, II [Göttingen, 1908], p. 151) remarks: 'On the contrary, we are of the opinion that even if there were no hope of eternal life, a life lived in faithfulness to the spirit of Jesus would be superior to and happier than, a life of uninterrupted sensuality.' To Christians who might be tempted to speak like this great theologian, who was also a great Christian, we would reply by this question: 'Is not this way of seeing life as a total sacrifice offered to Christ, the proof that you are, because of the resurrection of Christ and its shattering effects in the invisible world, already freed from the power of death and darkness? Then is not the hypothesis of your being engulfed by death, which you think of only as an unreal contingency, also quite impossible and even absurd?'

rule and every authority and power. (25) For he must reign until he has put all enemies beneath his feet, (26) and the last enemy which will be destroyed is death. (27) Indeed, 'God has subjected all the universe under his feet'. But when it is said: 'All is subjected', it is clear that it is with the exception of him who made the universe subject to him. (28) And when the universe has been subjected to him, then the Son himself will submit to the one who made the universe subject to him, that God may be present in the whole universe and completely.

synonymous with '*arrabōn*' = 'earnest', because the resurrection of others is still in the future. He will bring the resurrection of the new humanity, that is of Christians, the only ones for whom the word '*kekoimēmenoi*' = 'those who are asleep' is used, as Ed. Reuss points out.[26]

Much weight is sometimes given to the words '*pantes zōopoiothēsontai*' = 'all shall be restored to life' (15[22]) in order to assert the universality of the resurrection in Paul's teaching, that is, a resurrection of the elect and of all others. But we shall see that this interpretation utterly contradicts his eschatology. If we look more closely at the meaning of 15[20-2] we shall see that each of the two Adams acts as the head of a humanity—the old and the new. Now, not all men, but Christians only who belong to the body of Christ form the new humanity. That is the meaning of '*en*' (15[22]), which connotes the respective belonging to Adam or to Christ. Now, we repeat, all men are not 'in Christ'. So we are in the presence of two humanities, each one having an 'Adam' as its founder and head. '*Pantes*' should therefore be taken *cum grano salis* as 'all who depend on Christ'.[27] Naturally Christians belong also to the old humanity through their earthly birth. That is why some Christians have already died before the Lord's return (15[18]). But they too share in the resurrection through belonging to Christ. Conversely, those who belong to the first Adam only—this is the inevitable conclusion—will not rise again.

It is true that mention of a resurrection of non-Christians has been sought in the next verses. Let us look more closely at this passage (15[23-4]). The noun '*tagma*' can mean a troop or in a more general way a group occupying a particular rank.[28] But the fact is that the first group is constituted by Christ alone and we must therefore translate '*tagma*' by 'rank'.

The second rank is assigned to Christians who will rise at the

[26] *La Bible*, N.T., part 3, Epistles of Paul, Vol. I (Paris, 1878), p. 259. Cf. 7[39], 11[30], 15[6], 1 Thessalonians 4[13]; and also Matthew 27[52], Acts 7[60].
[27] 'When he says, "All shall have life in Christ", he cannot mean all human beings in general, for the simple reason that all are not in Christ; he means: all those who are in Christ shall have life, precisely because they are in Christ, who is the author or the cause of that life which is henceforth indestructible.' Ed. REUSS, ibid., p. 260.
[28] In the Epistle of Clement of Rome to the Corinthians, 37[3], we read: 'All are not generals or captains..., but each one is in his place' ('*ou pantes eisin eparchoi ē chiliarchoi . . ., all' hekastos en tō idiō tagmati*').

moment of the Parousia, that is at the Lord's coming. Then a mention of a third '*tagma*' might be expected. But, instead of speaking of it, the author puts in the third place—'the end', that is the events between the Parousia and the final establishment of the Kingdom of God (see **15²⁴ᵇ** from the first '*hotan*' as far as **15²⁸**). As verb for the subject '*telos*' = 'the end', '*estai*' must be added (we shall denote this translation by A).

Some scholars, such as Lietzmann, followed by J.W., attempt to dodge this point, which is misleading at first sight, by translating '*telos*' by 'the rest', i.e. 'the remainder of men' (translation B). In this case the verb understood would be '*zōopoiēthēsontai*'. But this translation seems impossible, because we have been unable to find a single text, sacred or secular, in which '*telos*' has this sense.[29]

A third translation (translation C), advanced by v. Hofmann[30] and used again by Karl Barth, takes '*to telos*' as an adverb (= 'finally'), as beginning a sentence which continues with '. . . *eschatos echthros*', etc. (**15²⁶**). **15²⁴ᵇ**, that is the two phrases beginning with '*hotan*', as well as the parenthesis of **15²⁵**, then merely lead up to '*katargeitai*' in **15²⁶**. It must be agreed that a complicated construction of this sort is not impossible in our author. The adverbial use of '*to telos*', is attested by 1 Peter 3⁸: '*to telos pantes homophrones*', etc. = 'Finally, be all of one mind', etc.

Since translation B ('*to telos*' = 'the rest') seems impossible, there remains the choice between A ('then will come the end') and C, which has just been outlined. But whatever our choice may be, it must be recognized that there is no question of the resurrection of the non-elect.[31] This fact will not surprise readers who meditate on the import of the explications which follow of what resurrection means (**15⁵¹⁻⁵**). These exclude radically any resurrection other than a resurrection in glory, the one which German theologians sometimes called 'the joyous resurrection'; and we further point out that the words '*apollumenoi*' = 'those who are going to destruction', is a synonym for unbelievers.[32]

[29] See the detailed demonstration in our article: 'Saint Paul a-t-il enseigné deux résurrections?' (*RHPR* [1932], pp. 300–20, and particularly p. 304, note 3).— ALLO came to the same conclusion; see his article in the *RB* (April 1932), called 'Saint Paul et la double résurrection corporelle'. He upheld this point of view in his commentary. And O. CULLMANN is similarly of our opinion; see his *Christology of the New Testament* (Tr. Filson, 1959).

[30] *Die heiligen Schriften des N.T.*, II.II.366–7. (Nordlingen, 1864).

[31] 'Paul is concerned utterly and only with those who will be called to the life of glory, in conformity with that of the risen Christ. Throughout this chapter, he leaves the damned in the shade. One would be hard put to understand whether he thinks that the unfortunate ones condemned to eternal death will be "given life in Christ". Consequently, and on this score alone, '*to telos*' has little chance of meaning "the others", that is to say those who do not belong to Christ and who, at the resurrection, will not obtain salvation.' ALLO, *RB* (1932), pp. 8–9.

[32] Judaism of the time had two conceptions of resurrection, namely: (*a*) resurrection of the elect alone; (*b*) resurrection of all men. In support of (*a*), 2 Maccabees 7⁹, ²³ (and doubtless 14⁴⁶ also) and Psalms of Solomon 14³⁻⁷ might be quoted. In support of (*b*) 2 Esdras 7³², Apocalypse of Baruch 50–1; Ethiopian

But why does the Apostle express himself in 15^{23a} in such a way as to lead us to believe in several '*tagmata*' (at least three)? We think that a third group really did exist in the author's mind, namely that mentioned in 1 Thessalonians 4^{16-17}. There events unfold in three stages: (*a*) the appearance of Christ, which presupposes naturally his resurrection and his ascension; (*b*) the resurrection of dead Christians; (*c*) the transformation of Christians still alive. But in 15^{24} the Apostle makes no express mention of the third group, because his thought is concentrated on the resurrection proper.[33] In any event, it seems clear that if the Apostle had believed in a resurrection of the non-elect, this would have been the time to mention them and this chapter the place!

It remains to choose between the two possible ways of construing the passage 15^{24-6}, and consequently between the two interpretations called A and C above. If after full reflection we opt for A,[34] that is, '*eita to telos estai*', it is because this is a simpler form of expression and has a parallel in 2 Esdras 7^{33} ('then shall come the end').[35] But we admit that it is to some extent a matter of personal opinion.

The succession of the two '*hotan*' is an aesthetic fault which none of the three translations can eradicate. The logical connection between the two subordinate clauses is as follows: the second '*hotan*' states the condition to be fulfilled before power is handed over to the Father, namely that the hostile powers which were already conquered on the Cross, must be finally destroyed. The parenthesis in 15^{25} is intended as explanation of this truth. The parenthesis is not superfluous, for it eliminates possible misunderstandings on the nature of the Kingdom of the Son, that is of the Messianic Kingdom according to Paul's thought. Its reason for existence is the destruction of enemies which oppose the effective power of God, and in so doing prevent the complete and visible coming of His Kingdom. When does this battle begin? At the Cross, as we have just been reminded, followed almost immediately by the resurrection and the ascension of the Son of God to Heaven, where He receives a title which He bore neither in His earthly life, nor in His pre-existence,

---

Enoch 51^1, and Testament of Benjamin 10. The Tannaim were divided over this much-discussed question (G. F. MOORE, *Judaism in the First Centuries of the Christian Era*, II.VII (Harvard U.P., 1927)). Jewish theology cannot, therefore, enlighten us on this point. Still less can we get support from the Revelation of John, whose eschatology is very different from Paul's; it teaches for instance, the coming in the future of a millenial kingdom, of which we can find no trace in the letters of Paul. The few texts in the Gospels, reproduce one or the other of the Jewish conceptions: for (*a*) see Luke 14^{14}, for (*b*) see Mark 12^{25-6} and par.

[33] A three-stage formula is indeed preserved in the Testament of Benjamin 10^{6-8}. We can give this summary of it: the resurrection of (1) the Patriarchs down to Jacob, (2) 'us' (the twelve tribes, no doubt), (3) 'all'.—A curious tripartite formula from the Parsees is preserved for us in the *Bundahish* 30^7, reproduced in note 8 of our article quoted above.

[34] With BACHMANN ('*dann der Abschluss*', p. 447).

[35] KAUTZSCH, p. 371; CHARLES, *Apocrypha and Pseudepigrapha*, II.583.

namey the title of '*kurios*'.[36] This Messianic Kingdom (and there is no other in Paul's thought) ends at the Parousia, or shortly afterwards, when death is destroyed. Why is the destruction of death specially proclaimed? Because the kingdom of death, that is Sheol or Hades, forms an obstacle to the all-mightiness of God. According to the Jewish conception it was as though His power ceased, indeed, at the gates of Hell. Thus it was said that the dead cannot praise God.[37]

The end of the empire of death (see the hymn of victory in 15^{55} below) precludes the possibility of something like 'everlasting torment'. What becomes of the rejected? It has already been said: together with our world, they will cease to exist and will share the fate of the 'hostile powers', which will be destroyed. 15^{25} quotes Psalm 109^1 (110^1), and 15^{27}, Psalm 8^7, freely be it said; this is to give scriptural support to the author's conception of the Messianic Kingdom, and to stress that nothing occurs without the powerful will of God. But 15^{25} and 15^{26} are worth the trouble of closer examination to find out what are the subjects of the verbs '*thē*' (15^{25}) = 'he has put' and '*hupetaxen*' (15^{27}) = 'he has subjected'. In 15^{27}, it can only be God: it is the Father who subjects the world to the Messiah. This interpretation is confirmed by 15^{28}, where the Son finally 'subjects Himself to Him who subjected the universe to Him', that is to God. This view is also that of the Psalmist. But in 15^{25} the subject of '*thē*' is perhaps Christ. Why stress the subordination of the Son to God, as also in 15^{27} and 15^{28}? Perhaps to make it clear that the Son is not a revolutionary god in the style of the Greek gods who oust the ancient gods—Saturn dethrones Uranus only to be ousted in his turn by Jupiter—and as the unknown God of Marcion dispossesses the God of the Old Testament. Moreover, it goes without saying that even the final extinction of the dignity of *Kurios*, to which He has been raised (Phil 2^9), in no way involves the loss of His nature as the Son of God and the Image of God, which He has had since His pre-existence.

What does 15^{28b} mean: '*hina ē Theos panta*' (or '*ta panta*' according to the Textus Receptus and ℵ) '*en pasin*'? '*En pasin*' must be neuter (on that point there is agreement) and mean 'in the whole universe'. But if '*panta*' is an attributive nominative, which is the usual interpretation, it must be translated as 'God is all in all'. However, we are not sure of the accuracy of this interpretation. '*Panta*' might easily be the Greek accusative, so that the sentence might mean: 'that God may be in every respect' (or 'completely') 'in the universe',—whereas at present His dominion is only partial. What makes us opt for this translation is that the first has two unsurmountable difficulties: (*a*) The equating of '*Theos*' ('God') with '*ta panta*' ('everything'), implicit in that rendering, would teach a pantheism unknown in the Bible (cf. our remarks on 8^6 on this topic). (*b*) If this equation were admitted,

[36] See the exegesis of Philippians 2^{6-11} in our article, 'Kyrios Anthropos' *RHPR* (1936), pp. 196–209.
[37] See especially Psalm 113^{25} (114^{17}), Isaiah 38^{18-19}; cf. Matthew 22^{32}.

(29) *Otherwise what will those who are baptized for the dead achieve?
If the dead have absolutely no resurrection, why are they still baptized
for them?* (30) *Why do we also risk dangers every hour?* (31) *Every day
I go to death, brothers, as truly as I boast of you in Christ Jesus our
Lord.* (32) *If, with a merely human outlook, I had fought against beasts
in Ephesus, what use would it have been to me? If the dead are not
raised, then 'let us eat and drink, for tomorrow we die'.*

the complement '*en pasin*' = 'in all' would be a stupid pleonasm. We
render it then: 'in the whole universe and completely.' It is 'pan-en-
theism', that is to say an affirmation of the total and visible
presence of the Kingdom of God.

15²⁹ has since ancient times given rise to various interpretations
(Godet has counted thirty), which it is impossible to list here.[38]
Following Tertullian, Ambrosiaster thought that some Christians
had themselves baptized (it should really be, re-baptized) on behalf
of others who had died suddenly without baptism, so that the latter
might participate equally in the grace bestowed by this sacrament.
Tertullian adds that this custom is mentioned by the Apostle though
he did not approve of it. Paul may simply have wished to show-up
the contradiction of those who while rejecting the resurrection, practised a rite which in that case was nonsensical. Further, baptism by
proxy was still practised by certain sects at a relatively late date,
particularly by the Marcionites, the Montanists and the Cerinthians.[39]

Lietzmann and J.W. suppose that it was indeed an early rite at first
tolerated in the Church, then forbidden, but surviving in some sects.

[38] As curios, here are a few of those interpretations which deny baptism by
proxy. LUTHER: 'What is meant is baptism on the tombs of the dead.' But '*huper*'
never has this locative sense in the New Testament. Besides it is difficult to see
the connection of these tombs with the resurrection.—CALVIN: 'Christians in
danger of dying called for baptism, in order to be baptized "as dead".' But then
it would be necessary to read '*hōs nekroi*'.—Similarly BENGEL: '*qui mox post
baptismum ad mortuos aggregabantur*.' This explanation is impossible for the same
reason.—BACHMANN: 'They have themselves baptized on their own behalf as
being about to die' ('*für sich als die künftig Toten*', p. 458). In this case the
omission of '*autōn*' or '*heautōn*' between '*huper*' and '*tōn nekrōn*' would be very
strange. Only '*huper autōn*' in 15²⁹ᵇ might, at a pinch, be explained in this way
(the correct reading of 15²⁹ᵇ is in fact '*huper autōn*').—W. SIGRIST (*Kirchenblatt
für die reformierte Schweiz* [1942], pp. 18ff) takes up Luther's interpretation.
again. But this opinion is contested by E. VISCHER (ibid. [1942], pp. 43ff), CHR.
MAURER (*ibid.* [1942], pp. 57ff) and K. L. SCHMIDT (*ibid.*, pp. 70ff).

[39] For the Marcionites, see TERTULLIAN, *Adversus Marcionem* 5.10 (*CSEL*
XLVII.605), as well as JOHN CHRYSOSTOM (*MPG* LXI, col. 347); for the Cerinthians
—EPIPHANIUS, *Haereses* 28 (*MPG* XLI, col. 384 C—385 A); for the Montanists—
PHILASTER, *Haereses* 49: '*hi mortuos baptizant*' (*MPL* XII, col. 1166 A). According
to ALBERT SCHWEITZER, *Mysticism of Paul the Apostle*, pp. 279, 285, this baptism,
as the sacraments generally, was to ensure the baptized of an early resurrection,
allowing them to share in the Messianic Kingdom. This Kingdom would be
followed by the general resurrection. It is a very ingenious interpretation, but
we do not think that Paul expected a Kingdom of the Son in the future. See our
commentary on 15²⁵⁻⁸ above, and note 29 p. 166.

This explanation raises no philological problems; for '*huper*' certainly has the sense of 'on behalf of' or even 'instead of'. Nor is it necessary to object that Paul would have had to protest against the rite, because, in his view, baptism can be granted only to those who already have faith. For nothing prevents the supposition that baptism by proxy was administered only in such cases. Yet it must be noted that any interpretation, whatever it be, encounters a quite serious grammatical difficulty in the fact that '*poiein*' = 'to do' is used in the future tense. Why does Paul not say: 'What are they doing, those who allow themselves to be baptized for the dead?' but 'What will they do . . .?' Von Hofmann takes this detail into account; also he attaches '*huper tōn nekrōn*' to '*poiēsousin*'. Then the sense would be: 'What will the baptized, i.e. the Christians, still be able to do for those who have died?' But why then have '*baptizomenoi*' ('present') and not '*baptisthentes*' or '*bebaptismenoi*' ('past')?[40] Godet also gives an interpretation which should do justice to the future '*poiēsousin*', and which is at first sight more attractive than von Hofmann's. 15³⁰⁻¹, in which the Apostle speaks insistently on the danger of death ('*kinduneuomen*' = 'we risk dangers', '*apothnēsko*' = 'I go to death', '*ethēriomachēsa*' = 'I fought beasts'), leads Godet to suppose that there is in 15²⁹ a reference to martyrdom, which Christians must be ready to face, and he recalls in this connection the well-known texts of Mark 10³⁸ and Luke 12⁵⁰, where baptism has this sense. Then it must be translated as 'to be baptized with a view to death', that is, to enter into communion not with the living, but with the dead. This explanation would be excellent, if '*huper*' could have the sense suggested—but unfortunately this seems quite impossible.[41]

We are then obliged to have recourse to the traditional explanation, which gives the preposition its usual sense. To explain the future, we must suppose that the verb '*poiein*' has a sense similar to '*ausrichten*' in German, that is 'What will they accomplish or achieve who . . .?' We have rendered it in this way, but openly admit that it is a rather desperate solution of the difficulty presented by the future tense.[42]

At bottom, we cannot eradicate the impression that the text is not quite in order. A verb form in the present tense might be expected, depending on '*baptizontai*' in 15²⁹ᵇ. As it is difficult to imagine the

[40] We do not mention the unexpected explanation of 15²⁹ᵇ by von Hofmann, who attaches it to 15³⁰.

[41] SCHLATTER (p. 423) also thinks in terms of martyrdom. But he retains the normal sense of '*huper nekrōn*': 'on behalf of the dead'. Yet we fail to see why the dead should gain any particular benefit from it.

[42] J.W. attempts to reassure the reader by speaking of a quite mysterious '*futurum logicum*'. But why then is '*baptizontai*' in 15²⁹ᵇ not put into the future also? Moreover the Greek grammar of KÜHNER (Leipzig, 1890–8), II.172–3 mentions a *futurum praesens* only as a form of politeness used particularly with verbs expressing a request ('I shall beg' for 'I beg'). The idea of giving the sense of a future perfect to the future simple might also be considered. Then it would be rendered as: 'What will they have done who . . .?' The understood answer would be: 'They will have wasted their time.' But this use of the future is doubtful.

mutation of 'poiousin' into 'poiēsousin',[43] the present of another verb would have to be postulated. We should like to think that the Apostle dictated 'pisteuousin' = 'what do they *believe* who are baptized for the dead', a verb which might easily have been corrupted to 'poiēsousin'. But it does not need to be said that this conjecture is to be taken as no more than a suggestion.

15[30-32] throw into clear relief the foolishness of the courage of Christians and of all progress in the struggle against the powers of evil, in the eventuality of death's having the last word.[44] In that case what would become of the Christian Church, as well as of the Kingdom of God? Would not God Himself come out of the great struggle defeated?

In 15[31] 'apothnēsko' must be a synonym of 'kinduneuomen' = 'to be in danger of death' (cf. 2 Cor 11[23ff]), but the use of this strong expression must also be explained by the fact that the Apostle envisaged his life as a crucifixion (Gal 5[24], 2 Cor 4[11]). 'Humetera kauchēsis' must denote some moral reality very dear to the Apostle. It can refer only to the foundation and existence of the Church of Corinth which—in spite of everything—is a matter for glorying (cf. 1 Thess 2[19-20], Phil 2[16], Rom 15[17]). 'Humeteros' denotes therefore the object and not the subject of the pride.

But the great stumbling-block is the phrase 'ei kata anthrōpon ethēriomachēsa en Ephesō'. 'Kata anthrōpon' = 'from the human viewpoint', with a horizon limited by earthly humanity, that is, without hope of resurrection. It goes without saying that this purely human attitude was not that of Paul; in any event an unfulfilled condition is involved: 'If I had fought in a purely human spirit, etc.' But we must ask whether a further hypothetical element is not introduced by 'ethēriomachēsa'. The sense would then be: 'Suppose that I had fought against beasts at Ephesus (which did not happen, though I was ready to go through with such a fight), and suppose that I had done so "kata anthrōpon", then . . .?' Such an interpretation is grammatically possible because the indicative can be used to indicate an unfulfilled condition. Further, it has not passed unnoticed that the

---

[43] That is why the reading 'poiousin' in F and G has no great value and must be accounted as an attempt to make the text more comprehensible.

[44] This side of the question, implicit in Paul, has received admirable treatment by the great philosopher VLADIMIR SOLOVIEV, who in his 'Entretiens sur la guerre, la morale et la religion' (French Tr., E. Tavernier, Paris, 1916, p. 157) puts into the mouth of Leon Tolstoi (introduced under the name of the 'Prince') the following words: 'Death . . . is outside our will. And that is why it cannot have in our view any moral importance. In this respect, the only respect that has any present importance, death is an unimportant fact, like bad weather, for example.' However, Mr Z (who represents the author himself, ibid., p. 154) declares: 'If the victory of this extreme physical evil must be considered as definite and absolute, then the supposed victory of good in the social realm or in the realm of moral personality would not deserve to be ranked amongst serious improvements. . . . Then, to protect us against extreme pessimism and despair, ethical literature would be of no service to us. . . . We have only one prop: the real resurrection.'

*(33) Do not deceive yourselves: bad company corrupts good morals.
(34) Wake up to a well-conducted life and do not sin! For some have
no knowledge of God—I speak to shame you.*

*(35) But someone will ask: How are the dead raised? With what
body do they return? (36) How foolish you are! What you sow returns
to life only after being dead. (37) And what you sow is not the future
body, but a naked germ, for example of wheat or some other plant.
(38) But God gives it a body according to his will, and to each seed its
particular type of body. (39) All flesh is not the same, but there is a
difference between that of men, that of beasts, that of birds, that of fish.
(40) Indeed, there are heavenly bodies and earthly bodies. But the
glorious substance of the heavenly bodies is different from that of the
earthly ones. (41) Moreover the glorious substance of the sun differs
from that of the moon and from that of the stars. For one star differs
from another in its substance.*

Apostle, being a Roman citizen, could not be submitted to this
ignominious punishment; yet this argument does not carry much
weight if it were the case of a riot (cf. Acts 19²³⁻⁴⁰). But what makes
us side finally with the idea of a conditional interpretation, is that
the famous catalogue of hardships in 2 Corinthians 11²³ᶠᶠ makes no
mention of such a fight against the beasts; and, last but not least, let
us not forget that de La Palice reminds us of a consideration
which is generally overlooked by scholars—the Apostle did not
die in Ephesus. So it can only refer to a danger of being thrown
to the beasts, one that did not actually happen, and of which only
a vague recollection is perhaps preserved in the account in Acts
19.⁴⁵ To take *'thēriomachesthai'* metaphorically, in the sense of
'struggling against men who behaved like beasts', has in our view
little ground for support in this context, where the danger of death
is in question. Our interpretation of *'ethēriomachēsa'*, as involving a
conditional construction, is shared also by J.W.

The quotation in **15³²ᵇ**, *'phagōmen . . . apothnēskomen'* = 'let us
eat, etc.' is borrowed from Isaiah 22¹³.⁴⁶ The iambuses in **15³³**:
'phtheirousin . . . kakai' = bad company, etc. are a proverb which is
also found in Menander's Thaïs.⁴⁷

How is it to be understood that the ethic approved (hypothetically)
in 15³² should be contested in 15³³⁻⁴, in which bad company obviously
means dealings with materialists? The best way of solving this
difficulty is to assume that in Corinth some elements ran the risk of

---

⁴⁵ Cf. the scene in the theatre in the Acts of the Martyrs of Vienne in EUSEBIUS,
Eccl. Hist., Bk 5, Ch. 1.

⁴⁶ Similar ideas will be found in Wisdom 2⁶ᶠᶠ; and to a certain extent in Proverbs
12¹⁻¹⁰.—Cf. the slogan recorded by SENECA, *Controverses* 14: '*Bibamus, moriendum
est.*'

⁴⁷ Fragments, ed. Meineke (Berlin, 1823), p. 75; Loeb Series (London 1921),
p. 356.

really falling into this practical materialism. 'Yes,' says the Apostle, 'I could well understand that you might do that. The danger is not an imaginary one. Already there are among you bad libertine elements, which you must shun.'—There is no need then to read into '*homiliai kakai*' in **15**[33] an allusion to keeping company with pagans. If our interpretation is correct, the point once again concerns a group with immoral tendencies within the Church, probably the predecessors of the Gnostic libertines, well known to the heresiographers; and this supposition seems to be confirmed by the word '*agnōsia*' = 'the opposite of knowledge', in **15**[34], which might well be satirizing some false Gnostics.

'*Dikaiōs*' in **15**[34] means nothing other than 'as is fitting'. **15**[34b] stresses the seriousness of the danger. Far from apologizing for his rather harsh manner, the Apostle emphasizes its pedagogical necessity.

15[35–41] introduce an objection of deniers of the resurrection and give a provisional but rational refutation which prepares the way for the revelation of **15**[42ff]. The objection arises from the prejudice that there is only one sort of body, just as there is only one sort of matter. Consequently if there is such a thing as resurrection, the Kingdom of God is a grossly materialistic conception, according to which men live in heaven with fleshly bodies. That was indeed a notion common among the Greeks for whom ideas of materiality and of heavenly bliss were absolutely incompatible. They could not imagine an embodiment other than a grossly materialistic one.

In his reply, the Apostle recalls that the transformation of a seed into a plant, an analogy of the resurrection, similarly presupposes a new creation which precludes qualitative identity between what dies and what later grows. This reasoning naturally loses its force among those who hold different biological concepts with regard to the nature of plants. But it must have made some impression on those Greeks, who perhaps under the influence of the mystery religions, conceived of the miracle of Spring vegetation in the same way as the Apostle.[48]

The author then declares that there is a host of different bodies actually present in nature, a remark calculated to prepare the minds of his opponents to accept the idea of a resurrection body as made of some special substance and not of flesh. It is true that, even with this reservation, the idea of bodily resurrection was difficult for the Greeks to accept. It can be seen in Origen, who is not even the most Greek of the Fathers, but who has the courage to carry his thought

[48] RICHARD REITZENSTEIN has written a commentary on Chapter **15** in the light of the mystery religions (*v. Die hellenistischen Mysterienreligionen* [2nd edn, Leipzig and Berlin, 1920], pp. 194–204). But in agreement with A. SCHWEITZER (works cited in our Introduction) we think that a direct influence of these religions on Paulinism is not demonstrable. This does not of course preclude influences from Persian religions on Jewish apocalyptic, which itself had profound influence on early Christianity.—K. L. SCHMIDT (*Der Apostel Paulus und die antike Welt*, in *Bibliothek*, WARBURG, lectures 1924–5, Leipzig, 1927) agrees on some matters of fact with REITZENSTEIN, but places the emphases very differently.

through to its logical conclusion, and who postulates at the end of time the dissolution of all bodies, even of the subtle resurrection bodies.[49] But even if the Apostle did not convince all his opponents in Corinth, he has done us the inestimable service of dispelling certain misunderstandings, by clearly indicating the difference and even the contrast between the nature of our present bodies and of resurrection bodies.

Matters of detail in 15[36-41]. 15[36]. '*Aphrōn*' is almost a synonym for 'godless', as in Psalm 13[1] (14[1]), '*Eipen aphrōn . . . ouk estin Theos*'. —The contrast between '*zōopoiein*' = 'make to live' and '*apothanein*' = 'to die', presupposes that the germination of the wheat is not thought of as a natural occurrence, but as an event requiring heavenly intervention.—15[37] is also very typical of the idea of vegetation assumed here. The plant is not preformed in the seed. God could in principle make any plant to grow from it ('*kathōs ēthelēsen*'), but in fact he regularly gives to each one the 'desired' body, in accordance with Genesis 1[11]. '*Gumnos kokkos*' = 'naked germ' must stress the neutral and 'unclad' character of seeds[50]—'*ei tuchoi*' = 'for example'. 15[39]. '*Sarx*' is unfortunately a word of many meanings for the Apostle. We have already met the following senses for it: (1) The carnal principle, in a moral sense (cf. the expression '*sophia sarkikē*' or '*sarkinē*'). (2) The racial sense. 'Carnal' kinship, i.e. natural, as opposed to kinship according to the promises, cf. 10[18]. (3) The biological sense: '*sarx*' = 'creature' = בָּשָׂר, cf. 1[29]. (4) The social sense: '*en sarki*' = 'in the external situation of life', cf.7[28].—Here we meet a fifth sense, which might be called (*cum grano salis*) the chemical sense: the sort of matter from which a body is composed. According to the notions of antiquity, this matter differs with the classes of animals.[51] Naturally the 'heavenly bodies', i.e. the living bodies of certain angels which appear to us in the form of stars, are of other matter than earthly bodies. Furthermore, the former differ among themselves as much as do the latter (15[41-2]). However, the author does not have the courage to speak of '*sarx*' in connection with heavenly bodies. He uses the word '*doxa*' = 'glory' to denote their luminous substance. Unfortunately this choice of words

---

[49] See DE FAYE, *Origène*, III.(Paris, Leroux, 1928).249ff.

[50] Cf. 2 Corinthians 5[3]. John 12[24] also supposes that the seed of wheat must die before germinating. The curious expression 'naked seed' also occurs in the Talmud. It is possible then that Paul borrowed it from Jewish tradition. According to Sanhedrin 90b (GOLDSCHMIDT, IX.31), Queen Cleopatra said to Rabbi Meir: 'I know that the dead will rise, for it is written (Ps 72[16] in the Hebrew Bible):"They will come out of the town as flowers come out of the ground." But will they rise naked or with clothes?' He answered her: 'The answer is given by a conclusion *a minore ad maius*, by taking a grain of wheat. If a grain of wheat which is buried naked, comes out of the ground abundantly clothed, how much more will the godly be dressed in their clothes!'

[51] It is thus that GALEN, *de constitutione artis medicae*, Ch. 9 (KÜHN, I.255), even insists on the difference between the flesh of lions and flesh of lambs.

(42) *So it is with the resurrection of the dead.*
   It is sown in corruption,
   it is raised in incorruptibility.
(43) *It is sown in wretchedness,*
   it is raised in glory;
   it is sown in weakness,
   it is raised in strength.
(44) *It is sown a natural body,*
   it is raised a supernatural body.

If there is a natural body, there is also a supernatural body. (45) *For this is what is written: 'The first Adam was created to have a living nature', the second Adam to be a life-giving spirit.* (46) *Yet, it was not the spiritual man who came first, but the natural man; then came the spiritual.* (47) *The first man was of earth. The second man came from heaven.* (48) *Such as was the man made of earth, so also are the earthy. As was the man from heaven, so also are the heavenly beings.* (49) *And as we have borne the image of the earthy, so also we shall bear the image of the heavenly.* (50) *But I declare to you, brothers: Flesh and blood cannot inherit the kingdom of God, nor can corruption inherit incorruptibility.*

accidentally carries with it (**15**[40b]) the use of '*doxa*' for earthly bodies too, because it is necessary to have a common denominator for both earthly and heavenly matter.

In **15**[42] '*houtōs*' = 'thus, so' provides a transition to what follows. The idea expressed in **15**[39–41] and used here is just this: there are many sorts of matter; the resurrection bodies must not therefore be represented as being of the same substance as the biological bodies of this aeon. But it would be wrong to ascribe to the Apostle the idea of seeking to rank purely and simply the resurrection bodies among the 'heavenly' bodies. Besides, the Apostle also recalls the parable of the wheat in **15**[36–8]. Here the analogy with the problem of the resurrection is more striking: the point of comparison is the opposition between what goes down into the earth and what will come up out of it.

15[42–44a] (from '*speiretai en phthora*' = 'it is sown in corruption' as far as '*egeiretai sōma psuchikon*' = 'it is raised a supernatural body') form a strophe composed of four clear, vigorous antitheses, rending the darkness of our ignorance as the bugles of victory break the silence of an anguished waiting. The first antithesis: '*phthora*' = 'corruption'—'*aphtharsia*' = 'incorruptibility', does more than express a hope, it clarifies that hope. It is not the immortality of the soul, and consequently the lack of a body as over against an embodied condition, that is promised by the Christian revelation, but a body freed from corruption, i.e. realizing the fullness of the eternal and completed life willed by the Creator. We might add without falsifying

the Apostle's thought: nor does it promise the abolition of time and space, which only a very clumsy Kantianism has been able to read into New Testament eschatology.[52] The second antithesis, '*atimia*' = 'wretchedness', '*doxa*' = 'glory', gives precision on the axiological plane to the opposition between the two modes of existence. Is it not a supreme shame for man to be saddled with a perishable animal body?[53]

Though modern thought tends to set this whole problem on one side because the mortal constitution of our body is 'natural', it forgets that nature itself becomes a problem for theology. Indeed, from the standpoint of the Kingdom of God, it is miracles which are natural, whereas the laws of nature are anti-natural.[54] The third antithesis, '*astheneia*' = 'weakness'—'*dunamis*' = 'strength', has both a physical and a moral meaning. This body 'of death' is subject to weakness and to the law of sin. It is (in the Calvinistic sense) 'disabled'. Further, the law of our bodily organs, that is to say the law of biological egoism, is in opposition to the law of God. The sense of '*dunamis*' arises from contrast to this.

The fourth antithesis introduces the notion towards which this proclamation is tending—namely the notion of '*sōma pneumatikon*'. The term is very well chosen; for it allows us to glimpse two qualities of resurrection bodies, which we have difficulty in imagining, but which the theology of Paul calls us to consider: namely, on the one hand the supernatural life granted by the Holy Spirit, and on the other the body's perfect submission to the spirit, which will truly make it his temple. If there is any Cartesian prejudice to the term 'spiritual body'—by which 'spiritual' would be equated with what lacks substance and extension, and would therefore be in contradiction to 'body'—then this must be overcome. We might avoid it by speaking of a 'supernatural body', a rendering further suggested by the contrasted term '*sōma psuchikon*' = 'principle of life', in which '*psuchikon*' (derived from '*psuchē*' = נֶפֶשׁ) is quite simply a synonym for 'natural'. It is certain moreover that practically speaking the natural body is confused with the body of flesh; for this natural body is precisely that which has fallen under the domination of the '*sarx*' (taken in its usual sense, i.e. of the principle of corruption and death).[55]

So we must soak ourselves in this truth that the resurrection body

[52] See HÉRING, *Le Royaume de Dieu, selon Jésus et l'apôtre Paul*, p. 214 and note 1.—O. CULLMANN, *Christ and Time* (Tr. Filson, London, 1951), passim.

[53] For any commentary we refer readers to the many texts cited and discussed by Wilfred Monod in his work *Le problème du bien*, especially in the first volume (Paris, 1934).

[54] 'Miracle is no anomaly in creation, but the establishment of its true order'— CHRISTOPH BLUMHARDT in *Vom Reiche Gottes* (pub. Furche), p. 8.

[55] See the important article by H. CLAVIER on 'La notion du *sōma pneumatikon*' in *The Background of the New Testament and its Eschatology* (ed. Davies and Daube, Cambridge, 1956), pp. 342ff.

is not immaterial. In Pauline language we should say: the risen person is not a naked seed, but is clad. This body is not endowed with a lesser reality than the present physical body; it has nothing in common with the spectral body of phantoms or ghostly apparitions (cf. Lk 24[37ff]). In one way, it is even more real than our corruptible body, because it is 'without weakness' and full of 'strength'. Furthermore Paul's conception is absolutely incompatible with the representation of the resurrection which has been popularized by medieval sculpture and which has unfortunately had a resurgence under the pen of a Charles Péguy;[56] in this the dead rise up with their fleshly bodies afflicted with all their weaknesses, to be glorified after the event if all goes well. According to the Apostle there is no other resurrection than the glorious resurrection. 'It is raised in glory.' That is why the resurrection of unbelievers is not mentioned in 15[24]. So there are neither two different resurrections, nor a neutral general resurrection leading to glory for some, and to eternal torment for others. All such speculations are completely foreign to Paul's teaching.

At the same time it is clearly very difficult to reconcile with the Apostle's eschatology, which denies the resurrection of the flesh, that of the Roman Creed (commonly called the 'Apostles' Creed') which affirms it.[57] We will leave that to the dogmatic theologians who consider this creed a happy summary of the Christian revelation.

Finally, there is a last question of interest to the theologian which is left somewhat in suspense. Is there numerical identity between the body of shame and the body of glory, despite their qualitative difference? It seems to us that an affirmative answer is the only reasonable one. For 15[51], as well as 1 Thessalonians 4[17] no doubt, teaches the transformation of the bodies of surviving Christians. By analogy, we might admit for the resurrected also identity between their two bodies, an identity represented indeed by the metaphor of the seed. Besides, we know that the new man already exists in a concealed way within each Christian; it is the well-known 'esō anthrōpos', the term denoting in Paul's work not the soul, or the spirit as opposed to the body, but something like the 'germ of the glorious future man'. This man is still invisible, but will be revealed at the end of time, according to Romans 8[18-19]. It is this that ensures the continuity of consciousness between the two states. (Cf. Rom 7[22], 2 Cor 4[16], Eph 3[16].)

The passage 15[44b-5] gives to the kerygma of the resurrection its Christological and therefore its anthropological basis, Christ being envisaged as the new Adam, who replaces the the old Adam. This

---

[56] See 'La résurrection des corps' in *Morceaux choisis, Poésie*, ed. N.R.F. pp. 146ff.

[57] 'No New Testament author has ever taught the resurrection of the flesh'— PHILIPPE-H. MENOUD, *CTAP*, IX.35; cf. W. BIEDER, *Auferstehung des Fleisches oder des Leibes? TZ* (1945), pp. 105-20.—As is known, the Nicene Creed passed over this question in silence. The Creed of Constantinople (381) speaks of an 'anastasis nekrōn', which is quite in the Pauline tradition.

doctrine of the two Adams is found neither in Jewish apocalyptic, nor in the Talmud,[58] nor in the Gospels, nor in Hellenistic or Mandaean speculations on Anthropos. But the summary of the doctrine of the Naassenes given by Hippolytus,[59] represents a slightly parallel scheme.

Furthermore, the speculations of Philo on the two creation narratives (Gen 1 and 2) are particularly instructive, because Paul seems to have known them in a somewhat similar form. According to the Alexandrine scholar,[60] the account in Genesis 1 tells of the creation of a heavenly man, called *'ouranios'* = 'heavenly' and *'aphthartos'* = 'incorruptible', whereas in Genesis 2 another man, earthy and corruptible, called *'gēïnos'* = 'earthy' and *'aisthētos'* = 'perceptible', is the subject of the narative. But the differences between the teaching of the Alexandrine scholars and of the man of Tarsus are very perceptible also. Not only is Philo obviously ignorant of any incarnation of the heavenly man, but he also speaks of him as *'asōmatos'* = 'incorporeal' and even as 'androgynous'—two traits unknown to Paul's doctrine.

In 15[45a] *'anthrōpos'* is a mere duplication of 'Adam'; but Adam is indispensable as a counterpart to 'Adam' in 15[45b], and therefore *'anthrōpos'* should be deleted; it has been added to make the text more like that of Genesis, in which the LXX says: *'kai egeneto ho anthrōpos eis psuchēn zōsan'* (נֶפֶשׁ חַיָּה) = 'and man was created a living being'. The Apostle contrasts the second Adam with the first, but without alluding to the other Genesis account (Ch 1), as Philo does. The second Adam is characterized as *'pneuma zōopoioun'* (רוּחַ מְחַיָּה) = 'a life-giving spirit'. The adjective *'eschatos'* = 'the last' is here synonymous with *'deuteros'* = 'the second'. *'Ultimus aeque atque alter'* (Bengel). Now, no Scriptural text is known on the last Adam. Nor is it necessary to postulate here a quotation from an apocryphal writing. The author, well launched into antitheses from 15[42], was well able to coin the term by analogy with 15[45a]. The second Adam is *'pneuma'*, because he is a spiritual creature, i.e. supernatural (in the sense of *'pneumatikon'*, 15[44]), whereas the first Adam is *'psuchē'*, i.e. a natural being (cf. the sense of *'psuchikon'* in 15[44]). In addition, he has within himself the source of all life, and more particularly the

---

[58] 'No trace'—STRACK-BILLERBECK, III.478.

[59] In his *Philosophumena or the Refutation of all Heresies*, (Tr. Legge, London, 1921), I.118-46). It is reproduced in REITZENSTEIN AND SCHAEDER, *Studien zum antiken Synkretismus in Iran und Griechenland* (Leipzig, 1926), pp. 104-53, 161-73. —In the Hermetic texts, contrast between the carnal man and the spiritual man is to be found. But this is merely a matter of two aspects (exterior and interior) of the earthly man, *v.* FESTUGIERE, *La révélation d'Hermes Trismégiste* I.269 (Paris, 1944).

[60] See especially *De opificio mundi*, §§134ff (COHN AND WENDLAND, ed. minor, I.38ff); *Legum allegoriae*, I.§§41-3 (ibid., 60ff); *De plantatione Noe*, §§44-5 (ibid., II.133); *De confusione linguarum*, §§62-4 (ibid., II.230ff).

source of eternal life,[61] whereas the first only shares in life in the manner of a natural being; *'non solum vivit, sed etiam vivificat'* (Bengel). Once more, as in Romans 5, and less obviously in Philippains 2[6ff], Christ is considered as the Second Man, head of a new humanity. We know, certainly, that His existence goes back to the time before creation. However (and this is the force of *'alla'* at the beginning of **15**[46]), His appearance on earth is later than that of the first Adam.

15[47] characterizes the two Men by a new antithesis: the First Man was made of earth, in a sense he came from the earth; the Second descended from heaven, *'ex ouranou, epouranios'* (cf. Jn 3[13], 6[62]). The adjective *'choïkos'* = 'made of earth' (**15**[47a]) is a duplication of *'ek gēs'* = 'of earth', and has no parallel in **15**[47b]. It is in its right place in **15**[48], from whence it must have crept into **15**[47] by mistake. Genesis 2[7] gives a slightly different text: *'kai eplasen ho Theos ton anthrōpon choun apo tēs gēs'* (*'chous'* = 'a heap of earth'). The earthly character is not therefore an effect of the Fall. It is inherent in the creation. Moreover the Fall is not in question here; but the doctrine of the Epistle to the Romans makes it clear that Adam was corruptible, i.e. likely to corrupt himself body and soul by a fall. Moreover, the ideal man, represented by the Second Adam, will be more than an earthly Adam restored—He will be incorruptible, made of heavenly substance, according to **15**[48ff]. If Philippians 2 reveals that the heavenly Adam, after His resurrection, was elevated to a place higher than the one He had in His pre-existence (*'huper-hupsōsen'*), this is also true *mutatis* of empirical men.

But the Apostle has no intention of giving here a complete anthropological scheme. He hastens to draw a practical conclusion from his revelations; we Christians are destined to become heavenly, in the image of the Heavenly Man, as we were earthly in the image of the first Adam. Is it only after the resurrection that we shall bear this image in us? If we read the future indicative *'phoresomen'* = 'we shall bear', we must answer in the affirmative; but the best manuscripts, P 46 and B among others, give the subjunctive. We suppose that this image may be already in us here below. It is a question of not refusing to accept it and of not falling back under the dominion of the *'sarx'*, which will not inherit the Kingdom of God (no resurrection of the flesh); in this sense it might be said in advance that Christians are already *'epouranioi'* = 'heavenly beings'. This shows moreover, that the appearance of the second Adam mentioned in **15**[45], is not the Parousia, but the incarnation. Concerning the

---

[61] See the Prologue of St John's Gospel, 1[4] (*'ho gegonen en autō zōē ēn'*). Cf. also the Johannine affirmations according to which all who have been born again have a spring of life within themselves: 4[14], 7[38]. They are the same as those who, in Pauline language, bear within themselves the image of the Second Adam.

(51) *Here is a mystery that I reveal to you: All of us will not die but all of us will be transformed, (52) in a moment, in the twinkling of an eye, at the last trumpet. For the trumpet will be sounded, the dead will be raised incorruptible, and we shall be transformed.* (53) *For it is necessary for this corruptible thing to put on incorruptibility and for this mortal thing to put on immortality.* (54) *But when this corruptible thing has put on incorruptibility and this mortal thing has put on immortality, then that word of Scripture will be fulfilled: 'Death has been swallowed up in victory.* (55) *O Death, where is your victory? O Death, where is your sting?'* (56) *Now the sting of death, is sin; and the power of sin is the Law.* (57) *But thanks be to God who has given us the victory through our Lord Jesus Christ.* (58) *So then, brothers, be steadfast, be immovable, unflagging in the work of the Lord, knowing that, thanks to the Lord, your labour is no baseless futility.*

expression '*sarx kai haima*' in **15**[50], we agree with M. Bornhäuser[62] that it may have been borrowed from Judaism, according to which only the bones could rise again. But again there is no trace of this idea in the Apostle's writings.

15[51] and **15**[52] add a new revelation of the highest importance. Not only will 'all of us' not be dead at the end of the world,[63] but those still living will not die at that moment. Like Enoch and Elijah they will be relieved of death. If the Apostle meant people of his own generation, he interpreted his revelation wrongly; for that generation is dead in its entirety. But 'we' can have a wider sense—'we men'— that is those among men still alive when that time comes. However, it goes without saying that those still alive will not be able to enter the Kingdom with their bodies of flesh. They will be transformed. The technical term for this metamorphosis is '*allattesthai*'. Those who

---

[62] 'Die Gebeine der Toten', *Beiträge zur Förderung christlicher Theologie*, XXVI.3(1921). KARL BARTH thinks it possible to express the idea of the spiritual body as a 'totally different future existence of man. Man as he is to his own self-knowledge has a reflection of himself held up in front of him in which he appears as a completely new man. And he now hears this reflection saying to him: You who here and now are *this*, will then and there be *that*' (*Credo*, Tr. McNab [London, 1936], pp. 161-2). This highly paradoxical statement shows the difficulty he faces by wanting at all costs to combine the affirmations of the so-called Apostles' Creed with the totally different Pauline texts.

[63] '*ou pantes*' would be a preferable reading to '*pantes ou*'. For '*pantes*', etc., would mean that no one of the Apostle's generation will die. However, on this point see the following note.—DIESTELMANN (*Jahrbücher für deutsche Theologie* [1865], p. 506) proposes the conjectural reading, '*pantes hoi ou koimēthēsometha, pantes de . . .* etc. *Alle die wir nicht entschlafen werden, werden wir doch alle verwandelt werden.*' As BALJON says, p. 130, this construction is as un-Greek as it is un-German.

see the Parousia will not pass through death.[64] As for the '*eschatē salpingx*', it is not necessarily the last of a series; the expression can also mean: 'the trumpet of the end of the world.' It was already part of the machinery of Jewish apocalyptic.[65]

15[53–55] form a kind of strophe composed of two parallel antitheses, followed by biblical quotations. It will be noticed that the author sets aside the terms for resurrection ('*egeiresthai*') and transformation ('*allattesthai*') in favour of the more neutral expression '*endusasthai aphtharsian*' or '*athanasian*' = 'to put on incorruptibility' or 'immortality'; what he is seeking to make clear, is what the two glorious facts have in common, namely victory over death and corruption. Further, '*endusasthai*' = 'to put on' is well chosen to suggest the idea of a new corporeal existence, which will, however, not be without a link with the old.

The expressions '*to phtharton touto*' and '*to thnēton touto*' (**15**[54]) are at first sight slightly awkward. But it is difficult to see how the author, without calling on technical philosophical terms, could have expressed himself more simply to denote 'our present mortal corruptible existence'.

15[55a]. '*katepothē*, etc.', is not a biblical quotation, and Nestlé is wrong to mark it as such. But it is a striking reply to Isaiah 25[8] '*katepien ho thanatos ischusas*'. 'Well,' says the Apostle, 'here is the revenge of life; death is engulfed in the victory of life.' In **15**[55b], in the quotation

---

[64] Did the Apostle seriously profess that in principle no Christian was likely to die before the Parousia, as '*pantes ou*' and '*pantes de*, etc.' (**15**[51]) suggest? Strange as it may seem to us, it is not impossible, if account is taken of the two following statements: first the author looked on the Parousia as imminent; and second, his primitive conception of baptism, still to be found in Colossians (2[12]) and later modified in the Epistle to the Romans (6[2]), and which saw in this sacrament the fulfilment of death and resurrection in Christ, must have favoured the idea that, apart from the violent deaths of martyrs, Christians in a way had already death behind them. This also helps in understanding the curious remark in 11[30]. Later, Christians had to admit that none of Paul's contemporaries saw the Parousia. This explains two other readings of **15**[51]: (*a*) '*pantes koimēthēsometha, ou pantes de allagēsometha*.' This would mean: all will be dead, but all will not be transformed. In this case, either '*allattesthai*' is synonymous with resurrection, which is not Pauline, or it means, 'all the dead will rise, but all will not share in the resurrection to glory', which is equally contradictory of Pauline eschatology—(*b*) '*pantes anastēsontai, ou pantes de allagēsometha*'; this reading again shows itself for what it really is, namely the intention to teach a conception of the resurrection, widespread later, but quite incompatible with Pauline thought. Both readings are valueless. Obviously the theological interest of these revelations on the transformation of those still living is not lessened by the fact that the Parousia and its consequences are delayed. Generally speaking, we have learned to distinguish in prophecy between the events predicted and the dates suggested for their fulfilment, in which subjective errors of perspective by the seer are always possible.—In dating the Epistle to the Colossians, we side with those who fix it at the time of the Ephesian imprisonment.

[65] See Targum Pseudo-Jonathan on Exodus 20[18] (ETHERIDGE, I.513), Zechariah 9[14], 2 Esdras 6[23] (KAUTZSCH, p. 368; CHARLES, II.576); cf. Matthew 24[31], 1 Thessalonians 4[16], and BOUSSET, *Der Antichrist* (Göttingen, 1895), pp. 166ff.

from the prophet Hosea (13¹⁴), '*nikos*' = 'victory' takes the place of
'*dikē*' = 'power to punish'. The second vocative '*thanate*' = 'O
death' (in 15⁵⁵ᵇ), given by Nestlé, following some ancient authorities,
does not occur in Hosea. The LXX reads '*hadē*' = 'O Hades'. The
Textus Receptus also gives '*hadē*' in our Epistle, doubtless to conform with the LXX. '*Kentron*' could mean the ox-driver's goad; but
it seems more likely that the author compared death to a harmful
creature equipped with a '*sting*' (a scorpion?).

15⁵⁶ adds the theological interpretation of the metaphor of the
sting: it denotes sin. Reference to Romans 5¹², so dear to commentators, explains little; for there death is presented as a result of sin,
here sin is death's weapon, and death injects men with the poison
which corrupts them and subjects them to its power. In one way or
another, sin obviously turns men away from God, who is the source
of all life. What is the role of the Law? The reader will understand
that we cannot embark here on a discussion of the Pauline conception
(or conceptions) of the Law, for this question, merely touched on
here, is to be treated in the commentaries on the Epistles to the
Romans and to the Galatians. Let us limit ourselves to recalling the
passage Romans 7⁷ᶠ (especially 7⁹), according to which sin increased
in power when the Law came. The exclamation in 15⁵⁷ is somewhat
reminiscent of the one in Romans 7²⁵ᵃ. It is also possible that 15⁵⁶ is
a gloss. 15⁵⁸ gives a practical conclusion to the teaching on resurrection by taking the opposite view to 15³². It is introduced by '*hōste*',
as are 3²¹, 4⁵, 7³⁸, 11³³ and 14³⁹. '*Ametakinētoi*' = 'immovable', like
'*mē metakinoumeoi*' in Colossians 1²³, has in view the Christian hope,
from which the Christian must not let himself be diverted; '*to ergen
tou kuriou*' = 'the work of the Lord' recalls the duty of active love;
'*hedraioi*' = 'steadfast' might then be an allusion to firmness in the
faith, which would take us back to 13¹³.—It will be noticed that the
Apostle gives no indication of the precise state of the departed prior
to the resurrection. So far as concerns souls untouched here below
by the preaching of the Gospel, one can, without being unfaithful
to the essential data of Pauline revelation, envisage as does Ph.-H.
Menoud, in *Le sort des trépassés d'après le N.T.*,[66] a preaching to the
dead, taking inspiration from 1 Peter 3¹⁹; perhaps even, as we do in
our *Royaume de Dieu*,[67] we can take account of the hypothesis of a
plurality of earthly lives in this aeon.—As for the 'dead in Christ',
one certainty will throw light on that provisional existence: it is that
'*neither life nor death*' will be able to separate them from the love of
God (cf. Rom 8³⁸⁻⁹).

⁶⁶ *CTAP*, No. 9.
⁶⁷ *EHPR*, No. 30, pp. 217-18.

CHAPTER XVI

(1) *In connection with the collection for the saints, act in your turn according to the recommendations which I gave to the Churches in Galatia:* (2) *On the first day of the week let each put on one side whatever he can succeed in saving, so that the collection is not made only when I come.* (3) *But when I do arrive, I will have your offering taken to Jerusalem by men of your choosing, accredited with letters.* (4) *And if it is desirable for me to go too, they shall go with me.*

(5) *Now I shall come to you when I have visited Macedonia.* (6) *For I shall pass through Macedonia, and I shall stay some time with you, or I may even spend the winter with you, in order that you may set me on the way I shall go.* (7) *Indeed, I do not want to see you merely as I pass through; for I hope to spend some time with you, if the Lord permits.* (8) *But I shall stay in Ephesus until Pentecost;* (9) *for a great opportunity of effective action has opened to me, even though there are many opponents.*

16¹. '*Logeia*' (written phonetically as '*logia*' in nearly all manuscripts) comes from '*legō*' = 'to collect'. '*Hoi hagioi*' = 'the saints' in the absolute sense, as in 2 Corinthians 8⁴, is here synonymous with '*hoi ptōchoi tōn hagiōn tōn en Hierousalēm*' = 'the poor among the saints in Jerusalem' (Rom 15²⁶). We know from Galatians 2¹⁰ that Paul promised the Church in Jerusalem to raise money for the relief of their poor. His conscientiousness in discharging this task is also shown in Acts 11²⁹⁻³⁰, 12²⁵, Romans 15²⁷, 2 Corinthians 8⁴⁻¹⁵.

The advice given in **16²** must have its explanation in some earlier tragi-comic experiences in Corinth or elsewhere. '*Euodōtai*' cannot mean 'to have earned, to have put on one side'. It must be allowed to keep its own meaning of 'succeed', and '*thēsaurizein*' = 'to put on one side' must be added as understood. 'Each one should collect by putting aside what he can manage to put aside.' It is true that this would not prevent the collection proper from being made at the last moment, but the money would be ready. '*To sabbaton*' = 'the week'; '*mia*' is a Semitism for '*hē prōtē*' = 'the first'. The first day of the week, as among the Jews, was Sunday. Does the Apostle propose it because it was a pay-day? We do not know. If there were some particularly important meetings on that day, it might be understood that the collection committee would then gather in the contributions; but we are not told that.

16³⁻⁴. In order to obviate any possibility of slander (we know from Chapters **3** and **9** how unscrupulous some opponents were), the Apostle does not propose himself as treasurer. '*Epistolai*' does not

(10) *But when Timothy comes, see that he can come among you without fear; for he is doing the Lord's work as I am.* (11) *Let no one scorn him therefore. Set him on his way in peace so that he may return to me. For I am waiting for him with the brothers.*

(12) *Concerning the brother Apollos, I strongly urged him to come to you with the brothers. But it was absolutely not the will (of God) that he should come now. However, he will come when he has time.*

(13) *Watch, remain steadfast in the faith, be manly, be strong.* (14) *Let all that you do be done in love.*

have the force of a singular sometimes found with *'epistolae'* in Latin. The meaning is that of several letters given respectively to the appointed delegates.

16⁵⁻⁹. The Apostle's travelling plans. The present *'dierchomai'* = 'I pass' might suggest the idea that this verse was written in Macedonia. But we know that *'erchomai'* often has a future force, replacing *'eleusomai'* or *'eimi'*, cf. Luke 23²⁹, John 4²¹, 5²⁸, 9⁴, 16²⁶, Jeremiah 38³¹ (31³¹). The reference to the land journey, longer than the sea journey across the Aegean, is perhaps to explain why his arrival in Corinth is not yet imminent. In compensation, he promises a prolonged stay, but adds 'if the Lord permits', in the same spirit which prompted the writing of James 4¹⁵. *'Propempein'* = 'to accompany a little way', e.g. as far as the boat, perhaps providing support for the journey.

According to Acts 18–19, the Apostle passed through Ephesus when travelling from Corinth to Jerusalem, at the end of what is usually called the Second Missionary Journey; then he returned to make a prolonged stay there.

'Pentekostē' is naturally the Jewish feast, since no Christian festival at this time yet existed. *'Thura'* has the sense of 'opportunities', 'providential possibilities'.

16¹⁰⁻¹¹. Paul's letter was naturally to go by the shortest route and to arrive in Corinth before Timothy, even if he had already set out for Macedonia with Erastus, as is recorded in Acts 19²². *'Ean'* = 'if' (conditional) instead of *'hotan'* = 'when' (temporal) is surprising. He may not be quite sure that Timothy will travel as far as Corinth. But why is the Apostle afraid of a snub to Timothy in Corinth? Doubtless because of his shyness (cf. 2 Tim 1⁷). An additional reason for the Corinthians to welcome him with respect.

Who are the *'adelphoi'* = 'brethren' with whom Timothy is to return (16¹¹)? First we should make sure whether *'meta tōn adelphōn'* goes with *'auton'* (Timothy will come 'with the brethren') or with *'ekdechomai'* (the brethren and I 'are waiting' for Timothy's return). In the first case, the more probable from the construction, it may mean the Corinthians in Ephesus, bearers of Paul's letter, who are to return with Timothy or with Erastus or other companions (Acts 19²²). In the second case, the Apostle means the Ephesians in general.

(15) *One further exhortation, brothers: you know that Stephanas and his family are the first-fruits in Greece and that they have dedicated themselves to the service of the Christians.* (16) *I desire you, on your side, to subordinate yourselves to such persons and to anyone who works and toils with them.* (17) *I rejoice, too, in the presence of Stephanas, Fortunatus and Achaicus, because they have filled the gap of your absence.* (18) *For they have brought soothing to me—as to you. Be grateful therefore for such persons.*

(19) *Greetings on behalf of the Churches in Asia. Many Christian greetings from Aquila, Prisca, and the congregation which meets in their house.* (20) *Greetings from all the brothers. Greet one another with the Christian kiss.*

(21) *My own greetings in my own hand, PAUL.* (22) *If anyone does not love the Lord, let him be anathema. Maranatha.* (23) *May the grace of the Lord Jesus be with you.* (24) *May my love be with you all, in fellowship with Christ Jesus.*

16¹². Apollos, who had left Ephesus for Corinth according to Acts 18²⁷–19¹, had returned. Paul clearly wishes to dispel any idea that he may have disapproved of his work in Corinth. That is why he insists on the fact that he has urged him to return. '*Meta tōn adelphōn*' may go with (*a*) the verb '*parekalesa*' = 'I urged'; or with (*b*) the subjunctive '*elthē*' = 'that he should go'—the more probable in our view, given such a construction. Apollos must have gone to Corinth either with Timothy and Erastus, or with the Corinthians of **16¹⁷**; as it may be supposed that the brethren in **16¹²** are the same as those in **16¹¹**, we opt for the first possibility.

'*Thelēma*' in Godet's view is the will of Apollos. But the end of **16¹²** speaks of circumstances beyond his will. We must therefore take '*thelēma*', although it has no '*tou Theou*' with it, as the will 'of God'; a similar thing occurs in Romans 2¹⁸, and in 1 Thessalonians 4³ according to some manuscripts; also 1 Maccabees 3⁶⁰ and Ecclesiasticus 43¹⁶ according to manuscript B.

16¹³⁻¹⁴. These exhortations end the letter proper. The expressions '*grēgorein*' = 'watch', like '*nēphein*' = 'be sober', form part of the metaphorical language of eschatology used by the Christians of earliest times; cf. Matthew 25¹³, 26⁴¹.—For '*stēkein en tē pistei*' = 'remain steadfast in the faith', cf. **15¹**, 2 Corinthians 1²⁴. For '*andrizesthai*' = 'be manly', and '*krataiousthai*' = 'be strong', cf. Psalm 30²⁵ (31²⁵). '*Panta humōn*' (**16¹⁴**) can mean only 'all that comes from you', i.e. 'all that you do'.

16¹⁵. For Stephanas, cf. **1¹⁶**.—'*Oidate*' with the accusative and followed by '*hoti*' is a good Greek construction for '*oidate hoti hē oikia estin*, etc.' = 'you know that the house (of Stephanas) is' . . . and presents no difficulty. Stephanas deserved the Church's respect in his double capacity as the first convert and as one dedicated to the

service (to the social service no doubt) of the brethren. It is true that *'diakonia'* = 'service' is not listed in Chapter 12 as a special charismatic gift; but the sense of the word is made clear by Acts 6[1ff]. We are in the presence here of the origins of the institutions of *'presbuteroi'* = 'elders' and of *'diakonoi'* = 'deacons'.

A Fortunatus is also named in the Epistle of Clement of Rome to the Corinthians 65[1] as the bearer of his letter, but we do not know whether it is the same man. We know nothing about Achaicus. As slaves were frequently called by the name of their country of origin, it might refer to a slave of Stephanas.

16[19-24]. Final greetings. Concerning Aquila and Prisca, see Acts 18[2,18,26]. *'Hē kat' oikon autōn ekklēsia'* = 'the congregation which meets in their house' (16[19]) seems to prove that in a great city like Ephesus, and perhaps in Corinth too, special meetings could be held in certain houses beside, but not necessarily apart from, the general gatherings. **16[20].** On the *'philēma hagion'* = 'holy kiss', see Romans 16[16], 2 Corinthians 13[12], 1 Thessalonians 5[26], cf. *'philēma agapēs'* = 'kiss of Christian love', 1 Peter 5[14].[1] Note that Justin Martyr[2] still knows of a Christian kiss in the Pauline sense. Likewise Clement of Alexandria, who calls it mystical (*'hoper echrēn mustikon einai'*),[3] also Tertullian,[4] whereas the Apostolic Constitutions (third century) forbids the *'philēma'* between men and women,[5] in order to obviate calumny and perhaps abuse.

16[23]. *'Maranatha'* preserved an Aramaic formula which was so ancient and venerable that no one had the heart to translate it (cf. *'amēn, allēlouïa, ōsanna'*). It may be an indicative (מָרָן אֲתָא) = 'the Lord comes', or an imperative (מָרָנָא תָ) = 'Our Lord, Come!' The second supposition can be supported by Revelation 22[20], which gives *'erchou, kurie Iēsou'* = 'come, Lord Jesus'. According to the Didache 10[6] this invocation had a set place at the end of the Eucharistic prayer, where it must have had the value of an epiclesis.

16[24] contains a greeting which is specifically Christian, bringing *'agapē'* to the fore and being somewhat reminiscent of the greeting in Ephesians 6[23] and 2 Corinthians 13[11]. *'En Christō Iēsou'* = 'in Christ Jesus', can go either with *'agapē'* = 'love' or with *'humōn'* (*'you'* Christians).

---

[1] Consult CABROL, *Dictionnaire d'antiquité chrétienne*, II.117ff.—The monograph by A. WÜNSCHE, *Der Kuss in Bibel, Talmud und Midrasch*, was not available to us.
[2] *Apol.*, I.65 (*MPG* VI, col. 428 A).
[3] *Paid.*, Bk III.xi.§81, STAEHLIN, I.281.
[4] *De oratione* 18 (*MPL* I, col. 1176-81).
[5] See II.57 and VIII.11 (*MPG* I, col. 736-7 and 1089 C).

In this exposition, we have not yet taken into account our division of 1 Corinthians into two letters, so as not to influence our exegesis by ideas which might seem prejudiced. But it will be permissible for us to explain briefly why in our opinion 16^{1-4} and 16^{10-14} go with letter A rather than with letter B (see Introduction).

(*a*) So far as the passage 16^{10-14} is concerned, it is indeed more natural to attach it to letter A, because Timothy's coming, also announced in 4^{17}, is in question.

(*b*) In 16^{1-4} Galatia is mentioned, a fact which can be easily explained if the Apostle's journey through those parts (Acts 19^1) is not yet too distant.

Furthermore, 16^{5-9}, which contradicts 4^{19} (cf. Introduction), should be attached to letter B.—Similarly, with 16^{15-18}, for there, Stephanas and his friends are in question, and there is no reference to them in 1^{11}, where only Chloe's people are mentioned as having come from Corinth. In addition, the transition from 16^{14} to 16^{15} is awkward. For 16^{14} seems to end the letter.

There can be some hesitation about the attribution of the salutations in 16^{19-24}. We think that they ended letter B, because 16^{19} follows 16^{18} very well.